Beside the
LAKE

By the same author – books for children:

Arkwright
Citizen Arkwright
Mallyroots' Pub at Misery Ponds
Featherbys
A Bit of a Hitch (short stories)
Tenterhooks

DEDICATION

This book is dedicated to the memory of my parents, to my family and to Margaret.

Beside the
LAKE

A Ballarat Childhood

Mary Steele

Mary Steele
with best wishes

HYLAND HOUSE

First published in Australia in 2000 by
Hyland House Publishing Pty Ltd
PO Box 122
Flemington
Victoria 3031

Copyright © Mary Steele 2000

This book is copyright. Apart from any fair dealing
for the purposes of private study, research, criticism
or review, as permitted under the Copyright Act, no
part may be reproduced by any process without
written permission. Enquiries should be addressed
to the publisher.

National Library of Australia
Cataloguing-in-publication data:

Steele, Mary.
   Beside the lake: a Ballarat childhood.

   Bibliography.
   Includes index.
   ISBN 1 86447 082 8.

   1. Steele, Mary. 2. Women – Australia – Biography. 3.
Ballarat (Vic.) – Biography. 4. Ballarat (Vic.) – Social
life and customs. I. Title.

920.72099457

Cover design by Rob Cowpe
Text design by Mary Steele
Edited by Bet Moore
Typeset in-house by Hyland House
Printed by Australian Print Group

Cover photograph View Point and Lake Wendouree, Ballarat,
from beside Gill's Boatshed, 1950s
Part I photograph (page 1) Summer on Lake Wendouree
Part II photograph (page 87) US battleships steam into action
in the Pacific, 1942 (BC 16.8.45)

Contents

PART ONE 1930-39 PEACE

A CATHEDRAL IN THE BACKYARD
Newcastle   2
Pantechnicon   11
Thumbnail portraits   13
Southward ho!   17

A COLONIAL BARCHESTER
We arrive in Ballarat   19
A tower   22
Servants   25
The old house   26
Hot and cold   31
Into the garden   32
The chapel   38

THE VIEW FROM WENDOUREE
Beyond the gate   41
Pleasure gardens   42
Gardens Botanical   45
Volcanos   47
Garden city   48

LESSONS IN LIVING
Serpents in Paradise	51
Margaret	54
Trams	55
The 'Pot of Gold'	59

FROM DIVINITY TO DAISY CHAINS
School	60
Onward and upward	63
Violin	66
The stage	68
Divinity	69
Playtime	71

THE SWEEP OF HISTORY
Centenary	74
Historical doorways	76
Kings and Queens	78
Empire	80
1939 – The Watershed	82

PART TWO 1939-45 WAR

TRANSPLANTED TO STURT STREET
The new house	88
My bedroom	90
Stairs	91
Design for living	92
Cracks in the design	92
Free-range kids	96

HOLY DAYS
Sundays 100
Hymns 104

UPHEAVAL
We are at war with Germany 107
The wireless 114
The domestic revolution 115

CHOOKS, AND MUCH ELSE, IN THE BACKYARD
Florrie 117
Pets 122
The facts of life 125
Sisterhood 127
Housework 127
'Over-dainting' 130
The backyard 131
The woodshed 134
Trees again 135
The wilderness next-door 137

THE BIGGEST INVASION SINCE THE GOLD RUSH
The Yanks are coming! 139
Flags 143
Dark days 145
War effort 149

A PORT ON THE YARROWEE
All around the town 154

SCHOOLING WITHOUT FRILLS
'Once again assembled here ...' 163
Education through thick and thin 166

Music	168
Battle songs	170
English and other languages	171
Listeners	174
Reading matter	175
'Creative' writing	178
Rebellion and discipline	180
Whatever would the neighbours think?	182
L'École de Vie	184
IN SICKNESS AND IN HEALTH, WITH VISITORS	
Visitors	188
Good plain cooking	193
Confined to bed	196
OUT AND ABOUT	
Beside the Lake	203
Hunters and gatherers	209
HOLIDAYS	
The Big Smoke	214
Rural rides	216
What Bird is That?	220
Bound for South Australia!	221
Portland	225
Christmas	231
THE END OF CHILDHOOD	
V for Victory	233
Epilogue	238
Bibliography	239
Conversion tables	240
Illustrations	241
Index	242

Preface

Beside the Lake is a period piece. It is about a particular place seen through the eyes of a child at a particular time. The child belonged to a particular family, so of course they come into it. Other people come and go, but birds and animals, trees, houses and landscapes are almost as important. School is there, but it is only one of the many kinds of education available to this child. This is the story of how her imagination was shaped and nourished.

I have concentrated on the years between 1936 and 1945, from the time we arrived in Ballarat to the end of the Second World War, which events provide convenient 'bookends' to my childhood. I was almost six at the beginning of this period and fourteen at the end. Earlier and later events of interest are referred to at times, but those ten years are the centrepiece.

My elder sister, Dorothy Graham, has lived with this project for a long time. As her memory stretches back a little further than mine, she has been able to correct details and fill in gaps, and I thank her for putting up with endless questions of the 'Do you remember if ... when ... who ... why ...?' variety. I am grateful for her patience and encouragement and for her willingness to read the work in progress. My younger sister, Elizabeth Wood, was spared much of this, being our junior by some years, but I thank her for her support and for some useful photos from her Box Brownie collection.

Margaret Rotheram, the friend who features large in the story, has also been very supportive, searching out old photos, memorabilia of the war, and a cache of my childhood letters to her. I wish hers to me had survived. I thank her for all of that, for reading the latest draft of the memoir, and for providing several memories of her own for inclusion.

Another long-time supporter of the book is Brenda Niall. She has read it at least twice in progressive drafts, with helpful suggestions, and has encouraged me to keep going, despite setbacks. At my request, my son Sam Steele read the latest draft as one of the younger generation and he made some useful comments, which I have acted upon. My husband, Bruce Steele, has been always at the ready to assist me with computer wizardry. I thank them all.

The Very Rev. Bill Edebohls provided copies of historic photos from the church archives, and Mr Jack Chisholm sent me a copy of the old sewerage plan on which I was able to base my 'map' of Old Bishopscourt. My thanks to them both for their interest.

Finally, I am grateful to my publishers, Hyland House – to Al Knight and Anne Godden in the lead-up time and now to Michael Schoo, who has generously agreed to bring the book into the light of day.

Mary Steele

PART ONE   1930 – 39

PEACE

A Cathedral in the Backyard

NEWCASTLE

My eyes opened to the world in Newcastle, New South Wales. From where we lived in the Deanery, it was a wide-angled scene, rather bare, windswept and rocky, its main features being the Ocean, the Port, the Steelworks, the Cathedral and the steeply angled streets. This was the first landscape imprinted on my mind.

Thanks to Father's position as Anglican Dean, we had a cathedral in our back yard instead of a shed, a fact I took entirely for granted. In England our 'back yard' would have been called the 'cathedral close'. Living in the shadow of the Cathedral was a bit like living at the foot of a small mountain or crag. It gave one a useful sense of scale.

My big sister Dorothy used the north side of the Cathedral as her hitting wall. As such it was more than adequate, except that balls tended to ricochet off the ornamental brickwork and fly downhill into the graveyard behind her. Lost balls had to be retrieved from among the gloomy vaults, which unnerved her because these were sometimes the haunt of vagrant men. Some balls bounced further, over the edge and into the streets below, for the Cathedral and its neighbours are perched on what is virtually a cliff, with the city centre at its foot. Stone steps lead down from the graveyard to the town level, and as a child I found the angle of the surrounding streets quite alarming. The steepest were furnished with handrails for puffing pedestrians. When tired, I felt as if I'd been carrying a wardrobe up Wolfe Street, I informed Mother. Wolfe Street, on the west side of the Cathedral, was the steepest.

When I was born in November, 1930, the family inhabited the 'Old Deanery', a two-storied house on Wolfe Street. Dorothy remembers her childhood there as solitary; she played on a piece of flat ground under a bush with a White Leghorn hen and her three make-believe 'sisters', Hifus, Lantus and Mundylardy. Her few toys included a prized India

A Cathedral in the Backyard   3

rubber ball which one day escaped into Wolfe Street and with ever-widening bounds vanished down into the main street of Newcastle, far below. Dorothy was inconsolable, but the ball was never replaced.

Other things careered down the hill. Storm water gathered in a dirty lane behind the old house and occasionally, during heavy rains, it poured through the back door and out the front, surging down the steps like the cascade of an old Roman villa. The carpets had to be hung out and hosed, while sinister patches of hairy black mould grew on the parlour walls. I was born in this house but have no memory of it, for soon after we moved into the 'New Deanery' on the opposite side of the Cathedral. Our younger sister, Elizabeth, was born there five years later.

Newcastle Cathedral, north side, from the city centre, c. 1930. 'Taken by Miss Street, the hairdresser.' Old Deanery chimneys at far top right. The belfry and graveyard also visible.

The Pacific Ocean rolled in at the end of Church Street to the east. When old enough, I was taken to play on the sand, from where I gazed at the towering green waves toppling towards the beach. Intrepid boys on surfboards rode those walls of water. Further round to the south was a wild, pounding, sucking blowhole, called the Bogey Hole, while to the north a narrow road ran along the causeway to the Nobbys Head at the mouth of the Hunter River and its port.

From our clifftop the view north looked straight across Port Hunter, with its channels, breakwaters and docks, its tugs and ferries and, on the skyline, the belching chimneys of the BHP steelworks. Over there

4 Beside the Lake

was the Industry which supported the whole region and coated everything in black grime. Down below us buzzed the Trade and Commerce of the city. The Cathedral was up on the Spiritual heights, visible for miles. Nature ruled down at the blowhole. Thus the great forces of life were plainly on show in Newcastle and the broad brush-strokes of that extensive backdrop remained indelibly in my mind, even though I left Newcastle at the age of five and didn't return for over fifty years. The smaller details of daily existence are much harder to recall.

The cathedral tower had not yet been built, but the nave was a massive structure of reddish brown brick, supported by flying buttresses and with a circular rose window at the west end. From inside and outside the building my eyes were drawn to the beautiful design of that window, although it was more like a daisy than a rose. In the grounds below it stood a rustic wooden belfry. Every Sunday, Billy, an old man from the nearby mental hospital, sat in the belfry pulling the bell rope to announce the services.

Newcastle Cathedral c. 1930. The rose window can be seen at the left end. The New Deanery was to the right, and Father's Whippet is parked in Church Street.

I escaped going to 'big' church very often, because of my age. Father was firm in his belief that a long service was no place for toddlers and he encouraged their removal before he had to preach the sermon. There was a children's service in one of the cathedral chapels early on Sunday mornings, and I was handed Sunday School stamps on these occasions. I enjoyed sticking these big, bright stamps in a book and studying them, for they included colourful portraits of bleeding martyrs, and in particular the Stoning of St Stephen. I understood that St Stephen was a good man and I wasn't sure what he had done to deserve this fate, but, whatever it was, my first memorable religious idea was that of being stoned to death.

Near the cathedral gate grew a very small tree; its limbs were low and spreading, and it aroused adventurous impulses. I went to our cook, Veta, and asked her to make me a squashed banana sandwich, with sugar. She was a very co-operative person and followed these instructions, which included wrapping the sandwich and putting it in a paper bag. I then set out on an expedition to the tree, all alone, climbed into it and ate my picnic, feeling brave and happy. Thus began a long career of tree climbing.

Squashed banana sandwiches, bread and butter sprinkled with sugar, and milk arrowroot biscuits were among my favourite foods, but I was a fussy eater otherwise. I approved of 'bar-cel' soup (made with barley and celery), and when my parents discovered that I would eat any soup called bar-cel, they were not above deceiving me. I developed a strange yearning for raw tripe. Realising that Veta would not be likely to give me raw tripe to eat, I invented a starving cat in the alley beside the house and, as Veta was cutting up tripe at that moment, could I please have a bit for puss? She fell for my sob-story and I escaped to the alley to enjoy a prolonged, leathery chew. This suggests that my powers of invention were already well developed; it also shows that deception could work both ways.

The alley was actually a very steep flight of cement steps down the side of the Deanery, because the house was built against the cliff. There were steps everywhere. The house had two storeys facing the street and one storey on the upper level, facing the cathedral. Owing to this peculiar arrangement, I find the inside disposition of the rooms very hard to recall. There was a carpeted flight of stairs with a security gate at the top for us children, and I think that most of our life was lived on the upper level, while Father's study or office was below, approached from Newcomen Street.

6   Beside the Lake

Upstairs on the ocean side there was a long, enclosed balcony where I played a lot. In the room where I slept, I can remember being in the cot, which had broad, brown bars and slats. Sometimes I was put into it out of the way while Mother and Doris, the maid, rolled up the carpet square and washed or swept the floor. When I was a bit older, and no longer cot-bound, I loved to crouch behind the carpet roll and pretend I was hiding in a foxhole or bunker. This strange pretence arose directly from a picture in a book – a drawing of three Bedouin warriors, with cartridge belts slung round their chests. They were sitting cosily in a deep foxhole in the desert, safe behind banked up mounds of sand draped with gorgeous rugs, and each had a rifle at the ready. Palm trees waved in the background. The appeal of this picture is a mystery, except that I craved the womb-like security of the foxhole.

Doris, the maid, lived with us in a room on the lower level. Doris and Veta were both young and attractive; Veta was married from the Deanery before we left Newcastle, a cathedral wedding with Doris as her bridesmaid, and Doris married later on. They were very kind to me and fond of playing practical jokes, such as bringing to the dining table a boiled egg which, when cracked, proved to be an empty shell. One of Doris's first tasks each morning was to clean the fireplaces and I trailed

A cathedral in our backyard. A recent photo of Newcastle Cathedral (now with tower). The New Deanery is at far left.

round after her watching, rapt, as she methodically swept up the ashes into a bucket, then sponged the hearth tiles with a soapy cloth and rinsed them until they shone. The daily routine, the tidiness, the gleaming green tiles, all were so reassuring. Black coal was used in the fires.

Other shadowy figures were a baby sitter, Mrs Percy, and a washerwoman who came once a week. I can see Mrs Percy as elderly, clad in black and always seated in an armchair. Did she never rise from her chair to deal with the demands of an energetic child and a baby? The washerwoman, Mrs Knowles, washed all the morning and ironed all the afternoon for ten shillings ($1). She did this five days a week in different houses and raised her family on that £2/10/- ($5), as her husband was unemployed.

The laundry was typical of its time, with a copper, a huge handwringer clamped to the trough and a ripply glass washboard on which stubborn stains were lathered and rubbed with bar soap. But one day an itinerant salesman called at the door, trying to interest the lady of the house in a miracle machine which washed clothes by itself. 'How much does it cost?' asked Mother, in amazement. 'Twenty-nine pounds, Madam.' Madam recoiled from such extravagance, but the salesman pleaded a chance to demonstrate the miracle in action and, providentially, Father appeared just in time to witness it. 'You must have it!' Father announced, being rather in favour of miracles, and we did. It remained in the family for at least twenty-five years, with scarcely a chip off its grey enamel.

Two other people came to the house on a regular basis. Miss Street came to cut our hair. After one of her visits the house was filled with an acrid smell, for she singed the ends of the newly cut locks with a taper. Miss Monahan was a dressmaker who would be engaged for several days at a time to make clothes for us and to alter and mend things. Girls didn't wear trousers and many of our garments were hand-me-downs. I didn't like any of my clothes much, then or later.

I was born at the height of the Great Depression, and in those years men often came to the door in search of work or money or food. Father set one of them to grow vegetables in the Deanery garden. Others were never turned away hungry, and I sometimes sat with them on a garden seat while they ate slabs of bread and jam and drank tea from enamel mugs. They rarely spoke and I wondered why they looked so sad, unshaven and shabby. Father visited destitute families living in shacks among the sand dunes along the Nobbys beach. Dorothy and I must have accompanied him sometimes, for she remembers the shack walls being made of flattened kerosene tins and other scrap materials, while I was intrigued by the little borders and boundaries of stones which the occupants laid in the sand between their 'properties'.

Father drove a 1928 Whippet, a chugging brown car with a square canvas top, wheezing horn, and flapping celluloid side-curtains which let in most of the draughts while obscuring the view. It often needed cranking to get it started. It also had 'running boards', wide steps below the doors, and for me the chief thrill of car travel was being allowed to ride for a short distance on the step. Travelling in the back seat of the Whippet was rather like being in a dark, padded box, bouncing about, unable to see, sometimes feeling sick. Water was apt to get into the engine, so Father cobbled together a white canvas cover which he lashed over the leaky bonnet. Dorothy was so embarrassed about driving around Newcastle in this grotesque vehicle that she claims it almost ruined her childhood. She remembered with affection the car which Father had driven in Adelaide; it had no side curtains to block her view. As they drove sedately along North Terrace and turned around the policeman on point duty, Father would say, 'Good morning, constable!' and the reply would come, 'Good morning, sir!'.

In Newcastle, picnics became legendary. One was to Glen Rock Lagoon, where Father parked the car on a steep incline. When departure time came and he started the engine, the Whippet began to roll backwards. Bravely, Father ordered the family out while he wrestled to engage first gear before the brakes slipped and the car sailed backwards into the lagoon. The high emotional temperature of this episode was set by Mother who, clutching her children around her and anticipating imminent widowhood, was having the vapours. Thereafter, the very name of Glen Rock Lagoon was doom-laden, even though Father and the Whippet survived.

The other outing was to Lake Macquarie, where we sometimes went to buy fish from a man Father had known in the army. On this occasion I fell off a jetty into the lake, where I floated face down until rescued by the fisherman. His wife lent me some dry clothes in which I paraded theatrically in front of Doris when we arrived home. It was easy to be brave after the event, but for many years I had a fear of jetties and the sight of water through cracks in the decking made me shake.

Dorothy was already at secondary school by the time I began my formal education. Across the street from the cathedral, and up yet more steps, was a small infant school run by Miss Buick in a church hall. It was known in our family as 'Boo's School'. There were writing lessons at Boo's, doing rows of pothooks and forming letters. At the edge of memory I can glimpse a school reader of the 'John and Betty' variety, but I have no sense of learning to read. The word 'hippopotamus' entranced me because of its length, its rolling syllables and the bizarre animal which it represented. Behind it float images of a visit to Taronga Park Zoo in Sydney and of an animal alphabet book at home, which included obscure creatures like the ibex and the quagga. Probably from this book I learned to spell 'hippopotamus' correctly, while pronouncing it 'hittopotamus'.

Boo lined all the children up at playtime, boys in one file and girls in another, and we were marched into a dank yard to the bleak toilets. There, one after another, we were expected 'to go'. My natural shyness and fastidiousness rebelled against this regime and on three consecutive days I said to Boo, in a well-rehearsed speech, 'I don't feel like going today, thank you.' I suppose she couldn't force the issue, but on those three days I went home in tears and wet pants. This is my most vivid memory of that first school; no wonder I didn't like it. I don't remember making any friends.

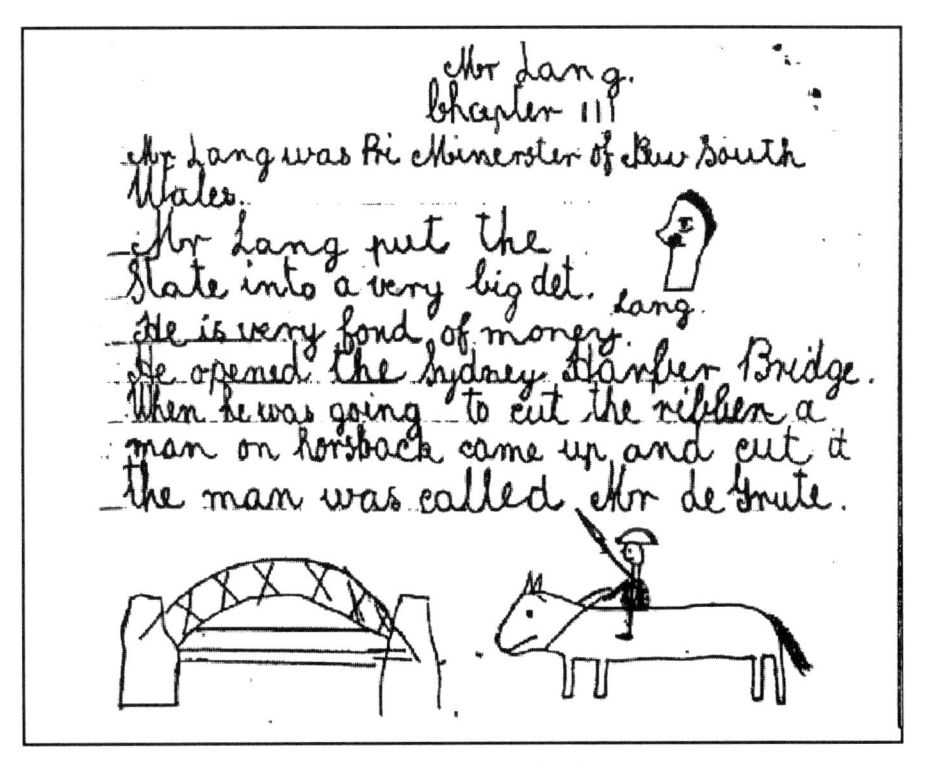

Dorothy (aged 8) tackles current affairs at Boo's School, 1932

Father, with his long thin legs, was very good at the bouncing-on-the knees game. After an unpredictable number of bounces to build up suspense, the knees would open wide and the child would fall through. But sitting on parental laps was also associated with books. Mother was keen on the poems of A.A. Milne. Dorothy's favourite must have been 'Tattoo was the mother of Pinkle Purr, A small black kitten without much fur ...', for she and Mother were known to each other as Pink and Tat for the rest of their lives. My own favourite was 'The King's Breakfast', with its cosy, domestic view of royalty and messages being passed down the line from the King to the Queen to the Dairymaid to the cow, and back again. The strong beat of 'James James Morrison Morrison Weatherby George Dupree ...' was irresistible, and E.H. Shepard's drawings of London pavements, with bears waiting to capture careless persons who trod on the lines, still flash across my mind as I walk on footpaths today, carefully avoiding the joins! London and the idea of monarchy were thus absorbed very early into my consciousness. So were the very satisfactory notions of rhyme, metre and the patterning of language.

Father was most partial to the Uncle Remus stories. As Mother and Dorothy had become Tat and Pink, he and I went through a season of being Brer Fox and Brer Rabbit. This little charade was ruined when a small boy at Boo's School rebuked me – 'You mustn't call the Dean a fox!' Father laughed, but I squirmed at having my private life intruded upon in this way.

J.M. Barrie's *Peter Pan and Wendy* was much in vogue at that time, and Mother made me a Peter Pan costume for some fancy dress affair. It was brown and yellow with a pointy, zig-zag hemline, and there was a little elvish cap. I drew many pictures of elves along these lines. Often they were wading through long grass, mainly because I discovered an efficient way to draw grass by using squirty pencil strokes moving upwards from the roots. But the really rousing characters in Peter Pan were Captain James Hook and Pirate Smee. I was hooked by the whole romantic tradition of piracy – black hats, earrings, twirling moustaches, eye-patches and missing limbs, swishing swords and cutlasses, the Jolly Roger, walking the plank, treasure chests, and maps proclaiming 'X marks the spot'.

There were other books such as *Winnie the Pooh*, and *The Just-so Stories* by Kipling. I relished 'the great grey-green, greasy Limpopo River, all set about with fever-trees' in 'The Elephant's Child' and the way Kipling addressed his reader as 'O best beloved!' Epaminondas and Little Black

Sambo were still politically acceptable then, as were golliwogs.

There were also other dressings-up; photos show me as a white rabbit and as the Mary who had a little lamb. Fancy dress parties must have been in vogue, and Mother obviously went to great trouble to make the costumes. I took no interest in dolls. There was a golliwog and perhaps a teddy bear, but my favourite toy and best friend was a fairly small but hideous orangutan called Binker.

Fancy Dress. Dorothy (left) on the steps of the Old Deanery, c. 1929. Me (right) as the White Rabbit, c. 1935.

PANTECHNICON

In 1936 Father announced that on a certain day the Pantechnicon would be coming, and from then on nobody thought of calling it a furniture van. Here was a noble word for my collection, even more imposing than hippopotamus! It encapsulated everything to do with our Move. Our lives were to be packed up into that word and trundled holus bolus to distant Victoria.

I don't remember much about the packing up, but after the Pantechnicon had driven away I made the dreadful discovery that

Binker had been packed in a tea chest and was well on his way interstate. I would have to endure the journey without him!

We drove south from Newcastle in a gleaming new car, a cream Ford V8, which had replaced the chugging Whippet just in time for the journey. (Its registration number, 248 096, and that of Father's next car are permanently engraved in my memory, yet I am hard put to remember the number of the car I drive today.) The Ford V8 was a streamlined marvel with a hard top, winding glass windows and a boot, but, although it promised to be the last word in modern motoring, our progress down the highway was not without setbacks. To drive from Newcastle to Ballarat in those days was a fairly intrepid thing to do, as there were no freeways, of course, and the highways were narrow and winding. Near Gosford it was necessary to take a car ferry, which slowed things down even more.

This was not my first experience of a long journey. A couple of years earlier we had travelled to Adelaide by sea, to visit grandmother Marmie, Father's mother. All I remember of the ship is the dark cabin, its bunks full of prostrate bodies – including mine. On arrival in Adelaide, I explained to Marmie that we had all had 'influenza' during the voyage.

Departure day in October 1936 was ferociously hot with a howling wind, and my best dress, hung out at the last minute to dry, blew away without trace. As we drove off through Newcastle, friends waved farewell from their gates and verandahs and Mother began to weep. Father said, with a touch of desperation, 'Now that we're off, we won't stop until we reach Sydney.' He was quite wrong, but at least Mother was soon diverted from her tears, for the baby, Elizabeth, was sick twelve times and bushfires haunted us all the way. And I was traumatised by the separation from Binker and not ready to forgive whoever had stowed him in a tea chest.

While this journey is in progress, let us take a closer look at the passengers in the car.

Binker

THUMBNAIL PORTRAITS

At the wheel was Father, William Herbert Johnson, aged forty-seven. He was driving all that way to Ballarat to become a bishop, not that I understood much about that. (The new car, and perhaps the washing machine, were signs of his new status and a rise in salary.)

He was born in Adelaide, South Australia, in 1889 and became an Anglican clergyman. Before I was born in 1930, he had become Dean of Newcastle, and at that time he was known variously as Mr Johnson, Mr Dean, Bill and Daddy. When he reached Ballarat and the bishopric, his official signature changed mysteriously to 'William Ballarat'. He was now called Bishop, His Lordship, My Lord, and still (by us) Bill, Daddy, Pa, Pop and Father. (Like most families, ours had a complex scheme of pet names, so to save confusion I shall henceforth refer to our parents as Father and Mother, and to my sisters by their given names.)

Father was tall, thin and balding. All his life he suffered from migraine headaches, but despite this he was energetic and gregarious. He was buoyed up by a great sense of humour, and he was going to need it in the years to come. A sense of humour was near the top of his catalogue of human virtues, it being a sign of optimism, tolerance and a generous spirit.

Father worked hard through terrible times, but he always made room for his family and never lost touch with his own childhood. He had a boyish enthusiasm for things like picnics, games of Rummy, circuses and pantomimes, yabbying, beach holidays and, on this occasion, for driving a thousand miles across Australia to his new job. He had grown up in the Adelaide suburb of Brighton, where his own father, Samuel Johnson, an Irishman from County Cork, was the superintendent of a school for blind and deaf children. The family had lived at the school, surrounded by gardens and orchards and the sandhills leading down to the beach; Father's childhood was free and happy, and he wanted the same for us. One tragic event of his boyhood, however, had been the death of his eleven-year-old elder brother from tetanus after cutting his hand with a knife. Father entertained us with tales of his own juvenile pranks and scrapes, and as an adult he never forgot that children, like young animals, need to let off steam and burn up energy.

Beside him in the passenger seat, drying her tears and nursing the car-sick baby, sat Mother, Frances Dymphna Johnson, née de Chair. She was known at home as Dym, Tat, Mummy, Ma, Mother, and abroad as Mrs Johnson. People often said to us in later life, 'Oh, your mother was a real lady', by which I think they meant that she had a natural dignity and charm. On the other hand, she hadn't a trace of vanity and hated having her photograph taken. She was attractive, with thick, wavy, brown hair which in later life became a halo of snow white.

Mother was born in 1894, in Brisbane, and her childhood was difficult. Her own mother, one of twelve children, came from the pioneering Yeates family in outback Queensland. Ten of the children had accompanied their parents on the overland trek of seven hundred miles from Bowen to far southwest Queensland in 1880. They travelled in covered wagons drawn by twenty-four working bullocks and took with them all their possessions, twelve hundred sheep and a milch cow. The youngest child was then one year old and my grandmother was fifteen.

However, Mother's father, Ernest de Chair, was an Englishman who had been in the Royal Navy before his marriage. His family boasted a crop of naval officers and two of them, admirals Rawson and de Chair, served as governors of New South Wales at different times. When Father's appointment to Ballarat was announced, much was made in the press of Mother's connection to the previous governor, her uncle Sir Dudley de Chair. The exotic name, the knighthood, the vice-regal status, the ties with 'the old country' and the Royal Navy all carried a lot of weight in that society of the 1930s, although they were quite irrelevant to Father's new job and really no more remarkable than the pioneering exploits of the Yeates family. Britannia still ruled the waves, however.

The difficult name de Chair was French Huguenot in origin, and we three girls were presented with it as our second name. Most girls I knew had second names like Jean or Anne, so I tried to suppress mine, especially as people would pronounce it 'dee Chair' as in armchair, and not 'd'Share' in the French way.

On his marriage certificate my grandfather Ernest de Chair described his occupation as 'gentleman', which doesn't sound very arduous. This union of two families on opposite sides of the world was not uncommon in those days, I suppose, when young Englishmen were sent out to the colonies to look around and be toughened up, but the two-way pull led to difficulties. Mother and her little sister were taken 'home' to visit their English grandparents in 1901. Mother (aged nearly seven) caught scarlet fever and was put in an isolation ward in a London hospital. One day she was visited by a strange woman wearing a mask. The woman, a family connection, had been sent to tell the child that her mother had died suddenly. I try to imagine this apparition, the masked Messenger of Death – surely the stuff of nightmares! Mother's mother had indeed died, of a clot, leaving these two small daughters. Their English granny coped for a while – there seemed to be no question of their father doing so, and in any case he also died a year or two later. Eventually the little girls were sent back to Australia by ship and thereafter were brought up by various kind Australian aunts and uncles. These early experiences didn't seem to have blighted Mother's life, beyond establishing in her a certain sense of insecurity; in fact, they made her a sympathetic and kindly person, very sensitive to other people's feelings and problems.

The family in 1936, just prior to leaving Newcastle. Mother holds a sleepy Elizabeth, while I hold Binker. My dirty shoes are a disgrace.

16   Beside the Lake

In her arms was Elizabeth, then about one year old and not yet walking. She had been a premature baby when born in Newcastle in 1935, and I had been unaware of her imminent arrival. When taken to visit Mother and baby in hospital, I was unimpressed by the sight of a very little sister (who looked suspiciously like a doll), but overjoyed to find a packet of Columbine Caramels on Mother's bedside table. Thereafter, visits to the hospital focussed on those caramels in their shiny blue wrapping. The name Elizabeth eluded my infant tongue, so I very soon shortened it to 'Lea' which has been her pet name ever since.

In the back seat of the car, twelve-year-old Dorothy (Dordy, Pink, Dotty, Dot, Dittle) was very excited about the journey south. She, likewise, had not been prepared for my arrival in the world five years earlier. On that occasion she was packed off to spend the day with Boo, and when told later that there was a surprise for her at home, she had exclaimed, 'Goody, is it my new wardrobe?' and was disappointed to find only a baby sister. Such were the demands of propriety in those days, at least in our family. We were shielded from such things as pregnancy and birth, and thus were quite unprepared for the sudden appearance of siblings.

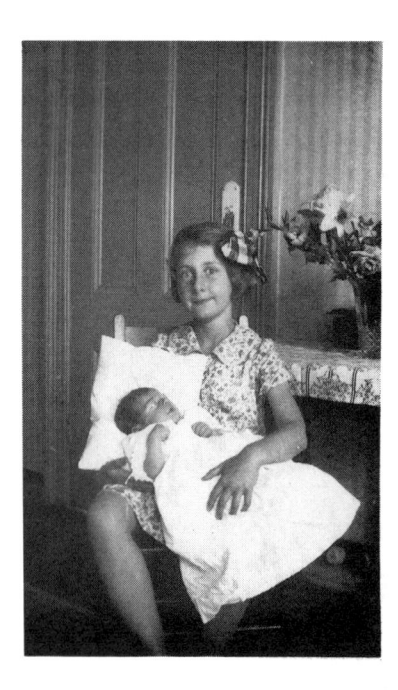

Unprepared for siblings. (Left) 1930 – Dorothy, grimacing, holds me. (Right) 1935 – I, unused to dolls, hold Elizabeth.

Dorothy herself had been born at home in an Adelaide rectory in 1924. Father and the housekeeper, waiting in the kitchen, heard the baby cry, but when no summons was forthcoming from the doctor, Father went to investigate. He found the baby growing cold on one bed while Mother was being attended to in the other, so he carried off his firstborn to revive her. His solution was to climb into his winter pyjamas, tuck the baby inside next to his chest, put his little fingertip in her mouth and go to bed. There they stayed cosily until next morning, well and truly bonded.

Also travelling with us in the back seat of the car was Doris, who was going to stay in Ballarat for a few weeks in order to help Mother settle into the new house. Being small, I was squashed into the middle of either the front or the back seat, depending on whose turn it was to endure my wriggling.

So, the Ford V8 was full. Every spare nook must have been filled with baby gear, including a pusher (although there would have been room for Binker). It took us over a week to reach Ballarat, staying overnight in hotels along the way, in a manner reminiscent of the old stage coach journeys.

SOUTHWARD HO!

On the way I behaved badly, partly because, like the Elephant's Child, I had a 'satiable curtiosity'(sic). I suppose, too, that I felt insecure because of this disruption to our lives. In North Sydney, I eluded the adults and darted into the road to sit on the 'silent cop', a metal hemisphere which marked the centre of a large intersection – I was attracted to it because it looked like a giant poached egg. In Albury I tipped the baby out of her pusher, while in Seymour I released the handbrake of the car when it was angle-parked on a steep kerb, because I wanted to know how the handbrake worked. Luckily Father arrived just in time to prevent us from pranging a light pole. Somehow, we managed to complete the journey to Melbourne. On our first halt there to do some shopping, Mother was mortified to see the baby's potty roll out of the car into the heart of Kew Junction. That, at least, was not my fault.

In Melbourne, relatives had begun to gather, first for the service in St Paul's Cathedral at which the new bishop was to be consecrated, and then, next day, for the Enthronement service in Christ Church Cathedral, Ballarat. (Elizabeth and I were not present at either, which was a wise decision.) Before these ceremonies took place, I think our parents must have gone to Ballarat for a day, taking Doris and leaving

18   Beside the Lake

us in the care of relatives in Melbourne. How else could the logistical problems have been overcome – those of receiving the pantechnicon and its contents, arranging furniture, having the house and larder ready for the influx of children, staff and several relatives who were coming to stay? And between the two ceremonies, one in Melbourne, the second next day in Ballarat, Father had to drive the rest of us up that narrow, winding road onto the Ballarat plateau. He must have been very tired at the end of that week.

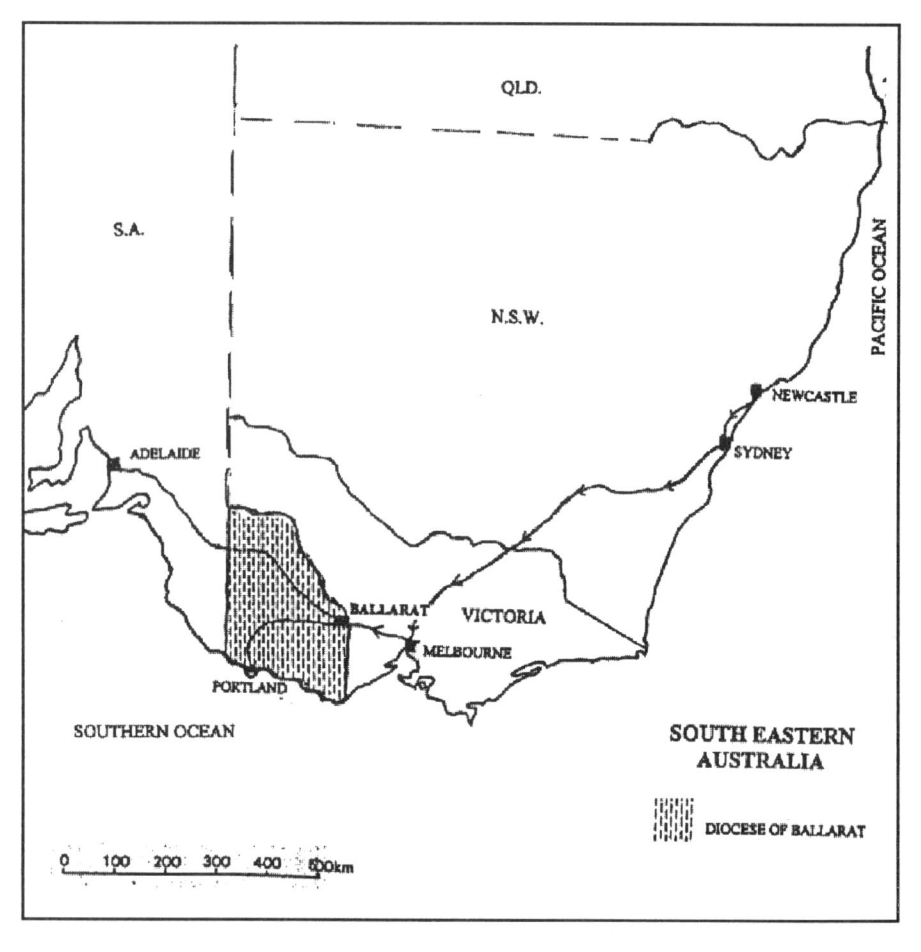

Route map to the south.

Opposite Sturt Street, Ballarat, looking west. An early view showing the towers, flags and tramway. Father drove up the right-hand carriageway. (SHGM postcard)

A Colonial Barchester

WE ARRIVE IN BALLARAT

Before we set out for our new home, my elders had no doubt been briefed about the climate and topography of Ballarat, and the fame of its gold-fields, but I grasped none of these facts except that there was going to be a lake. Remembering the close shave in Lake Macquarie, I wondered if a lake would be much good.

Dorothy was mortified by our manner of arrival in our new home town. Father negotiated the busy bottleneck of Bridge Street (now a pedestrian mall), only to find himself adrift in the enormous arena at the other end, facing one of Australia's finest streets, the grand dual carriageway of Sturt Street with its divided one-way traffic system. Confused, he headed into the right-hand carriageway and advanced doggedly up the wrong side of the main thoroughfare. The fact that nobody took much notice of our eccentric progress suggests that Ballarat was a sleepy hollow, with minimal traffic. I was probably so glad to arrive that I didn't mind which side of the street we used to reach our goal (and Binker), and I don't remember the incident.

My first clear memory is of the horse-drawn cabs which stood in a funereal rank outside the railway station when we went to meet the relations who were steaming up from Melbourne that same day. Dorothy and I persuaded our indulgent Uncle Hal to hire one of these lugubrious, black-hooded vehicles. We crammed into the dark interior, snibbed the little flapping door behind us and set off along Lydiard Street in gales of giggles at the driver's back. The old cab turned right and lurched up the full, regal length of Sturt Street, passing grand and weighty buildings with towers or lace balconies, then turned into Wendouree Parade beside the lake – there it was – big! We swung into a driveway under huge, dark cypress trees, and finally clattered to a halt at the front steps of our new home. Despite our giddy behaviour, we had chosen by far the most fitting manner of arrival, for the grand old house, with its carriage sweep around the fountain, had long known the swish of wheels and the clatter of hooves. One really needed a carriage and four to bowl up the drive to Bishopscourt, but even a one-horse cab was a more appropriate conveyance than the Ford V8.

Bowling up the drive to our new home, Bishopscourt, Ballarat 1936

From the moment of our arrival, the grown-ups were all extremely busy. For example, three days in succession were set aside for 'At Homes', so that people could call at Bishopscourt to meet our parents and to leave their visiting cards in the brass tray in the hall. These cards entitled our parents to a return visit.

A few years later when Elizabeth started school, she was asked to describe her father's occupation. The question had to be rephrased – 'What sort of work does he do, dear?' (as if they didn't know!). 'Oh!' said she, airily, 'my father doesn't work, he's a bishop.'

Father himself was mightily amused by this, realising that his small daughter was confused by the fact that he didn't go 'out' to work each day, driving trams or selling fruit and vegetables. But this 'idle' cleric had many occupations – as pastor, preacher, administrator of a large diocese, civic leader, host, diplomat and adviser. He conducted confirmation services and regularly visited parishes all over western Victoria. He presided over councils and committees and attended bishops' meetings in Melbourne and Sydney. He worried about diocesan finances, clergy problems and appointments, and he presided over the two diocesan school councils. He was a communicator, editing the Church Chronicle, writing to the newspapers and broadcasting. An endless stream of letters flowed from his desk, and he read a lot, keeping up with politics and current affairs.

Like all clergy wives in those days (and often today), Mother was expected to devote herself to church affairs, by serving on or presiding over committees in organisations like the Mothers' Union, the Girls' Friendly Society, the Missions to Seamen, the Travellers' Aid Society (in Melbourne) and, later, the Red Cross. She provided hospitality for official visitors, accompanied Father on his round of church and civic duties, visited the sick, answered the phone, ran the household and so on. I heard a new word, 'auxiliary', usually applied to groups of women. In many areas, the 'ladies' auxiliary' existed to raise funds, but women parishioners were also expected (like housewives) to provide tea and cakes, to wash up, to do the flowers, to launder church linen, to clean the brass. Although, as bishop's wife, Mother didn't have to help in these ways at parish level, she nevertheless did the same sorts of things as Father's auxiliary. This didn't leave her much time for her children.

At the end of 1936 Dorothy was sent to school for the remainder of the term, but, as it was by then November, and I was only just six, it was decided that my schooling could wait until the new year.

So, Dorothy went to school; Elizabeth couldn't yet walk and was in charge of a nurse; and I went mildly feral.

A TOWER

Our new home was vast. It had about twenty-five rooms and its grounds covered eight acres (over three hectares). That did not mean that we were wealthy landowners: the house did not belong to us, but to the Anglican Church. Clergymen were rarely well off (usually the opposite), but they were apt to find themselves living in large, rambling mansions, especially in older places like Ballarat, and bishops' houses rambled in an even more extravagant manner than vicarages.

I became an explorer. This was a much more romantic house than the modern one we had left behind in Newcastle. Most obviously, there was a tower! I already associated towers with stories of imprisoned damsels and wicked goings-on, which suggests some knowledge of fairy tales, and naturally I headed for this tower soon after arrival. It was a disappointment – no dusty treasure chests, no cracked mirrors, no sleeping princesses, not even bats. A doorway near the kitchen led to it, up a narrow wooden staircase. A box-room halfway up smelt musty and the tower-room itself was empty, small and unromantic. It was, after all, only a lookout. Its original purpose, I suppose, had been to command the fine view across the lake, but by 1936 this view had vanished behind the screen of trees in front of the house, although there still remained a good overview of the estate.

'Old' Bishopscourt, taken in 1939 after the garden beds in front had been cleared. The main entrance was behind the urns and the large bay with steps was the study. (CFE)

At the front was the driveway up which our horse-cab had clattered, over-arched by those huge, gothic cypresses. At the end of the drive, just in front of the house, was a large, sandy-coloured fountain in the centre of a circular carriage sweep. To the left side of the tower lay the main lawns and shrubberies, with a neglected orchard and vegetable garden hedged in towards the front fence. To the right side were various out-buildings, stables and paddocks, relics from the days of horse-drawn bishops. A large fowl-run (with resident chooks) lay against the far fence and the Ford V8 slumbered in a garage near the distant stables. On this same side, towards the lake, were the empty buildings of a disused theological college, St Aidan's, and the Warden's House, which had been leased out. Next to our house stood a red-brick chapel and its tall wooden belfry. The college and the chapel made up, slightly, for the lack of a cathedral in the backyard.

From the rear windows of the tower could be seen the bulk of the house itself, with its squadron of ornamental brick chimneys, and beyond that the service driveway to the sheds and garage, the back gate into Gregory Street, and a geometrical flower garden where blooms were produced for use indoors. Roses climbed on rustic arches and below them grew what seemed to us a floral profusion, after the wind-swept seaboard of Newcastle. Dahlias were abundant and I particularly remember little borders of linaria and mignonette.

I have since tried to visualise this estate in earlier, more spacious days – a carriage or two in a coach house and horses in the stables, with a groom to manage them; several gardeners to produce fruit, vegetables and flowers for the house, and to keep the enormous expanses of gravel and lawns in trim; St Aidan's College occupied by the theological students, with the Warden and his family in their house; the bell summoning the students to prayer in the chapel or to meals, for in earlier days part of the chapel was a refectory; visitors bowling up the driveway in their gigs and carriages; and numbers of servants to keep the house running smoothly. Anthony Trollope, the English novelist, had visited Ballarat in 1871 and been impressed by what he saw. As the author of the celebrated 'Barchester' novels, which dealt with clerical life in the English provinces, he would have felt reasonably at home had he called at Bishopscourt, Ballarat, a decade or so later, for here was a veritable colonial 'Barchester'!

The old mansion, formerly called Strathalbyn House, had been built in the 1860s. The original owner was said to have made his fortune from gold (and lost it again), and his was surely the sort of house which Henry

24 Beside the Lake

Handel Richardson described in *The Fortunes of Richard Mahony*, where people such as Henry Ocock lived in opulence 'on the farther side of Yuille's Swamp' (which became Lake Wendouree). Ballarat's first Anglican bishop, Samuel Thornton, had arrived from England in 1875 to find that he had nowhere suitable to live. For the next few years he regularly reminded his diocese of this fact until, in 1879, this property (valued at £8000) was acquired cheaply for £4500 as the bishop's residence. Still in the garden in our day was a small marble tombstone engraved DEAR TIP AGED 13 1892, presumably the first episcopal pet. (There was a legend, perhaps apocryphal, that Dear Tip had once attacked the Dean as he walked up the drive, and torn the seat out of his pants. The Dean, it was said, retired behind a bush until suitable help arrived.)

Thornton's successor, Bishop A.V. Green (1900 – 17), left more substantial landmarks behind him. The house was extended, St Aidan's College was built and opened in 1903, and the chapel was erected.

A colonial Barchester! Christmas at Bishopscourt, 1888. Bishop and Mrs Thornton on verandah at left, with more horse-drawn visitors approaching up the drive. Visible are the urns, the box hedges and the fountain, but where are the ladies? (DBA)

SERVANTS

It will be clear that I was born into a society where the idea of domestic service was taken for granted. The very existence of such an estate as Bishopscourt depended on the presence and labour of staff. Bishop and Mrs Maxwell-Gumbleton (1917 – 27) had four staff for the house and four more for the outside work, we were told. And when they went on tour round the diocese, they went in a chauffeur-driven car; the chauffeur doubled as a valet and Mrs Maxwell-Gumbleton took a personal maid. I believe that this sort of royal progress didn't go down very well in Australian country hotels. The Maxwell-Gumbletons were English.

In those earlier days the students at St Aidan's were another source of manpower when needed. There were no students for us to call on, for the college had closed in 1932, a victim of the Depression. In 1936, we started off with Doris, and Mother had asked Jean, a former parishioner from Adelaide, to come and be the baby's nurse. Mr Scruse, who lived out, was already employed as the sole gardener. He sometimes turned into a chauffeur for Mother (who didn't drive), by putting on a peaked cap and a dust-coat, and in moments of crisis his wife provided additional help in the house. She was there at the outset and fairly often thereafter, for the image of gracious living in the style of Barchester died hard. Despite the bleak economic climate of the times, an effort had to be made to keep up appearances; bishops, after all, lived in Courts and Palaces!

However, the supply of well-trained servants seemed to be waning, and during our first years in Ballarat, up to 1939, there was a fairly regular turnover in our cooks and housemaids. The first cook had a husband attached, so they were employed as a 'married couple', although I don't think his duties were very clearly defined (and he had a bad temper). Her culinary repertoire was extremely limited, soggy meat fritters being her main standby, especially for breakfast. She was followed fairly rapidly by Nellie, a very Irish Irishwoman of great personality. Once, when the entire household was being rounded up to look at a superlative rainbow over the lake, Nellie replied, 'Oh no, thank you, Oi 've seen one of dose!' And on a dark night when she had walked home alone up the drive beneath the black trees, 'Glory be to God!' she shrieked, on arrival. 'Oi came up dat droive with me bag in one hand and me heart in the other!' By 1939, perhaps on account of her nerves, Nellie had been replaced by Lilian. A housemaid called Thelma was with us for some of that period, after Doris had returned north.

The domestic service system was of course a product (and a reinforcer) of the class system, and while class divisions in Australia were, mercifully, never as rigid as those in England, a sort of hierarchy nevertheless existed. The master and the mistress of the house gave the orders and the staff carried them out. The state of relationships between the two camps depended very much on the attitude of the employers, and also on the touchiness of the staff. At times, I think, Mother found it quite a strain to keep a happy equilibrium, but on the whole my parents were kind and co-operative employers, added to which they were Australians. (Previous bishops had been imported from England, with their English ways.) While the domestic service 'industry' then provided many with employment, being in service must often have been a drab and lonely life, especially in an isolated house like Bishopscourt.

In our family it seemed that the nurse had her own place in the hierarchy, for she ate her meals with us and at night she would often sit with Mother. It seemed to be customary to call the unmarried staff by their given names (Jean, Nellie), whereas the married ones were accorded the dignity of their titles (Mr and Mrs Scruse). I'm not sure, even now, if that was accidental or discriminatory. In any case, I didn't understand the subtle boundaries and spent some of my time in the kitchen or following the servants about, watching them perform their tasks, as I had been used to doing in Newcastle. But I missed the cameraderie of Doris and Veta.

THE OLD HOUSE

The servant system had a marked effect on domestic architecture, for a house which was large enough to need one or more servants inevitably grew even larger to accommodate them. While in England the servants' quarters would usually be 'below stairs' or in an attic, out here the division was mostly between back and front. Visitors came to the front door, tradesmen went to the back. There was often a label on a side or a back gate saying Tradesmen's Entrance. The servants' wing, containing bedrooms, a bathroom and perhaps a sitting-room, would be at the rear near the kitchen and the back door.

From the tower above, Bishopscourt was seen to be built as a square with a hole in the middle. This 'hole' was a square central courtyard, but it boasted none of today's chic courtyard accessories; its function was partly to provide light for the inner rooms and also for practical

A Colonial Barchester   27

affairs like airing the bedding. It was distinctly down-at-heel.

The front of the house, however, was clearly designed for gracious living. The drawing-room and the dining-room stretched across its full width, with their long sash windows looking across a wide verandah to the fountain and the drive. A Japanese wisteria, pure white, twined about the elegant iron pillars of the verandah, and in the springtime it was as though the elderly house appeared annually in a bridal veil, like Dickens's Miss Havisham in *Great Expectations*. Mother was moved to measure one of the white racemes at random: it was twenty-eight inches (seventy-one centimetres) long.

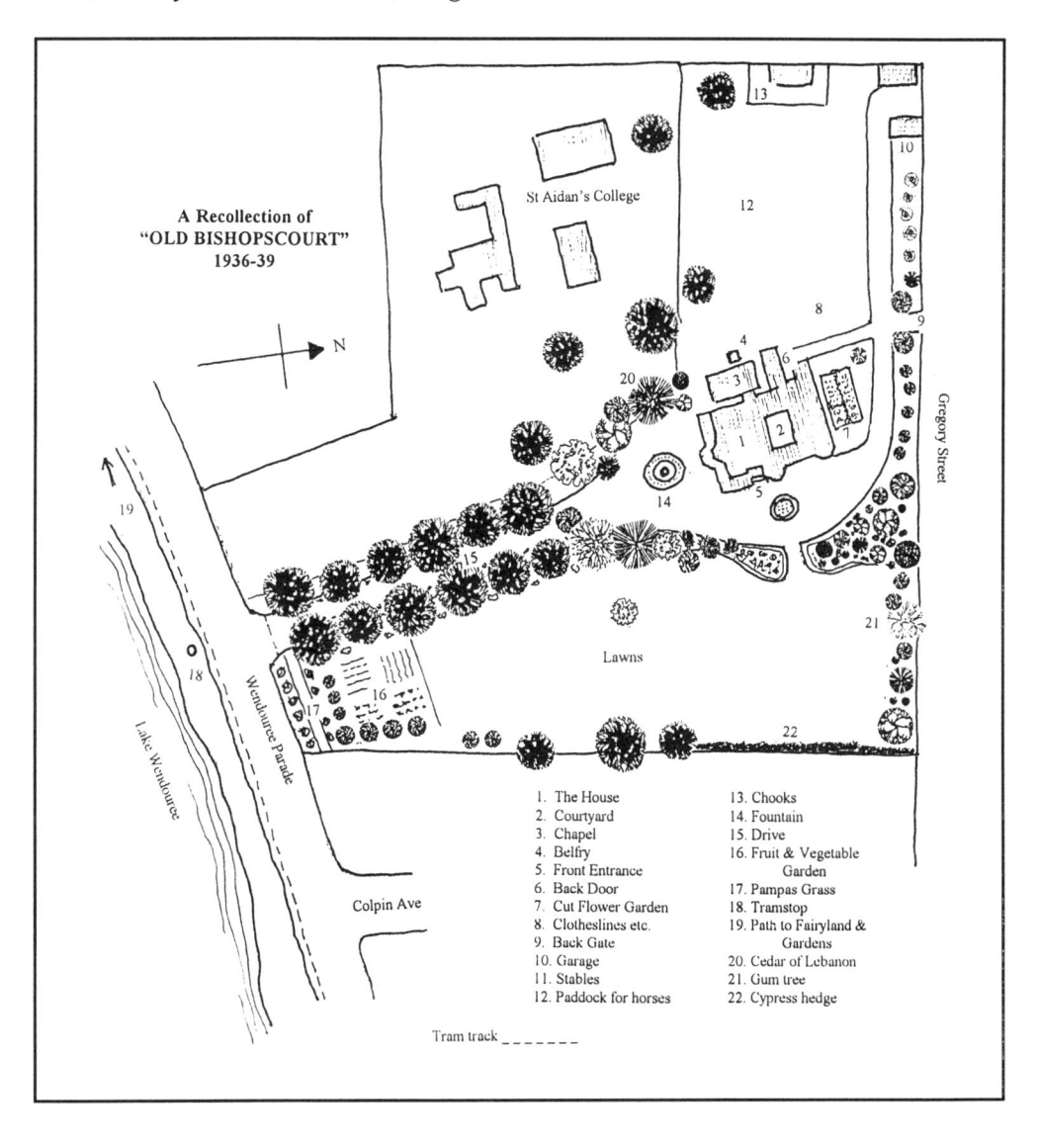

A Recollection of
"OLD BISHOPSCOURT"
1936-39

1. The House
2. Courtyard
3. Chapel
4. Belfry
5. Front Entrance
6. Back Door
7. Cut Flower Garden
8. Clotheslines etc.
9. Back Gate
10. Garage
11. Stables
12. Paddock for horses
13. Chooks
14. Fountain
15. Drive
16. Fruit & Vegetable Garden
17. Pampas Grass
18. Tramstop
19. Path to Fairyland & Gardens
20. Cedar of Lebanon
21. Gum tree
22. Cypress hedge

Tram track _ _ _ _ _ _ _

The verandah continued round to the east side where broad stone steps led up, between urns, to the main entrance. This faced out to another carriage sweep and the enormous lawns beyond. This gravel sweep and the other one around the fountain must have provided an efficient system of roundabouts to avert horse-drawn traffic jams in bygone days.

The entrance hall, running alongside the front reception rooms, was from memory something like twelve metres x three metres, with a beautiful floor of Victorian tiles, tan, blue and cream, in a geometric pattern. In later years, when this floor was removed, the tiles were found to be set straight on to banked up bare earth, with no form of grouting to secure them. Elizabeth, just learning to walk then, still remembers the pattern of this floor, and I loved skating on it in my socks. Each week or so the housemaid, on hands and knees and equipped with an iron bucket and sandsoap, scrubbed the floor from end to end.

At the far end of the hall there was a 'flower room', where all those cut flowers from the back garden were arranged for the house and where urns and vases were stored. Of the various small, specialised rooms to be found in this house, the flower room was one of the most useful. It also helped to keep the peace with whichever cook, who would not have welcomed swags of dahlias and snapdragons dumped on her kitchen draining board.

The drawing-room was a double room divided by a wide arch, and with very high ceilings. It swallowed up with ease innumerable couches and armchairs, occasional tables and the walnut piano. There were two elegant fireplaces with white marble mantels. The problems of heating the drawing-room did not become apparent to us until 1937, when we encountered our first Ballarat winter. The two elegant fireplaces with their cramped iron grates were no match for the lofty ceilings, seven long windows, and the arctic chill of the tiled entrance hall hard by. Primitive electric radiators, with pine-cone shaped elements, were used to supplement the fires, but to almost no effect, so we spent much of the time huddled in Father's study or in a small sitting-room next to it, both of which were more cosy, or in the dining-room where there was a ravenous, coke-eating Esse stove. The dining-room also contained a lot of oak furniture and a huge Turkey carpet.

In the summer, the drawing-room came into its own. The windows were shaded by the wide verandah, the green wisteria leaves filtered the glare, and the cool tiles of the hall were a blessing to hot, bare feet. Even baby Elizabeth found the mood relaxing; one summer's day she was found lying in the centre of the drawing-room's cream carpet, her legs waving lazily in the air, and her attention riveted to a book entitled *How to Conduct a Public Meeting*. This volume had no doubt been left lying about by Mother, who was trying to school herself to meet her official duties.

Across the entrance hall and facing into the shabby courtyard was a large guest-room with an equally large bathroom alongside, like a mid-Victorian en suite.

After the front part of the house, the eastern block was next in status. Just to the right of the main entrance, and with an outer door of its own, was a handsome, book-lined study, where Father spent much of his time closeted with sermons and documents and with the many visitors who came and went through that outer door. Further along that passage and facing on to the garden were the small green sitting-room, then two bathrooms, one of which we children used. The other belonged to the very large master bedroom at the end of the passage.

The passage itself ended with a door which led into a palatial lavatory; there were only two lavatories in the house and the other one was for the servants. Ours had an entrance hall, so to speak, then another door into the inner sanctum. During the great drought of 1938-39, an edict came down from on high that chains were not to be pulled 'every time' – in fact only once a day, if possible. Even in those relatively unplumbed days, I found this a very alarming situation, probably because it was my first experience of a state of emergency. The lavatory was also the scene of another emergency when Elizabeth, crawling, got her head wedged under the door of the inner sanctum. Almost the entire family and staff assembled to deal with this crisis and, despite the crowded conditions, managed to free the victim without needing to call the fire brigade.

At this corner one turned into the back wing, where there was a warren of about six small bedrooms, inhabited by children, the nurse and minor visitors, and at the far end were the servants' sitting-room and bathroom and, a relic of bygone days, a 'boot-room'. We actually used the latter for its proper purpose, but it was generally the owner of the shoes who applied the polish as nobody on the staff was officially a boot black. In our next house, years later, when we had no boot-room and no resident staff at all, an occasional overnight guest was still known to place shoes outside the bedroom door at night. When all was dark, the bishop (Father), with true Christian humility, would spirit them away and clean them himself!

The fourth side of the house, on the south, contained the kitchen department, more servants' quarters (which I never entered) and a large ironing-room. In the latter sat a vast ironing table, while a capacious clothes hoist attached to the ceiling by ropes and pulleys was usually festooned with airing sheets and table cloths.

In the dark, barn-like kitchen were three deal tables, a triple-fronted dresser and a big black range. A sink with wooden draining board lurked in one corner, surmounted by a plate rack. Next door in the china pantry was another sink and storage cupboards for china and glass. Off each of these rooms a door led to a 'breezeway' coolroom, which was set between the walls of the house and the chapel. Its sides were clad in flywire and food was put on the shelves in this wind tunnel to keep cool. As the icy gales tore through the breezeway in winter, it might have been possible to make ice-cream on the open shelves, although we didn't try. Not until ten years later did we buy our first refrigerator, but there was an ice-chest for the hottest part of the summer when, even in the breezeway, the butter gave up the struggle and the milk turned sour. Heatwaves meant regular visits from the ice-man, who ran in carrying a dripping block of ice in a hessian bag with handles and dumped it in the top of the chest. Even better were trips to the ice-works to collect our own blocks, for there we could watch the man splitting the ice with his pick and carrying it with spiked tongs to the boot of the car, where it was wrapped in sacks for the trip home.

There was a small gas stove in the kitchen, but most of the cooking was done on the big range, and this was also the source, supposedly, of hot water for the entire household. With four bathrooms and a laundry in various far-flung corners of the house and with a minimum of eight or nine people using them, it is little wonder that one of our persistent family memories is that of miserably lukewarm water. In a house of that size and layout and in a Ballarat winter, only a blast furnace could have supplied water hot enough to weather the voyage along the pipes to the distant taps. Not only that – the bathrooms were built on the ballroom scale, vast and bare and draughty, so washing was rarely a pleasure, save in summer. In the drought year there was little water to spare for baths anyway: we were asked to limit them to the depth of one inch.

Yet a shallow, tepid bath was preferable to that other prevailing custom of washing in the bedroom. Bedrooms were furnished with a washstand, a towel horse and a little cupboard by the bed for a chamber pot. Washstands were usually topped by a marble slab on which sat the 'set' of basin, jug and soap-dish. If one had a maid, it was she who filled the jug with hot water, carried it to the the bedroom and covered it with a towel ready for the sponging ritual – and I suppose it was her job, too, to empty the chamber pots. I recall several white porcelain buckets with cane handles which were part of that unpleasant ritual. Bishopscourt still had its quota of washstands, although the main bedrooms had basins with running water. In the move to the next house, the washstands were somehow eliminated, but Mother clung on to the towel horses which, as she rightly said, were among the most useful items of furniture ever invented. The grand old jugs and basins (now collectors' pieces) usually found their way into kitchen service for holding lemon barleywater or fruit soaking for jam.

Close to our kitchen where the stairs led up to the tower, another flight descended to a dank cellar which had evidently been designed for cool storage, to supplement the breezeway. (There were no wine racks in evidence, only the odd table or shelf.) The cellar was never used in our day, for in wet weather it filled steadily with chilly water. When this first happened, we found that the siphon-tap was on the far wall of the cellar, opposite the stairs! As the water level rose relentlessly towards the ground floor, our nurse Jean heroically donned her bathing suit and more or less swam across to set the siphon going. We soon came to appreciate the problems of the Ballarat gold miners whose shafts were flooded by the merciless seepage.

HOT AND COLD

Bishopscourt was typical of many an Australian house built in the last century and later. Every sign of planning and forethought was directed towards defeating the fearful bogey of the Australian summer – shady verandahs, high ceilings, tiled floors, large airy bathrooms and kitchens, cellars, cypress hedge barriers against the north winds, huge shady trees, and so on. Such measures were often very successful in beating the heat and glare but they usually ensured that the houses were retreats of rheumatism and gloom in the winter. We might better understand this if we consider the stuffy, formal garments worn by our forebears and the problem of food storage without refrigeration. Summers must have been dominated by the difficulty of keeping themselves cool and their food edible. In these ways, winter would have been less of a challenge. Nevertheless, visitors who survived one winter stay in the guest chambers at Bishopscourt were known to prepare themselves for subsequent ordeals with layers of insulating newspapers to put between the blankets.

While my elders recalled the bitter cold of those years with some emotion, I recall the facts but little of the misery. In Ballarat I first discovered the phenomenon of Seasons, and the things I best remember about those first winters were not shuddering in draughty bathrooms, but skimming a tennis ball across the partially frozen lake, crunching in boots over the white, frosty lawns, breaking the ice in the fountain, skating on frozen puddles, watching the wind thrashing through the cypresses, and having to use the back gate when the lake flooded across Wendouree Parade and overflowed into our drive. Looking like Christopher Robin in gumboots and sou'wester, I tested the flood level each day. Winter was an adventure and frost was so pretty!

It soon became apparent that Bishopscourt was a very isolated and lonely place, surrounded as it was by acres of unlit land and overshadowed by great trees. Even inside, especially when Father was away at night, we were often startled by bumps in the roof and unexplained doorbells ringing late, and unnerved by the notion of the empty tower and the long, ghostly passages. Jean, the nurse, came to my bedside on the first night to tell me not to be frightened of strange noises. (If she hadn't alerted me, I wouldn't have been aware of them!) Eventually, Father had the belfry moved from the far side of the chapel to a site outside the kitchen window. The dangling bell-rope was passed in through this window so that in a beleaguered state we could summon the distant neighbours to our aid. However, the bell was never tolled in that context, for it was decided that bumps and doorbells in the night were caused by possums larking in the roof.

INTO THE GARDEN

Ballarat and our new home sent my imagination into orbit. I was at that crucial age when the imagination needs rich nourishment if it is to survive and grow. This new environment was very different from the one I'd known, and therefore not to be taken for granted; it was also enormously stimulating. As a bonus, I had three months to myself, free of school and able to roam about the huge estate uninterrupted.

While the house was intriguing, what lay outside was a child's paradise. Snapshots from that time show that I was nearly always attired for guerrilla warfare, dressed as a soldier, or a pirate (after Captain Hook), or a Red Indian (after Hiawatha), or an Arab, and armed to the teeth with a wooden sword, or home-made bow-and-arrows, or a toy air rifle. Many of these accoutrements were birthday or Christmas presents.

Father helped to make the swords and bows-and-arrows, and he seemed happy to encourage me in my tomboy pursuits, which no doubt reminded him of his own boyhood and made up in some ways for the absence of a son. Mother, although disappointed about my disdain for dolls and frilly things, went along with Father's policy, but the best presents I ever received were chosen, I feel sure, by him. I wore the soldier suit to bed, and the rifle was a constant companion in garden expeditions for many years. 'Six-shooters' with explosive caps were also popular.

Armed to the teeth   Arabs

I suppose it was unusual for a small girl to brandish toy firearms, but the gun culture was strong in those days, fed by world wars, popular stories and films of the wild west and big game hunting. In addition, many people grew up on the land, or indulged in shooting as a pastime. Father owned a shotgun. My toy guns were very seductive, lovely to handle. They offered a small, timid child a line of defence and a sense of empowerment, even if only imaginary. I have never handled a real gun since then, so the addiction to firearms didn't outlast childhood.

A small red two-wheeler bike was under the Christmas tree for me in 1936, and in the vast spaces of the estate I soon learned to ride it. After rain, the drive beneath the cypresses developed smooth, shiny wheel-tracks where I could work up exhilarating bursts of speed down to the front gate, then swish round through the two puddles just outside before flying back in a victory sprint to the fountain. My legs grew long, like Father's.

The garden lent itself readily to siege battles, big-game hunts, jungle safaris and stealthy tracking, especially in the overgrown shrubberies or along the drive, where the massive trunks of the cypresses provided good cover. Many an innocent visitor walked up the drive unaware that he was being shadowed by a heavily armed tracker, darting from tree to tree. Inside the front fence there was a row of pampas grass clumps. The waving plumes made wonderful 'banners' for processions, or 'flaming torches' for cannibal feasts or to keep tigers at bay.

Botanically, the Bishopscourt garden was what would now be termed 'old-fashioned' or, more correctly, Victorian. Native plants were rare and accidental, but one of my favourite trees was a lone eucalypt which had sneaked into a shrubbery and grown to a great height, dropping long scrolls of bark around its feet. This tree was midway along a secret tunnel between the shrubs and the back fence, and I frequently stopped there to stroke its smooth white trunk and to handle and admire the crunchy bark. Of all the trees in the garden, this was the exotic specimen, yet strangely it was the one I felt drawn to. Grouped around the house were larches, sequoias and a 'monkey puzzle' tree, while a swing hung from a weeping elm on the lawn. All these trees were elderly giants, in keeping with the scale of the garden.

Our predecessors, Bishop and Mrs Crick, with the episcopal car fleet, 1932. The Cedar of Lebanon is at the centre, with the Warden's House low to its right. Another dog is present – perhaps he, and not Dear Tip, assaulted the Dean!

The most aristocratic specimen was a mighty Cedar of Lebanon in front of the chapel. My elders regarded this tree with some reverence, although nobody informed me then that King Solomon had built his temple from such timber. Nevertheless, I admired the tree's bluish silky needles, its beehive-shaped cones and its resounding name, and I sensed that there was more to this plant than just its great size and dignity. Who, what or where was Lebanon?

Flanking the back gate grew two laburnums, dripping gold, while the shrubberies harboured viburnum and laurustinus, agapanthus and red hot pokers. Out towards the boundaries were some giant aloes and the pampas grass. I especially liked the garden beds between the house and the lawns, because these were neatly hemmed in with miniature box hedges, silky and aromatic. Probably Scruse did not share my enthusiasm, for he had to stoop very close to the ground to clip them. The scent of box sweeps me back to that garden, still.

The trees were companions in my solitary games. To a child, trees resemble large people and can often be treated in the same way. They have arms and fingers and necks and trunks; you can sit on them or lean against them, you can hit them or hug them or stroke them or hide behind them. They behave in all manner of ways. But they have one advantage over people – they stay rooted to the spot and don't go off to meetings or to talk on the telephone. You can generally rely on a tree to be where you left it yesterday and in much the same mood. But not always! A large cypress on the far side of the lawn gave up the ghost with a terrifying crack (it was said) and thundered to the earth. It must have happened at night, for I didn't witness the crash. However, this calamity caused everyone to regard the trees above the drive in a new light. Had the time come when they, too, would start crashing?

The size and age of the Bishopscourt trees meant that tree-climbing had to be postponed. They were all too big, their branches out of reach. But there were many other things to do. Often I plodded to and fro with Scruse as he mowed the acre of lawn. In earlier times, horses and sometimes sheep had helped to trim the grass, but it took Scruse an entire working day or longer to achieve this with his hand mower. Shocked by this fact, Father at once bought a petrol mower and, thanks to this mechanical marvel, Scruse then reduced the task to half a day of plodding and emptying the grass catcher at the end of each row. There was still the gravel for him to deal with, the drive, the carriage sweeps and stretches of pathway in numerous directions, all to be chipped and raked. The once broad paths for promenading around the perimeter of

36   Beside the Lake

the garden had long been abandoned to weeds and grass, and poor Scruse never caught up with the overgrown shrubberies.

On one raised area of the lawn there were net-posts, suggesting games of tennis there in earlier times, although the absence of boundary fences around the 'court' made one wonder about the state of clerical tempers as balls whizzed for miles across the lawns with nothing to halt them. But it seems that bygone tennis parties were waited on by ball-boys press-ganged (with promises of cake?) from the nearby Grammar School. While tennis was played on this upper level, croquet matches went ahead on the grass below. The levels were separated by a smooth grassy bank, wonderful, I soon found, for somersaults and the bike.

We were given a croquet set by a thoughtful great-aunt, Auntie Flo, and whenever our parents had a spare half hour and the weather was fine, this devious game became a family pastime.

Croquet, a devious game, c. 1937; Dorothy scowls as I address the ball. Looking east towards the weedy shrubberies.

The fountain, 1937.
Elizabeth (centre) with
visiting friends, one
of them wearing
Father's military cap.

The fountain in front of the house was decorated by three enormous stone fish, or dolphins, at the base of its central column. They wore stern expressions, which is hardly surprising for they were forced to balance on their chins while waving their tails in the air to support a massive stone dish. Above this a smaller dish was supported by some fish spun into a barley-sugar twirl, and in this smaller dish stood a person balancing a modest saucer on his head. Had the fountain played, the jet would have shot up from this saucer and cascaded into the dishes below, but the mechanism must have failed for we never saw it in action. In the great bowl at the base of the fountain grew water lilies, beneath which swam a large family of Japanese carp. They led a precarious life, not only because of our childish attempts at angling. When winter came and the lilies died down, the carp sometimes found themselves walled up under a giant ice-block which we had to smash with sticks. Worst of all, when severe water rationing during the famous drought reduced the water level in the fountain to just a few inches, the hapless carp were found to be swimming on their sides! They survived all such perils, and as far as I can remember none of us fell into the fountain, either, although teetering round its flat, stone rim was an everyday challenge.

Mother added a large green china frog to the fountain, and it sat on the centrepiece among the dolphin faces looking remarkably life-like. One day, through a window, she watched a small errand boy pick up a stone and fire it with deadly accuracy at the frog, expecting it, no doubt, to spring into the water. Instead it smashed into a dozen pieces and it was the boy who performed the startled leap, on to his bike and off down the drive in a whirl of pedalling legs. 'Poor child,' commented Mother. 'Anyone could have made the same mistake – it looked so real!' She was very forgiving.

Having our own chooks was another bonus and finding clutches of their warm eggs in the straw was one of the wonders of the world. The same inspired aunt of the croquet set gave us a wonderful card game called 'Chook Chook'. The cards represented different breeds of fowl, settings of eggs (some addled), batches of chickens, poultry diseases and pests, and the game involved buying and selling, breeding and taking risks, rather along the lines of 'Monopoly'.

The tone of our chook yard soared when we were given a peacock, sent in from one of the grand homesteads of the Western District. This bird was intended to saunter ornamentally about the lawns, contributing to the general air of gracious living, but he was soon relegated to the fowl run, where he scratched about with the homespun old hens and occasionally gave them a thrill by displaying his sensational tail. I picked up the gorgeous feathers which he so carelessly dropped and stuck them in vases in my bedroom, transforming it into a romantic bower.

THE CHAPEL

On rainy days there was always the chapel to investigate. I soon found out where the key was kept so that I could let myself in. The interior smelt richly of wood and furniture polish, and in the little gallery sat an amazing contraption called a harmonium, like a tiny, wheezing organ. The double-hinged lid opened to reveal the keyboard and a row of stops above it, mysteriously labelled in gothic script – Diapason, Viola, Flute, Vox Humana, Vox Celeste, Clarionet, Octave Coupler ... The player had to push hard on two large pedals to supply wind to the pipes, but at my age I had barely enough power to do so, for my legs were still too short. By pumping desperately and gripping the seat, I could raise just enough wind to start the music, but as soon as I let go of the seat to play notes on the keyboard, I usually slithered weakly on to the floor, while the harmonium gasped into silence.

The chapel was a feast for the eyes as well as for the nose. When Archdeacon Julian Bickersteth came to Australia to raise funds for the restoration of Canterbury Cathedral after the bombing of the Second World War, Mother took him into the chapel, where, Father reported in the Church Chronicle (2.8.'48), '... he stood in amazed silence. When he had recovered his speech he said, 'I didn't know there was such a beautiful bishop's chapel as this in Australia, and as a matter of fact there are not many to equal it in England.' (I remember the Archdeacon with some awe because he presented Elizabeth and me each with a £1 note – a huge gift. I suppose we should have donated it back to the Canterbury Cathedral fabric fund, but we didn't.)

Up in the gallery one was close to the splendid cross-braced oak beams supporting the roof. Downstairs had been designed in the collegiate style, with panelled oak stalls round three sides. Three heraldic coats of arms surmounted the stalls and added brilliant colour to the dark woodwork – the arms were those of the Commonwealth of Australia, the Diocese of Ballarat and of Bishop Maxwell-Gumbleton. It had been his idea to remodel the interior after the pattern of the chapel of Peterhouse, Cambridge – his own college. This had been built by Sir Matthew Wren (uncle of Sir Christopher), who was Master of Peterhouse from 1626-34. The Jacobean style interior of our chapel was designed in England by Sir Harold Brakespear, and the money was provided in memory of the Hon. James Chester Manifold MP by his brothers, William and Edward.

I slipped in and out of the stalls, stroking the woodwork, and stacking the slim red kneelers into tall piles on the floor. Each stall was furnished with a big prayerbook, bound in red and printed in both red and black. The print was large and generous, on fine paper, and each prayer began with a rich red capital letter. Mysterious words like 'Vouchsafe' and 'Dearly beloved brethren' leapt from the pages. The altar was also made of oak and it had a canopy rather like that of a fourposter bed. Several altar frontals for the different seasons hung in a special cupboard near the front door and the processional cross and altar pieces were of brass. So too was the candle snuffer, which leaned rather drunkenly in a corner.

The tall wooden belfry reminded me of the one outside Newcastle Cathedral. It housed one modest bell (our alarm bell) and its long, dangling rope was a constant temptation, as were the criss-cross beams of the belfry itself, which were ideal for climbing and made up a bit for the unsuitable trees. I also discovered that the far wall of the chapel (again like its big cathedral brother in Newcastle) offered a large expanse of red brick on the edge of an open space, another hitting wall, and here I began to learn tennis, concentrating mainly on the volley as the ground was rather bumpy.

The chapel would have been in regular use in the days of the theological college, but in our time its function was confined to private services, an occasional wedding, and to those times when clergy 'in retreat' were staying with us or young men were being prepared for ordination to the ministry. We found ourselves having breakfast with men in black cassocks.

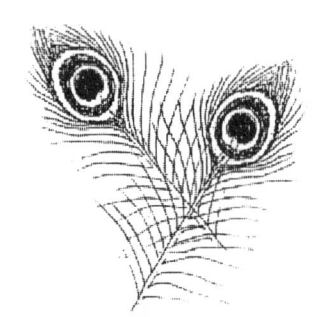

The View from Wendouree

BEYOND THE GATE

The scene beyond the back gate was semi-rural, for Wendouree was more of a village than a suburb. Gregory Street was a country track of yellow gravel and rich, ochre puddles, with ditches concealed in the long grass of the verges. We sometimes walked to the general store in Howitt Street on the far side of the railway line. This took us past the important landmarks of Wendouree – the railway gates across Forest Street, the Boys' Grammar School, St Matthew's Church (a pretty weatherboard in those days), and the Bluebell Hotel, which we passed by on the other side. Beyond these lay a few houses, but open fields for the most part, leading to Mount Rowan. The Monastery, wrapped in mystery, loomed at the end of Howitt Street. At the store we bought soap or stamps and a penny ice-cream to lick on the walk home.

Otherwise I don't recall much shopping, as food was ordered by telephone and delivered by a procession of errand boys on bikes or men in vans and carts. The butcher's boy barged his way through the back gate with a huge square basket on the front of his bike, and the milkman measured out milk into a large billycan on the back step. One of our favourite callers was Mr Smith, the postman, who pushed his red bike up the drive twice a day to hand in letters at the door. As Christmas approached, large sacks of His Majesty's mail were left on our verandah so that Smithy could reload. (I was awed that we were chosen to guard the bulging mailbags. Had the King chosen us?) By Christmas Eve, Smithy wouldn't arrive for his second delivery until about eleven o'clock at night, by which time he was very mellow and, with his cherubic red face, could easily have been mistaken for Santa Claus himself, although in navy serge.

When relatives came to stay in summer, one of the customary things to do in the evening was to walk in a large and straggling party to the tiny Wendouree Railway Station to watch the Adelaide Express go through. We would all line up on the midget platform, straining to hear the approaching rumble of the great train, and then cling breathlessly to one another as it thundered past only inches away. This became an even more elaborate game when there were visitors to be put on the express for Adelaide. We would drive the travellers to the main Ballarat Railway Station and wait until the sweating monster came in from Melbourne, we children up on the footbridge above the platforms to peer down into the funnels and to savour the full belch of warm steam and smoke in our faces as the engines hissed by below. The exhilarating drama of the steam age reverberated around the great stone cavern – puffings and explosions, clanks, shouts, whistles and banging doors – as the passengers were helped aboard into their sleepers. Then we would rush back to the car and urge Father to drive recklessly to Wendouree. Here we would line up on the platform and wave frantically to the travellers as they flashed by to South Australia, although it was hardly possible to identify them as the ribbon of lighted windows streamed past.

Apart from that excitement via the back gate, our walks far more often took us to the front. The front fence was a high wooden structure of rhubarb red, with a strip of ornamental ironwork inset near the top. The gates were of cast iron and a copper plate was fixed to either side, one saying BISHOPS and the other saying COURT in art nouveau lettering. We all took our turn at cleaning those copper plates in subsequent years, but in those days it was no doubt the housemaid who had to hike down the drive with her polishing rags and the Brasso tin.

PLEASURE GARDENS

Straight across the road from the gates was a perfectly shaped willow tree and beyond it gleamed the lake. Walks from the front gate inevitably took us to the right, towards the Botanical Gardens. The lakeside path meandered along that part of the shoreline known as 'Fairyland', which began most obligingly almost opposite our gateway. Fairyland was to some extent man-made, but it had developed a healthy wildness over time. The path led over rustic bridges and willowy causeways, it lingered beside tadpole ponds and backwaters lush with water lilies and reeds, and it closely overlooked islands where waterbirds preened and nested. I usually rode the red bike through Fairyland, bumping across the wooden bridges, teetering rather nervously along the causeway, braking suddenly in the face of some rampant swan, then swishing through the weeping willow fronds to skim onto the lovely smooth asphalt of the landing stage in front of the Gardens Kiosk.

The landing stage was edged with white mooring posts for rowing boats and for the paddle steamers which plied to and fro across the lake in summer, just as they must have done in Queen Victoria's day. These gracious old steamers, 'The Gem', 'The Lord Roberts' and 'The Golden City', were almost as impressive to me as ocean liners, as we sailed on them across to View Point and back, waving to the passing yachts and watching the paddles churning and foaming. Any doubts I might have had about living beside a lake were quelled.

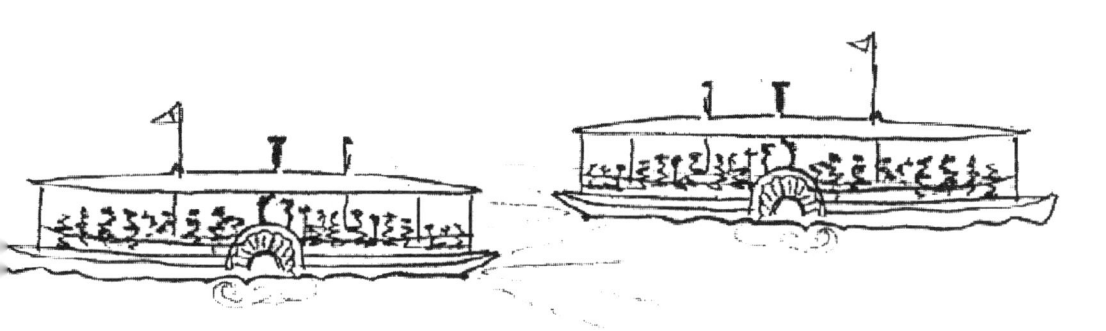

Most passengers joined the steamers on the other side of the lake and made the leisurely voyage across to the Gardens for tea at the elegant Kiosk and a stroll through Fairyland or among the flowers. They might also have had a fling on the swing-boats, for, as distinct from Botanical Gardens, there were Pleasure Gardens as well, an odd assortment of attractions grouped in the parkland near the fernery. For history-lovers, Adam Lindsay Gordon's cottage cowered there beneath a giant gum tree. Much more exciting to my mind were the swing-boats, which we weren't allowed to ride on without an adult for they looked as if they might loop-the-loop and tip us all out on our heads. The Maze was safer and more decorous, a larger than life puzzle made out of neatly clipped hedges. The aim was to find your way to the little tower in the centre, from where you could jeer at those lost in the labyrinth below. I didn't see another maze until twenty years later, at Hampton Court.

Cricket was sometimes in progress on a rustic, tree-ringed oval nearby, and behind this was the zoo. The sign over the entrance said ZOOLOGICAL GARDENS. Here was another impressive word, especially as it began with Z. We were taken to the zoo fairly often because of our age and also, perhaps, because of the novelty of having a zoo next door. We had been to Taronga Park Zoo in Sydney, but that had involved an immense journey from Newcastle. This Ballarat Zoo was almost in our own garden. However, it was a most modest menagerie, with nothing in it which could qualify as big game. Most of the residents were native animals, birds and reptiles, save for a few monkeys and deer, and one smelly, moth-eaten camel. There seemed to be strong local feeling against the zoo and most of this focussed upon the hapless camel, who was indeed a poor advertisement for large animals held in captivity.

There was a certain morbid fascination about peering at the camel while holding one's nose, but on the whole it was far pleasanter to watch the wildfowl swimming free on the lake or strolling under the trees near the Kiosk. The Eastern Swamp-hens, with their royal blue breasts and red faces, thought nothing of crossing Wendouree Parade and the tram-tracks in their search for snacks around the picnic pavilion near the swing-boats.

Yet the stars among the waterfowl were, without doubt, the white mute swans, of which there were several pairs on the lake. A couple of pairs patrolled the Fairyland region to keep the lesser breeds in order, skimming proudly among the willows, their snowy wings frothed up over their backs. They were obviously born to rule. The black swans looped their necks a good deal, but they were homely, colonial creatures with little of the majestic demeanour of their royal white cousins. White or black, they all did very well from our bags of bread.

Swings, slides and see-saws were grouped here and there under the parkland trees, but far more interesting to most children were the cannons around the Kiosk. There were four small ones near the tramstop, worth a quick inspection and good for a limber-up. The king cannon, however, was the big fellow round behind the Kiosk, with its barrel aimed straight across the lake. It had once been on the 'Cerberus' and it looked powerful enough to sink a battleship, let alone a fleet of steamboats. This gun was horizontal, smooth, slippery, with a back like a draught horse; it was more than a gun, it was a monolith or an animal. It was for climbing on, stroking, straddling, riding, slithering along, swinging under, jumping off. Had the book of Isaiah been written in the age of artillery, the verse (2:4) might have run, '... and they shall beat their swords into ploughshares and their spears into pruning hooks ... and their heavy cannon into playground equipment ...'

GARDENS BOTANICAL

To live alongside not only Zoological, but also Botanical Gardens, seemed almost too much. They were like an extension of our own garden, without the work. Here we were in the Garden City, and Mother was in seventh heaven. She may have wept upon leaving Newcastle, but she could not readily forget the humidity and the salty east winds which frustrated all her efforts at gardening on the cathedral crag. Her delight in this new environment infected us all. It was also a relief to live on a horizontal plane, after the steps and steeps of Newcastle.

During those first three years in Ballarat, we found every excuse to stroll along the willowy path to the Gardens – to take the baby for a walk, to show visitors the sights, to feed the swans, to catch a tram, to stretch our already-stretched legs. The Gardens then were fenced behind iron railings, and the rear boundary along Gillies Street was further enclosed by a dense bank of trees which created an illusion of depth and distance. One long pathway of fine brown gravel led straight across the Gardens from the fish hatchery at one end to the cool fernery at the other. Along the path were seasonal splashes of colour – a great square bed of massed dahlias; ribbon flower beds; the clear, hot, primary colours of the famous Rex begonias in the conservatory; the horse chestnuts, providers of pink flower-candles or gleaming conkers; thick, heavily-scented carpets of phlox; the darting goldfish in the long lily pond. In the lofty, gothic fernery you could run a figure-of-eight among the cool fronds.

There were classical marble figures placed strategically among the trees, and we grew up knowing that special beauty which statuary can impart to a landscape. My childish preference in statues was for the two marble lions flanking the entrance gates and for stout-hearted Wallace, nearby. He was a noble, uncomplicated figure, and I coveted his gigantic metal sword.

Many of the trees were of similar size and appearance to those at Bishopscourt, and nearly every one wore a label on its chest, like a delegate to an international conference, informing us of its name (in Latin and English) and its place of origin – China, South America, California, Northern Europe ... I read all these and soon learned to identify golden ashes at a hundred paces and sequoias at half a mile. The educational purpose of a botanic garden was being fulfilled. Especially majestic was a group of monumental conifers with names to match their stature – the Noble Spruce, the Heavy Pine (*Pinus Ponderosa*), the Mammoth Tree (*Sequoia Gigantea*). This, I now suppose, is what the Victorian gardeners would have called a Pinetum. I was discovering Latin, and some of its words made a sort of sense, like the Vox Humana stop on the harmonium.

Grandmother Marmie, sitting peacefully under a sequoia, was the first of us to meet a 'Ballarat' squirrel. It sat beside her on the seat to munch an ice-cream cone, before bounding back aloft into the Californian branches. The introduced grey squirrels added an exquisite touch of Beatrix Potter to the scene as they frisked, light as thistledown, across the lawns, waving their feathery tails and munching the pine nuts and acorns. They could be seen as far afield as Sturt Street.

Botanical Gardens with guardian lions. The Statuary at left and the fernery beyond.

Mount Warrenheip

VOLCANOS

One port of call in the Gardens was the statuary pavilion, where I liked to go to look at The Flight from Pompeii, the largest and most intriguing of the sculptures – a family group wearing very few clothes and running away from some unimaginable horror. The marble man held his billowing marble cloak over them as a defence, and the mother clutched a baby as she ran. What was it all about? I asked questions. What's Pompeii? I was told about the volcano, Mount Vesuvius, erupting and raining ash and lava down on the town of Pompeii. Where is it? In Italy, near Naples. I knew about Italy on the map because it looked like a boot, and I was relieved to know that Pompeii wasn't in the Ballarat region. I didn't ask why the fleeing figures had no clothes on, but I supposed it was hot living near a volcano. Have you ever seen a volcano? Well, there are two over there, across the lake. You mean those two hills!? Are they going to blow up? No, of course not. They did that millions of years ago – they're extinct. What's extinct mean? Dead. Are you sure? Yes, quite sure.

Walking along the lake's edge we were very much aware of those two landmarks on the eastern skyline. They were Mount Warrenheip and Mount Buninyong, the twin volcanic humps which guard the southern and eastern approaches to the city. We had already passed them on the journey up from Melbourne; when we reached our new home, there they were again, gazing steadily at us across the water. We had not expected a view of retired volcanos from our front gate. I was at first a bit anxious – would there one day be a Flight from Wendouree in the statuary?

But no, Buninyong and Warrenheip were safely extinct and we quickly became devoted to them. For us younger ones they were almost as important in our universe as the sun and the moon, like spirits of the land to an Aborigine. Returning to Ballarat after journeys elsewhere, we watched for those two familiar humps on the horizon, Bunny and Warry, like friendly, reliable watchdogs who had been left in charge during our absence and were now waiting to welcome us home. (In shape, Warry was more like a cat, neat and compact, but Bunny had a doggy sprawl.)

Mount Buninyong

Bunny and Warry were peculiarly our own, but there were other weird hills crouching in pairs or small groups on the surrounding plateau. The rural skyline was adorned by the smooth-backed shapes of giant green elephants and whales, dromedaries and dinosaurs. Our city was ringed by an ancient landscape whose remote volcanic upheavals had contributed bountifully to Ballarat's estate, from the rich chocolate soil of the potato fields to the solid bluestone buildings which dignified the district in every guise from barn to cathedral.

Mount Elephant, near Camperdown, among the weird shapes on the rural skyline

I learned quite early that bluestone was volcanic rock. It was an eerie experience to drive on the narrow dirt road through the ancient crater of Mount Buninyong among the tumbled piles of mossy rocks. Had our pet volcanos vomited forth the stones of the Ballarat Town Hall a million years before?

GARDEN CITY

As we arrived in Ballarat in high spring, it was in its role as the Garden City, rather than as the Golden City, that it first captivated us. In every direction there were trees, in avenues along the streets, in private gardens, in the Botanical Gardens, in layers around Lake Wendouree – enormous trees, small trees, some covered in blossom, others in new leaf. There were flower beds and statues and band rotundas and seats among the trees, and in the middle of it all was the lake. Swans and waterfowl and white sails were an everyday part of the scene.

The only trees I remembered from Newcastle were the Norfolk Island pines, but there were none of those here; nor were there many gum trees in this novel landscape. Many of the trees were very large, and so often did they grow in ranks and rows and avenues that it was fairly evident that behind all this natural beauty there lay a plan. At the time I wasn't very interested in the plan, but now I can record my admiration for those nineteenth century pioneers who planted not for themselves but for future generations. By 1936, some of the trees were already seventy years old, or more.

We should be astonished at how much was accomplished in the early days, especially in the decades between 1851-71. In that brief time, Ballarat grew from a few huts to a fully fledged city. In 1858, only seven years after the first gold was found, a hundred acres of land were set aside for Botanical Gardens. In the 1860s began the transformation of the swamp into a lake, and the first regatta took place on its shallow waters in 1864. Those early settlers who so quickly created an oasis in the heart of the Australian bush must have had enviable stores of energy and imagination, and no doubt the ugliness and destruction of the diggings drove them to extra efforts in creating more attractive and familiar scenes further west. The Ballarat which developed was a testimony to their longing for English woods and lakes, for Cornish boats and harbours, for the fashionable parks and pastimes of Europe.

Yet some of the finest features of the city today are partly the result of happy accident or practical necessity. How fortunate it was to have a swamp so conveniently placed, with land available nearby for the Gardens. In his initial survey, W.S. Urquhart laid down a width of two chains (about 40 metres) for most streets and three chains for Sturt Street. He might have been a man of vision, but old timers told us that Sturt Street owed its impressive width to its origins as a stock route: it was wide enough to accommodate a U-turn with a team of bullocks!

The tree-planting tradition lived on into the new century, and the most startling evidence of this was the Avenue of Honour, which set out from the western extremity of Sturt Street and marched along the Western Highway for fourteen miles or so, until the road veered around Lake Burrumbeet and headed off to Beaufort. As we drove along this

The Arch of Victory, grand entrance to the Avenue of Honour with its 4,000 trees

apparently endless avenue, I often tried to count the trees as they flashed by, but I soon grew dizzy and lost the place. In later years I used more advanced mathematics; I totted up the number of trees on one side of the road between two milestones, doubled it, and then tried to multiply by fourteen. This was very difficult to do in one's head at a tender age and in a moving vehicle, and I never reached the same answer twice. But never mind, there were thousands of trees (4000, actually) – poplars, rowans, elms, ashes, some already leaning away from the prevailing wind and many with magpie nests in their topknots. Father told us that each tree represented a soldier, a man from the Ballarat district, who had marched off to the war, the Great War of 1914-18, just as these thousands of trees marched in a double column for miles across the plain. Father's uniform from the Great War was at home in a cupboard. Have you got a tree, Daddy? No, I didn't live in Ballarat then. But one day we stopped somewhere along the avenue and by extraordinary chance found a tree labelled 'W. Johnson', so in a sort of way he did have a tree after all.

The Ballarat trees, above all, defined the place. They were exotic trees, European, foreign. This was a European and particularly English oasis in an ancient Australian landscape. Blue gums had once been planted in Sturt Street, but only as a temporary measure until the English oaks had reached a mature size. Then the gums were grubbed out and the parrots left Sturt Street to the introduced blackbirds, goldfinches and thrushes. The white English swans ruled the lake and the willows wept into its waters.

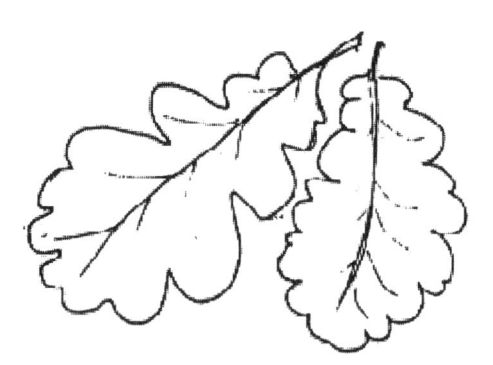

Lessons in Living

SERPENTS IN PARADISE

Memories of those first three years at the first Bishopscourt are rather dream-like and blurred, as though life was self-enclosed and timeless. I remember the seasonal moods of the lake – how it flooded or iced over or nearly dried up – but I am unable to date these events exactly.

Soon after our arrival, Father began to travel around his new diocese and I can see now why he needed a new car. The Ballarat Diocese was extensive, and everybody in it wanted to meet the new bishop and tell him their problems. There were big centres like Warrnambool and Horsham, but also many far flung farming communities who congregated in tiny wooden churches in the middle of nowhere. He set out to visit them all and often he was away from home for weeks at a time. His 'rural rides' were a feature of his life for the next twenty-five years, and he notched up hundreds of thousands of miles. Mother rarely went with him while we were small, but in the 1950s she travelled with him a lot, typing his letters on her knee in the car. As he explored his territory in those first years, he came home telling of places with alluring names – Rainbow, Edenhope, Swan Marsh, Mount Elephant, Drik Drik, Dimboola, Apollo Bay. Mother was always relieved when he returned safely from the Otway Ranges, as he told us of fogs and landslides and the perils of meeting logging trucks on dangerous bends of Wild Dog and Skene's Creek Roads. On his first trip there, he was entertained by a garage-man's wife with a snapshot collection of 'people who didn't get through', cars which had gone over the edge, some down three hundred feet, and drivers whom her husband had to rescue.

Apart from the drought and the freezing winters, there were other serpents in this paradise. There was a frightening epidemic of poliomyelitis, or infantile paralysis as we called it more bluntly in those days. Schools were closed for many weeks and victims in cots or wheelchairs were a not uncommon sight in the streets for years after. We all took the matter of isolation very seriously and were almost afraid to breathe in public places. Children were kept away from the beaches, and shops and cinemas were strictly avoided. Families of our generation had no benefit from Salk Vaccine or Triple Antigen, which were yet to be developed. I had whooping cough and barked violently for several months, dashing for the bathroom whenever I felt a paroxysm coming on, in case I vomited. Diphtheria was a disease which obviously terrified grown-ups. Fifty years later, in a graveyard in country Tasmania, I understood why; there on two adjoining nineteenth century tombstones were the names of nine children in two families of first cousins, who had all died within two weeks during a diphtheria epidemic.

I also cut three of my fingers to the bone by slithering down a trellis and catching my hand on a nail. Wounds were likewise taken very seriously (especially with our uncle's death from tetanus in mind), and, as I was by then at school, I made daily visits to the school matron to have the dressings changed. Disinfectant, iodine and boracic powder were our only weapons against blood poisoning. Elizabeth fell out of a cart which I was towing around behind my bike, and cracked her arm. The doctor came and diagnosed a 'greenstick' fracture, and I was surprised to learn that babies had green sticks instead of bones. She also hacked off a good half of her fluffy curls with a large pair of scissors, just before departing to a party. To Mother this was far more mortifying than the fractured arm.

It was, in fact, the peak time for children's parties, including one for my birthday to which all my class-mates came and played games on the lawns. I was then invited back to their parties. The Wattle Tearooms and the Misses Brazenor's Alexandria Tearooms (both in Lydiard Street) specialised in children's parties and followed the time-honoured formula of peanut hunts, musical chairs, Oranges and Lemons, Tail on the Donkey, raspberry vinegar, hundreds and thousands on white bread and butter, meringues and jelly. I didn't much enjoy parties, and I wonder how many children did? Perhaps they were designed to cultivate the social graces in the young, but in actual fact they encouraged anti-social behaviour – the competitive (games), the acquisitive (prizes and presents) and the gluttonous (meringues)! As well, one had to wear a frilly dress, which might have encouraged vanity, though not in me. I would much rather have worn my soldier's uniform or the Red Indian head-dress, but fancy dress parties seemed to be rare in Ballarat.

Staying with us on one occasion were a rather headstrong girl and her mother. This girl was a little older than me and she saw great possibilities for adventure in the Bishopscourt grounds and soon enlisted me as her accomplice. We broke a window, damaged the croquet set, and – worst of all – cut off all the flower heads in the garden and presented them to Mother in a carton. I could tell that Mother was distressed, but unable to say much because the other mother was her guest. I felt guilty and miserable, too, but was too young to cope with divided loyalties.

Soon after this unhappy affair we were visited by Aunt Nettie, from Adelaide. She was really an elder cousin of Mother's, but always went by the honorary title of Aunt, being one of the relatives who had taken Mother under her wing in earlier years. Aunt Nettie dressed in black and spoke her mind as Adelaide matrons did. It was reported to me that Aunt Nettie, having heard of my recent misdemeanours, had made a pronouncement: 'Mary is the failure of the family.' Being told this after Aunt Nettie's departure, I had no way of knowing if it was a final

Christmas 1937, with young partygoers on the front steps of Bishopscourt. A contrast to the photo on p.24. (CFE)

judgement which damned me for ever. I am now inclined to think that she spoke those words with a twinkle in her eye, but at the time I had no proof of that and her reported remark undermined my confidence for years.

So, by the age of six, circumstances had made me a rather solitary child. The positive side to this solitude was an ability, learned very early, to enjoy my own company and to live a rich imaginative life. My curiosity about the world around me was endlessly challenged, so that I rarely felt that there was 'nothing to do.' However, I was anti-social, wary of strangers and ill at ease with other children.

It was at this stage that I was introduced to Margaret.

MARGARET

Someone must have decided that I needed a friend. Bishopscourt was so isolated that there was no chance of hobnobbing with neighbours over the fence or meeting kids in the street. Even had there been, I think other children would have been wary of me for, by definition, a bishop's daughter would be a goody-goody.

I don't know who initiated the move to socialise me, but one day late in 1936 I was taken to meet Margaret as she was walking home from school. We waited by arrangement on a street corner and I saw, coming towards us, what looked like a mushroom on two legs, for Margaret was wearing a large white straw hat, part of her school uniform. Various adults had decided that we were well suited to become friends, as I would soon be attending the same school, in the same class, and (of course this came into it) Margaret belonged to an Anglican family. Adults are often mistaken in these matters, but in this case they were dead right and Margaret and I were to become lifelong friends.

Arrangements were made for us to play together now and then, but the glowing occasions were summery picnics to Lake Burrumbeet with Margaret's family. They would collect me in their cream two-door Ford. Waiting at the gate was the most trying part of outings, because I was always in position half an hour too early, but eventually the car would appear and I would climb into the deep leathery back seat with Margaret, her young brother and his friend – no seat belts, of course, just a seething heap of excited children. The Wilsons had discovered a perfect picnic spot. We set off along the Avenue of Honour, turned left at the little old Windermere Hotel and followed a trail along back roads and bumpy tracks, through paddocks and gates until we reached the far shore of the lake, far away from the official picnic ground beside the highway. Sometimes a couple of other families were there too, their cars parked under the gums just above the sandy-grassy 'beach'. Margaret's parents relaxed in the shade while we children romped and splashed in the warm shallows and chased the shoals of silvery, black-eyed 'whitebait' which swirled past us in the milky, brackish water. The bottom was a curious mixture of sand and warm, clammy mud. Afternoon tea under the gums consisted of raspberry vinegar, plain cake and a thermos of tea.

This new word 'brackish' represented a scientific discovery. Brackish water was halfway to salty sea water. Lake Burrumbeet was much more like the seaside than Lake Wendouree. It had sand and fish, rather than water weed and leeches, and above the beach were those lovely gum trees, instead of willows. The two lakes could have been on different continents, and the pleasures they offered were entirely unalike.

TRAMS

Early in 1937, when I started school, I became a tram traveller. Opposite our front gate there was a tramstop. The sign was a wide red band with white borders, painted on the power pole, and this was where I usually embarked, although on sunny days, if we were early, Mother and I would walk round to the stop by the Gardens. On the way, in autumn, I picked up leaves of brilliant shapes and colours to be dried and pasted into a scrap book – poplar leaves as yellow and shiny as country butter, and the heraldic shapes of the scarlet oaks. Jewels of this kind had not existed in Newcastle.

Dorothy vanished round the lake each morning on her bicycle, so Mother or Jean must have accompanied me to school several times to initiate me into the mysteries of the tram journey, but very soon I went solo. The trip covered something over two miles, and the half-fare was a penny-halfpenny (two cents), although I economised on that amount by using a Scholar's monthly concession ticket which I wore on a string round my neck. As the first concession ticket approached its expiry date, I wasn't sure what to do; I didn't like to bother my parents when they were so busy, but like most children I suffered agonies of apprehension over breaking the law. The dreaded day came and I went so far as to smudge the date stamped on the ticket – on one count or the other I would surely go to gaol! But the conductor barely glanced at it and in due course a new ticket arrived.

When I became a tram traveller, I was pushed out of the nest to join the wider world. Trams were civilising. To begin with, they had rules. They ran to time, on rails, and one needed a valid ticket. I had to learn which bell to ring. A high standard of behaviour was expected among the passengers. If necessary, children gave up their seats to adults without question. People were not allowed to spit, or to throw rubbish about, or to get off the tram while it was 'in motion', or to meddle with the trolley pole. The drivers and conductors were imperturbable, fatherly men, who kept an eye on things. They wore forest green uniforms and green mittens in the winter. Their faces soon became very familiar to me, and my parents evidently had no qualms about trusting a lone six-year old to their care.

The trams I rode in were the authentic Ballarat trams of that period, green and gold, fat and dumpy, skimming and waddling about the town like a family of well-fed ducks. The earliest trams, introduced in the 1890s, had been horse-drawn, with electric trams following in 1904. The larger trams which joined the fleet in the 1940s were Melbourne cast-offs, hand-me-downs from the brash metropolis, but the Ballarat tram of my youth had a single central cabin enclosed by sliding doors and a breezy open section at each end. It was usual for ladies in hats to seal themselves inside the central cabin, leaving the outer compartments to men and their pipes. The driver's cabin was open on one side to this outer compartment, which enabled passengers or the conductor to pass the time of day with him, despite stern notices forbidding this dangerous practice while the tram was in motion. (Some rules were bent.) Towards journey's end, when the tram was almost empty, I would slip into the little space beside the driver and watch him at work. Tram-driving looked easier than driving the Ford V8 and the controls made seductive clicking and hissing noises. The driver rested his weight on a small collapsible leather seat, and he kept his lunch (or something) in a black tin box. Sometimes he had to clamber out to change the points with an iron bar or to rescue the overhead trolley pole when it bounced off the power cable in a flurry of sparks, and when we lurched onto a loop there was always time to chat to the crew of the oncoming tram.

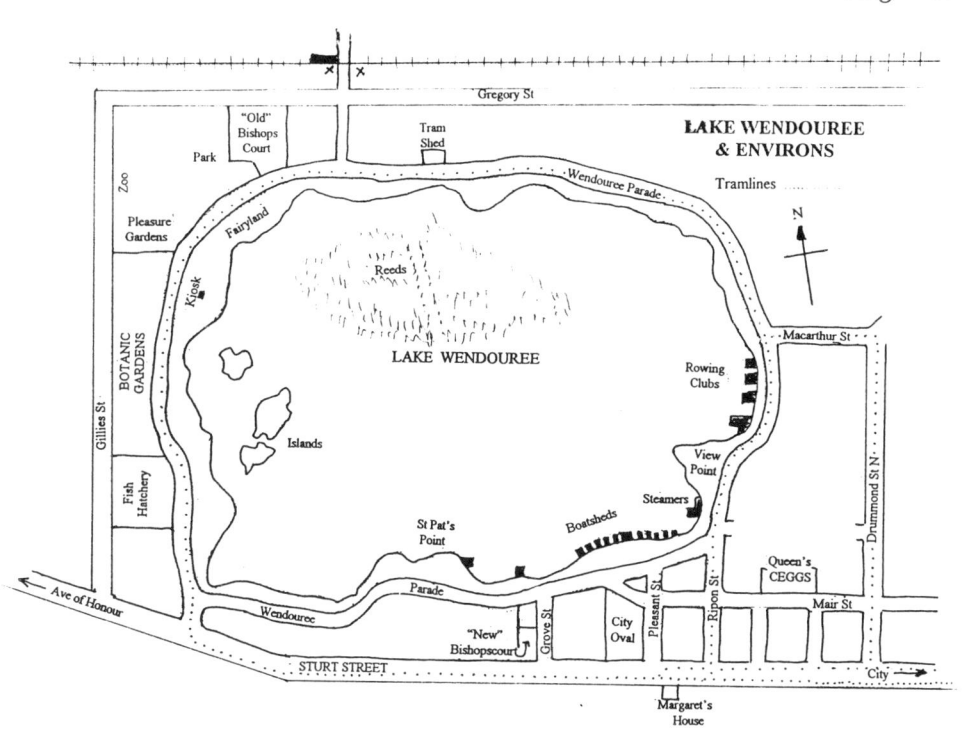

In spite of winter gales, it must have been a pleasant calling, that of a Ballarat 'trammie'. There was little traffic to disturb those delectable journeys along the lakeside, up and down the avenues of Sturt Street, Drummond Street, Victoria Street, through the brief bustle of Bridge Street in the city, on to destinations called Mount Pleasant, Sebastopol, View Point, Gardens. At night the trams retired to a grand abode on Wendouree Parade not far from Bishopscourt, flanked by gracious old houses and sharing their view across the lake, a charming piece of real estate which had no chance, of course, of remaining a trams' rest home forever.

Like all Ballarat traffic, the trams moved at a sedate pace, stopping frequently and rarely gathering any speed beyond the familiar rocking and creaking gait. This early-learnt patience in traffic immunised me against road rage in later life, I feel sure. There was time to learn how to 'ride' a tram, how to strap-hang or to balance 'no hands', when to pull the bell, how to open the doors and windows, how to swing on and off the step in a daring manner while the tram was (almost) still in motion.

58   Beside the Lake

When I was the only passenger left, I could roam about, slide to and fro on the slippery seats (worn smooth by countless bottoms), enjoy being catapulted into the far cabin by sudden stops or rare bursts of speed, sit on the empty driving seat at the back and imagine that I was in control, although going backwards.

Then there were the other passengers to observe. Discreet staring or eavesdropping was possible because the seats faced across. One girl from a rival school collected all discarded tickets from the floor, sorted them into coloured piles and then stowed them in her pocket. Could she have been papering her bedroom walls? I, too, began to collect tickets and one day I silently offered her my hoard. She seemed astounded by my gesture and for the first and only time in our acquaintance she spoke.'Golly, thanks!' said she. 'That's all right,' said I. I was too shy to speak to anyone else.

There were two mishaps. Coming home one wet afternoon I saw Scruse waiting in the car at the gate, to save me being drenched in the long trudge up the drive. I swung boldly off the tram and ran behind it and across the road; an oncoming car screeched to a halt and the white-faced driver wound down his window and, with good reason, swore picturesquely in my direction. Scruse looked equally pale, and on reaching home and Mother I burst into tears of shock. The shock was not so much the close shave, as the foul language! Anyway, that was another lesson learned for life.

The other mishap was the result of my finding sixpence (five cents) on the footpath as I left school one day. This was an enormous sum, two week's pocket money at least, and near the tramstop was a small shop with a fatally attractive sweet counter. (The word 'lolly' was considered vulgar, I somehow sensed). With the sixpence burning a hole in my glove I entered the shop to make my choice from among the array of chocolate frogs, licorice blocks, jelly babies, pink musk sticks, chocolate buddies, aniseed balls, sherbert suckers, sweethearts and clinkers. I retreated with my bulging bag, only to see the tram vanishing into the distance. I had missed it! There would not be another for twenty minutes and my frantic mother would soon be ringing the police. I stood by the tramstop in a hot and cold turmoil of guilt, shame and panic – but greed, of course, conquered every other feeling and all the way home in the follow-up tram I ate every last sweet and left the bag as litter under the seat. Then I spun a touching yarn to my anxious mother – I had stopped to assist a 'wounded dog' in the street, and had so missed my tram. Luckily, she didn't press for details about the dog's condition – this unconvincing narrative, together with my licorice stained teeth, probably told her all she needed to know.

When in later years the tramway system was dismantled, the character of Ballarat was sadly diminished.

THE 'POT OF GOLD'

In legends and pirate stories, rich rewards came in the form of treasure chests spilling forth jewels and gold coins, or as the Pot of Gold at the end of the rainbow. Experiment soon proved that the end of every rainbow evaporated as I moved towards it, so I realised that the Pot of Gold was a con trick; yet dreams of golden wealth persisted. Finding a stray coin in the gutter or the gravel, as I had done on my way to the tramstop, was the nearest I came to buried treasure, but there was always a stab of excitement as I pounced on the prize.

The coinage children dealt in was usually copper, or small silver. Befitting their great size, the copper pennies had real purchasing power – a chocolate frog or a penny ice-cream. A silver threepence (pronounced variously, 'thripence', 'thrupence' or 'thripenny' bit) was tiny and lost itself in the corners of pockets, but it was valuable, the sixpence even more so. I regularly extracted coins from my money box by manoeuvring them through the slit on a knife blade, in order to count them and to gloat.

Weekly pocket money became available in principle after I began school, but my parents were forgetful about such things and I usually had to ask for it. It was threepence to start with, rising slowly to sixpence, and perhaps to a shilling or two in my last school years. It was spent mostly on sweets, and later on milk drinks at the Dairy or comics, but substantial gifts of 2/6 or even 5/- were deposited in the money box and saved for a special purchase. Money was real coinage; it was also scarce and to be treated with respect. If you couldn't afford something, you did without or saved up for it. Some people did this 'on the lay-by' – the retailer held the goods while the customer paid by instalments and took possession only when the goods were fully paid off. Father had a horror of hire purchase or any form of debt (except perhaps a modest mortgage). There was another side to all this. A good many things in life were free, or cheap, and people often did things for nothing.

Actual size

From Divinity to Daisy Chains

SCHOOL

There was never any doubt about where to get off the tram for school, for on that corner of Mair and Drummond Streets stood the imposing white hospital of St John of God Convent. Today it cringes beneath the high modern additions behind it, but then it stood proud and alone in its grounds. It wasn't as old as Bishopscourt, but being two-storied it was very imposing, with its arrogant square tower and its sweeping upper balconies. I walked past daily, feeling very small and C. of E., and peeped sideways through the iron railings to see if I could glimpse any nuns. Our lives were divided not only by the horizontal class structure, but also by the vertical walls of sectarianism. Nuns floating about in their black or white habits were to me mysterious and somewhat alarming beings.

The school in Mair Street to which I was heading was Queen's Church

Manifold House. The 'Cubes' to the left housed the older girls. (MAG 1940)

of England Girls' Grammar School, known to everyone as Queen's. It already had a history going back sixty years, having started in Dana Street in 1876. By 1937 it occupied relatively spacious grounds in terms of girls-per-acre, for there were only about 130 pupils, if that. Of these about a third were boarders, girls from the country or interstate.

Manifold House where the boarders lived was a two-storied Victorian mansion which, despite rather pedestrian additions at the rear, bestowed an air of dignity upon the whole property. This was enhanced by the curved drive and the fine old garden in front of the house and by the Oak Tree, a giant which grew on the dividing line between the garden and the quadrangle, around which were grouped the red brick classrooms and the assembly hall. Queen's had both the advantages and the drawbacks of a small school.

I started in the room called 'Kinder' with Miss Jenkin ('Jenks') as my first teacher. Kinder had a black circle painted on the floor, three long, low, linoleum-topped tables with midget chairs around them, two low blackboards, a piano, and a screened, open fireplace in one corner for winter warmth. Outside there was a dingy cloakroom housing washbasins and clothes-hooks, a draughty lobby where there were lockers against the wall, and a tiny wood-room where the firewood was stacked.

Kinder was a neat and tidy room and not, like many classrooms today, festooned with juvenile art works, forests of mobiles and 'projects'. Order, discipline and tidiness were certainly ideals to be aimed at in those days, but austerity came into it, too.

The three tables represented the three earliest grades – Preparatory (or Play Class), One and Two – but we called them Bottom, Middle and Top tables. To those of us at Middle or Top, the denizens of Bottom represented a very low form of life. To make matters worse, there were usually boys amongst them, and I decided they were a great nuisance, being rather rough and rude and ganging up against us in the playground. I was not at all used to boys.

Jenks was in the dark about my educational standard, so she set me to copy 'pothooks' and 'ones' into an exercise book as a first step in learning to write. I did this diligently for about a week, in silence, before she discovered that I could already read and write fairly competently, as well as being able to spell 'hippopotamus' correctly, without drawing breath. Whether I could spell anything more useful is not recorded, but nevertheless I was installed in glory at the Top table with several other girls (including Margaret) and here we carried on with our work in pursuit of red stars (stamped on), three of which were worth a coveted gold star (stuck on). Those stars in my work book filled me with pride and a glowing sense of achievement as I turned back the pages to gloat over them.

From time to time we would leave our tables at Jenks's command and coalesce around the black circle on the floor. Here we stood to sing the morning hymn or other songs; here we did exercises, prancing or skipping round the ring or sitting on it to point our toes into the middle. The most exciting sessions involved the percussion band, when we rattled and thumped and twangled and beat castanets, tambourines, bells and triangles, and in turn one of us was chosen to wield the baton, while Jenks played the piano. Jenks managed to conjure up the aura of the famed conductor Dr Malcolm Sargent in our midst, for Dr Sargent had dazzled Australian audiences (including Jenks) during his first visit here in 1936. On a portable gramophone she played us one or two of his recordings to inspire us, then, through the back of her head, she watched our performances for any signs of slackness or inattention.

'You are not watching the conductor!' she would cry, while the piano continued on its merry way. 'You must watch the baton and never speak a word!' Pom-tee-pom. 'Whatever would happen if Dr Sargent's orchestra missed the beat?' Rum-tum. Magnetised by the legendary Dr Sargent, we stood there around our magic circle, thumping and tinkling and drumming in the noble tradition of London's Albert Hall.

A portion of the 'Kinder' room, showing the Top Table (Grade 2) and a glimpse of the 'circle' on the floor. (MAG 1940)

At lunchtime, most day girls went home for a meal, but Dorothy and I, who lived so far away, marched off to hot dinners in the boarders' dining-room, where I sat at Jenks's table. There were four or five long, white-draped tables and a round one where the Headmistress and several other teachers sat, and the floors were covered in shiny brown linoleum. The room echoed to the clatter of feet and cutlery and chattering girls. Jenks asked me to pass the cruets. What was this new word? Crimson with ignorance, I said to her, 'Please, what did you say?' 'The cruets, dear, the salt and pepper; and next time say "I beg your pardon".' I felt so ashamed, but the puddings made up for the wretched cruets. Ambrosial milk puddings in huge enamel baking dishes were borne in – baked sago or tapioca or rice, swimming thickly under a top layer of succulent brown skin. For some reason the boarders did not share my rather piggish delight in these dishes, but they certainly helped to build me up after my bout of whooping cough.

Sports Day was an ordeal in Kinder, for we little ones were put through a torture known as 'The Early Morning Rush'. This race appeared to have two purposes; it was a severe test of our very limited manual skills, and it was hilarious fun for the larger onlookers. We lined up and when the whistle blew we had to run to a point where a jumbled heap of clothing awaited each of us. In full view of all those mooing adults, we had to change from sandshoes to school shoes, tying the laces to perfection, then struggle into hat, gloves and coat, doing up the buttons, and finally erect an umbrella. Only then could we labour on to the finishing line. One umbrella after another would shoot up all around me, but it was no use – I was always left behind, humiliated, because I couldn't tie my shoelaces.

ONWARD AND UPWARD

In 1938, those of us at Top table in Kinder graduated upwards into Remove which was in the room next door, sharing the same cloakroom and woodheap. Nobody ever explained why it was called Remove. The transition was made easy because Jenks (re)moved up with us, and a new teacher arrived to take over the Kinder.

Remove was proper school; it consisted of three rows of double desks representing Grades 3, 4 and 5. We started in Remove C next to the window and worked our way up, during three years, through Remove B in the middle row to the pinnacle of Remove A which was, appropriately, nearest the door. Our new elevated status in Remove was symbolised by those two important pieces of furniture, the desk and the inkwell.

Each double desk was fitted with two porcelain inkwells which were filled regularly from a huge bottle. They also became clogged up with soggy pellets of blotting paper, pencil shavings and other rubbish, and ink stains spread over and into the desks and onto fingers, faces, tongues and knees. The smell of ink was pervasive, as was its astringent, bitter taste, and our mothers had cause to be thankful that our uniforms were of navy blue. We learned to use pens made up of wooden handles, metal nib-holders and gold relief nibs. Nibs were accident-prone. Pens rolled about on the floor and were trodden on, they were thrown as darts, and jabbed into inkwells or the bottom of the girl in front, or used to excavate holes in the desk-top. Nibs were broken, bent, twisted and crossed, or adorned with fluff and hairs, so that our books were decorated with blots and smears and smudges. The most essential item in our educational armoury was probably the eight-fold sheet of blotting paper, which swabbed up the mess as we went along. In Kinder we used pencils, and before that, I suppose at Boo's School, I had used a slate.

There were small seductive pleasures; the pure, virgin pages of a new exercise book; ruling up; the occasional triumph of a whole page completed correctly, without blot or error; the swinging chorus of the Times Tables, and the gradual recognition of their numerical patterns. Our very first textbook was the Speller, long, narrow and brown, with its unadorned lists of words, ten of which we learned each night for homework – and we were beyond the cat on the mat stuff; in Remove I remember mastering words like 'accommodation' and 'fuchsia'.

Jenks (and later Miss Hiller, whom we called Hillerino) carried out with apparent ease the daunting task of teaching three grades at once in this multi-age system. Our grounding in the Three Rs was thorough and lasting. The overlapping of grades was a positive advantage in this; a curious child in Remove C was bound to soak up interesting items from the other side of the room, and the process could work in reverse for the Remove A dreamer who needed reminding about the ways of multiplication or how to spell 'their'. It was a practical mixture of extension and consolidation.

Handwriting lessons continued and Jenks decorated the top of the blackboard with a permanent frieze of the alphabet all looped together. Each morning we rehearsed our spelling and copied down dictation, we did mental arithmetic and ordinary arithmetic, and we ritually chanted our Tables.

'Now, girls, rule up for ten mental and ten spelling ... ready? What is 2+3+5+7-4? What is 9 times 7? How many eggs in two and a half dozen? How do you spell "diphtheria"? How do you spell it? ... yes, phth ...' One needed to know how to spell diphtheria in those days, just as one needed to know that whooping cough began with a W. Before learning to spell it I had once asked Mother, 'Do horses hoof when they have hoofing cough?', which just went to show how important spelling was if you weren't to make a fool of yourself.

Our training in the examination system began early. Every Friday morning we had a Test consisting of ten spelling, dictation, ten mental and five sums. Jenks would correct our Test books over the weekend and on Mondays they were handed back by the headmistress herself, Miss Victoria Krome. The moment of her arrival was unpredictable, but as she entered the room a shiver of apprehension ran round the class. Miss Krome seemed enormously tall in her black gown. She had piercing, but humorous, black eyes and she was an expert at prolonging the agony of handing back our work.

Being read to at the parental knee was largely a thing of the past, because our parents were now too busy. This didn't much matter to me as I could now read for myself and I was given books – fairy tales, Bible stories, *Alice in Wonderland*, *The Wind in the Willows*, *Doctor Dolittle*. Jenks read them at school, too, and Hiawatha was also much in vogue in the classroom.

With Margaret (right) in 1939. Taken by Jenks in the school garden. Our tunic hems obviously 'allowed for growth'.

In Remove we were introduced to elementary grammar. This involved ruling up our books for 'Subject and Predicate' and parsing exercises. I was quite interested to find out about the parts of speech and how sentences worked, but within the next twenty years it was decided by educational experts that grammatical concepts are beyond the grasp of young children. Within a generation or so there were few teachers who knew much about grammar either!

Although we were acquainted with adverbs and pronouns we had little or no experience of standing in front of easels and expressing ourselves in swirls and splashes of paint. For us, Art consisted of pastels, grey pastel books and technicolour dust. As for craft, I recall weaving a native hut out of raffia, and shaping lumps of plasticine, but little more. Dr Sargent and the band had been left behind in Kinder, but by now I was learning the violin as an extra.

VIOLIN

I think the violin was Mother's idea. I found myself being presented with a half-size fiddle and being taken to meet Miss Rehfisch. Miss Rehfisch travelled up from Melbourne once a week to give violin lessons in Ballarat, and although I had no previous experience of music teachers as a race, I knew at once that she was a special sort of person. She combined a warm and enthusiastic personality with deep musical feeling and readiness in giving praise, all of which are necessary to extract any response from small, shy children. Before I had progressed much beyond the open string stage, I found myself in a violin quartet, counting grimly at No 3 desk and glowing with triumph at finishing on the right note at the right time. This fact did not escape Miss Rehfisch (how could it?), who was warm in her praise for each of us. The first violinist in the group, and the best, was Master Bobby Cooper, one of Ballarat's golden boys, who went on to become Concert Master of the South Australian Symphony Orchestra.

Far less enjoyable were school concerts. I was told that I would be performing and Miss Rehfisch came to the school hall beforehand to put me through my paces. I cannot remember what I played, but I clearly recall the misery of standing alone on the stage, dressed in a horrid white frock with pearl buttons, while out in the dark hall rows of faces stared and simpered at me. It was long past my bedtime; I felt weak and hopeless and unable to control bow or fingering, but I must have scraped through to the end for the worst moment came with the applause. Mingled with the clapping was the distinct sound of laughter. They thought I was a joke! I was too young to recognise the fond laughter of adults melting at the sight of infant performers. After the concert, the family found me near the car, sitting in the gutter, crying. Being laughed at can be humiliating for a child, and I hated it. Once, in Newcastle, I rounded on some well-intentioned visitor who had committed this offence and shouted, 'Don't you laugh at Mary!!'

Music exams were less distressing than the school concert. The audience was one fatherly gentleman, who certainly didn't laugh. There wasn't much to laugh about, but Miss Rehfisch's pupils were given great moral and musical support by the piano accompanist, Miss Murphy. She stiffened our resolve in the waiting room and steered us through our set pieces like a guardian angel (in a hat). She repeated this service during ordeals at the Alfred Hall, when we competed at the South Street Competitions. This again was no laughing matter: it was the cut throat world of the eisteddfod. As in England and Wales, mining and music had developed side by side in Ballarat.

The Alfred Hall was huge and ramshackle, with an iron roof and weatherboard walls. Church-like, it had a nave flanked by side aisles; theatre-like, it had a gallery, and it could hold about 5000 people. I expect that very few of Ballarat's musical young have escaped the South Street Comps, and at the age of seven I found myself in this cavernous hall competing with other small fiddlers in the Violin Solo (under 10) – 1st Prize £1, 2nd Prize 10/-. The hall was largely empty save for a scattering of hawk-eyed mothers near the front. In the dim distance sat the adjudicator, ghostly in the glow of his little reading lamp and wearing a green eye-shade. The stage sloped alarmingly towards the front. Miss Murphy was my lifeline as I wiped my bow across the strings, and the strains of Handel's long-suffering Bourrée wailed out for the umpteenth time that morning. Applause was polite but thin. When the adjudicator climbed down from his perch and up to the stage to give his verdict, I found that I had achieved an Honourable Mention. It was not £1, nor even 10/-, but it sounded rather grand and Mother was delighted.

THE STAGE

The school hall was less alarming, but its stage furnishings were primitive, consisting of dark brown curtains hanging from metal bars around the three sides, with a drop curtain at the front. At one side of the stage there was an empty space, at the lower floor level, where the actors milled about, waiting to 'go on'. The only way to reach the stage was via a moveable set of wooden steps and then through the brown curtains. In my Remove years our classes were involved in two dramatic presentations in the hall, both adapted from Lewis Carroll. In 'The Mad Hatter's Tea Party' I played the March Hare, with cardboard ears which kept falling over into my teacup, and although the Dormouse was played by a small girl she wasn't really small enough to fit into the teapot, which was a weak spot in the production. In 'The Duchess's Croquet Party' I was cast as the Cheshire Cat or, rather, as a disembodied grin leering through the brown curtains at the rear. I didn't have to speak, but my jaws ached for ages afterwards. These plays were attended loyally by parents and caused great hilarity, very possibly for the wrong reasons, but they were much more fun than playing solo in school concerts.

We were first introduced to the school hall in Remove C, for another sign of our superiority over the Kinder kids was our daily attendance at assembly with the big girls. Each morning we lined up and marched across the quadrangle to the hall, where we sat in the front row clutching our new hymn books. Miss Krome would sweep in, black gown afloat, and conduct proceedings from the stage, assisted by a sixth-former who read a passage from the Bible. Under such eagle eyes we could do little but behave ourselves and try to sing the hymns with some appearance of comprehension – not easy for seven-year-olds when grappling, for instance, with ...

> Our Shield and Defender, the Ancient of days,
> Pavilion'd in splendour, and girded with praise.

However, although the meaning was inscrutable, the words were noble, resounding, with a tune to match.

Sometimes there were special visitors to entertain us or to address us in assembly. The most intriguing of these performances was the Lantern Lecture – ancestor of the slide evening. Lantern lectures seemed to be the speciality of missionaries, and if they were to take place at school in the daytime the assembly hall had to be blacked out. This was achieved, in some degree, by masking the tall windows with assorted rugs, which must have been stripped from the boarders' beds and which lent to the hall a ghostly and inappropriate aura of gay tartan and check. The lecturer sometimes operated the massive lantern himself, pushing the big glass slides in and out; more often someone did it for him, while he stood at the front with a long stick and pointed out features of interest on the screen. The 'screen' was a cotton sheet pinned to the stage curtain, which gave a rather undulating effect to the image, and the pictures were black and white, save for those which had been hand-tinted in unnaturally bright colours. There seemed to be many pictures of clergymen and native huts, Africans with wide smiles and Papuans with wonderfully frizzy hair. On these occasions we often sang hymn number 358:

> From Greenland's icy mountains
> From India's coral strand,
> Where Afric's sunny fountains
> Roll down their golden sand ...

I wondered about the eccentric behaviour of those African 'fountains' rolling about (our own fountain did no such thing), but otherwise the words evoked wonderful impressions of light and colour and far places, of soft spicy breezes and palmy plains, and my imagination was so busy with these that I failed to grasp the main theme of the hymn – that every prospect pleases and only man is vile, with its further implication that some men (heathens), through no fault of their own, are viler than others. Hence the need for missionaries.

DIVINITY

There were certain lessons which all three grades in Remove took together, such as Divinity. To take lessons in Divinity seems now a bit presumptuous, but that's what they were called then, and one of our annual tasks was to draw a plan of The Church's Year. This took the form of a big wheel divided into fifty-two weekly segments which were then coloured in – purple for Advent and Lent, white for Christmas, Easter and Ascension, red for Whitsun, green for Epiphany and then the endless green plains of Trinity which quite upset the artistic balance of the whole. Drawing maps of Palestine and the Middle East was another regular part of Divinity, with little blue fringes to represent the Mediterranean seaboard.

I had books of Bible stories at home, and Jenks also read them to us at school in Divinity. These narratives were enthralling, especially those selected from the Old Testament. Many of the tales were about children – the sacrifice of Isaac, Joseph and his brothers, David and Goliath, Moses in the bulrushes – which gave us young readers an immediate foothold. I wished very much to know the technology of David's slingshot, and the pattern of Joseph's coat of many colours. Isaac's story was a heart-stopper, made bearable only by the knowledge that God relented just as Abraham was raising his knife! But the saga of the Israelites in Egypt and the Exodus probably gave us our first taste of the grandeur of the human story, mixed as it was with myth, legend and mystery. This is thrilling stuff in its sweep of history, dealing with the struggles of the human condition, temporal and spiritual power, slavery and tyranny, plagues and slaughter, loyalty and treachery. Each episode is told simply but provides great scope for young imaginations; plagues of frogs, the Nile turning to blood, the angel of the Lord daubing the lintels with blood for the Passover, the Burning Bush, Pharoah's chariots thundering in pursuit of the Israelites, only to be engulfed by the Red Sea. Even Cecil B. de Mille was unable to do it justice.

In one Divinity lesson Jenks used the word 'excruciating'. She didn't explain it, but she didn't need to as she was describing the crucifixion at the time, in grim detail, and she asked us to try to imagine the 'excruciating pain'. We couldn't, of course, but the word was gouged into my brain. This sort of instruction, rather than the Easter bunny, was our lead up to the Easter season, for the latter was not to be divorced from Lent. Self-denial was emphasised and the main methods for exercising this were by putting pennies in small cardboard money boxes (distributed by the Australian Board of Missions) and by giving up chocolate and sweets for Lent. We also sang a long and dismal item called 'The Story of the Cross' in assembly every Friday during Lent.

Although the Easter bunny myth had little place in our family customs, Easter eggs were well to the fore. We hoarded them in our bedroom drawers and practised self-denial while drooling over the hoard. This sort of Lenten self-denial was rather pleasurable, as one could feel virtuous during the abstinence while anticipating a chocolate binge on Easter Day. Margaret was once given a rich, dark chocolate bear of immense proportions. He lay wrapped in cellophane in a box among her jumpers and we gazed at him in dribbling awe. When the orgy began it was necessary for me to stay the night at Margaret's to help her with the task. This must have been very early in the war years before the chocolate famine. In fact, the war brought with it real self-denial.

PLAYTIME

Most of our games were played in the quadrangle, which was a large gravelled space with school buildings on three sides and the Oak Tree on the fourth. The Oak was a significant tree which must have affected generations of girls as they passed through the school. It transformed an otherwise dull yard into a place of character, and there was something reassuring about its size, its enduring presence and its regular seasonal changes. Its canopy sheltered us from sun and rain, and we waded through the fallen brown leaves and collected the fat acorns for 'ammo' or to make into little hatted men with matchstick arms and legs. We played chasey and hidey around it and its massive trunk was 'home', or the anchor for big skipping ropes. It was probably smaller than it seemed to me then, but I remember it as a giant among trees. Its branches were certainly beyond the reach of climbers.

The school had no conventional playground equipment and I doubt if we missed it. In the quad was a small tree with one suitable and long-suffering branch which was rarely without a small body suspended upside down from the knees and displaying a generous view of navy bloomers. Otherwise we passed the time in a variety of ways, most of them ruinous to shoes – teetering along rock edgings, scratching in the gravel, playing hopscotch, hidey, chasey, statues, skipping '...All in together, this fine weather ...' getting faster and faster as the rope gathered momentum and the dust flew '... Salt, mustard, vinegar, PEPPER! ...'

Playtime was unsupervised, but the traditional games of childhood were magically passed on from one generation to the next, and we shared our own meagre resources of balls, hoops and skipping ropes. Pieter Brueghel's sixteenth century painting 'Children's Games' shows activities which persist to this day – blindman's buff, leapfrogging, marbles, jacks, stilts, piggyback rides and so on. Wherever these games originated, they provide rich opportunities for counting, balance, muscular development, co-ordination, manual skills (jacks, cat's cradle, yoyos), observation, concentration, taking turns, obeying rules and so on. While having fun, we had taught ourselves a lot about teamwork and rules long before we reached the age of organised sports.

Thanks to the gravel of the quad, life was a succession of grazed knees, bleeding shins and visits to Matron to be patched up. Matron was Miss Violet Larkins, a small, grey-bunned lady who resembled Mrs Tiggywinkle. At about that time, Larks astonished the school community by acquiring a tiny black car, which became known as 'the Puddlejumper'. Very little of Larks could be seen above the dashboard as she chugged off down the drive, and when she peered down in search of the clutch she disappeared from view entirely. Not many women drove, let alone owned, a car in those days.

The school hockey field was usually frost bound in the winter, but when it grew lush in the late spring and summer we would roll in the long grass, making cape-weed daisy chains of ludicrous length and closely examining the bees and beetles at work. After a mowing, we scooped up piles of fragrant grass and had weak, giggly grass fights, or buried one another, and then returned to the classroom with daisy chains about our necks, and green knees. Up behind the boarding house there was a woodheap where we could climb and jump, and when we tired of that we could make secret nests in the long grass growing at the back. Sometimes we would find a screaming circular saw in action, with two men feeding the logs into the flashing blade. Then we would sit on the woodheap, wide-eyed and wincing, and watch the monster slicing up the fuel for our winter fires.

Next to the woodheap stood the Fort. This square, brick stronghold, screened on two sides by worn, straggly hedges, was the school toilet block. A request to 'leave the room' during lessons was never treated lightly by teachers, for a journey to the Fort could be prolonged almost indefinitely as one set out on that long trek. On the other hand, conditions at the Fort were pretty bleak, so that pupils thought twice about attempting the journey in winter, and the reasons for leaving the room had to be fairly pressing, one way or another. Understandably, one hymn which was never heard at school assemblies was 'Hold the fort, for I am coming'.

Beyond the woodheap and strictly Out of Bounds, was an overgrown, vacant allotment called 'Pringles'. There was a much coveted mulberry tree in Pringles and sometimes, when the silkworm season was in full swing, we were granted special permission to break the bounds in order to pick some mulberry leaves. Once there, of course, we found the other attractions of Pringles irresistible. There were warm nests in the long grass, and a pine tree with low-growing boughs supporting a platform of planks, rather like somebody's house in the Hundred Acre Wood. Christopher Robin would have felt entirely at home. What a hideout!

Who had put it there? How unjust to declare such a place Out of Bounds.

The rules of the school were even more complex than those of the Tramways Board. There were those boundaries, such as Pringles, which no-one dared overstep. Like the trams, the school ran strictly to time, measured out by bells. There was a uniform with sub-rules of its own – hats and gloves to be worn in the street at all times, and bloomers to be navy. Our very movements were regulated – no riding bikes in the school grounds or on footpaths; no climbing out of windows; no running in the corridor; 'Single file please girls!'; no talking in assembly after the silence bells; no eating in the street or in class; no chewing gum at any time. We obeyed this code of behaviour fairly well, or at least tried not to get caught, for no-one enjoyed a Talking-to. Little homilies on disobedience or unmannerly behaviour sometimes included the unanswerable question, 'Would you do such a thing in your mother's drawing-room, dear?' Detentions were not meted out until one reached the middle school, and corporal punishment was largely unknown.

And so, schooldays drifted on within their framework of timetables and bells, of Friday tests and trams, of *Hymns Ancient & Modern* and hopscotch, of rice puddings and gravel rash, of daisy chains and Divinity, disturbed only by the occasional illness or epidemic or half holiday. But great events were unfolding in the background.

The school classrooms seen across the hockey field. The oak tree peeps over the central roof. Manifold House is beyond with tennis courts to the right.

The Sweep of History

CENTENARY

Before we had been in Ballarat for long, the word 'centenary' was suddenly on everybody's lips. At school the opportunity was seized to instruct us in the wonders of Latin Roots. The citizens of Ballarat were trumpeting this word, it turned out, because our city was about to be one hundred years old (Latin *centum* = hundred, *centenarius* = of a hundred). This sort of thing reminded me of the tree labels in the Botanical Gardens, and now I was adding 'centenary' to my word collection.

In my childish way, I supposed that the city as I then saw it, with its solid banks and its bluestone churches, its trams and wide streets, the majestic railway station and the Town Hall clock tower – that all this had been plonked down in this spot one hundred years earlier and had been going about its business ever since. But what, in fact, we were about to celebrate was the arrival in 1838 of the Yuille cousins and other settlers and, most importantly, their sheep. Some of these historic creatures were set to graze on the fringes of the Great Swamp, which soon became known as Yuille's Swamp as the two men took up more land around its shores and settled down as the first pastoralists there, naming their tract of land the 'Ballaarat Run'. Thus, it was reasoned, they became the first 'citizens' of Ballarat.

My memories of the Centenary Celebrations in March 1938 are blurred but exceedingly flowery. The city, as always, put on its finest floral garb, and buildings and monuments were decorated with waxed or crêpe paper flowers and fairy lights. Among the bands, processions and floats, the decorated streets and flower-bedecked trams, I especially recall a giant floral carpet in the Alfred Hall. At night there were outings to see the floodlit buildings and the fairy lights; by day we were marched in crocodile formation from school to take part in the fiesta, and this in itself was a thrill, for daygirls rarely had the opportunity to be part of the crocodile. Boarders were used to it, especially on Sundays when they marched in reptilian formation to the Cathedral.

The year 1938 was the first centenary for Ballarat. In 1951 there was to be another one to mark the discovery of gold, with yet another in 1954 to commemorate the miners' uprising at Eureka. As newcomers in 1936, we had been taken in hand (especially by Archdeacon Best) and told about the stirring days of the gold rush and shown those parts of the town still scarred with mullock heaps and the messy remains of the mining operations. We drove to the top of Black Hill to see the excavations and the view across the city, and from there it was easy to see the strange contrast between the well-planned streets of the western township, up on its hill, and the muddled confusion of streets winding about below along the old gold-bearing gullies of Canadian, Eureka and Mount Pleasant, with historic Main Street wandering off towards Buninyong and Geelong. We visited the monument on the supposed site of the Eureka Stockade and I climbed on the cannons around its base, assuming (wrongly) that the battle at Eureka had been fought on an epic scale with cannon balls.

The deserted mullock heaps, the rusted machinery, the empty shafts and the lumpy mounds of yellow clay and white quartz – what did they all mean? They certainly did not evoke the feverish atmosphere of the diggings in the 1850s. What remained was, if anything, sinister, and I suppose many of Ballarat's children grew up under the vague cloud of menace which hangs over any mining district. We were told to beware of bottomless pits and suffocating earth-falls, not to mention the danger of drowning in the murk of waterlogged shafts.

Then, during the Celebrations, I saw a replica of the Welcome Nugget and I began to realise what all the fuss was about. This golden prize was dug up in 1858 and weighed in at 2217 ounces. I was ever afterwards hopeful of stubbing a toe on a similar prize or at least of scooping up a handful of egg-sized nuggets from the clay. One always kept an eye open for the tell-tale gleam. At school, very little was made of that turbulent episode of history which lay on our very doorstep, for the gold rush was probably considered a rough and unsavoury field of study for young persons. Whatever the reason, as I moved up the school we touched briefly in our history lessons on the manly figures of the early explorers, and then had our attention whisked away to the supposedly more dignified annals of British History.

Fortunately this solemn subject was counterbalanced by a slim volume which we, and many others, had on the bookself at home: *1066 And All That*, by Sellar and Yeatman, first published in 1930. Our 1937 edition was the twenty-fifth in seven years, which showed that the ability of the English to laugh at themselves was one of their most endearing (and perhaps unexpected) traits. In the 'Compulsory Preface' the authors state: 'History is not what you thought. It is what you can remember. All other history defeats itself.'

While this was a very unsound basis for historical study, such an attitude did at least liven things up; *1066 And All That* also demonstrated that the more one knew of the real facts, the funnier the joke became.

SCHOOLGIRL WISDOM.

....The masculine of vixen is vicar.

....A synonym is a word used when you don't know how to spell the one you first thought of.

....An abstract noun is the name of something which has no existence as—goodness.

....An epistle is the wife of an apostle.

....Marconi is the stuff out of which puddings are made.

....In 1620, the pilgrims crossed the ocean. This is known as Pilgrim's Progress.

....Lollards were lazy people who always wanted to rest against something.

....Joan of Arc was Noah's wife.

....Julius Caesar was renowned for his great strength. He threw a bridge across the Rhine.

....A grass widow is the wife of a dead vegetarian.

....A damsel is a small plum.

....Many Crusaders died of salvation.

....A dirge is a song a man sings when he is dead.

....A glazier is a man who runs down mountains.

....People in Iceland are called Equinoxes.

In the tradition of *1066 and All That*. From the school magazine 1937. (MAG)

HISTORICAL DOORWAYS

Doors offering glimpses into the realms of history were all around us, but rarely were they pushed open wide. Old Testament stories and classical statues sketched in a hazy backdrop of ancient civilisations, and of course there was obvious evidence of the local past in the diggings, the Eureka Stockade monument, the Chinese Joss house. The bandstand at the foot of Sturt Street was a memorial to the heroic bandsmen on the 'Titanic', with a tiny replica of the doomed ship on its weather vane. The Avenue of Honour, rolls of honour, adult anecdote and limbless men were reminders of the Great War, as were Anzac Day and Armistice Day. The Spanish influenza epidemic was often mentioned by our elders, and there were other small items of personal history – Father's binoculars which he had picked up on a battlefield in France, and the big woollen rug he took to the Great War, and which I still have. These items and his uniform proved that Father had gone to that war, but he never talked about it to us.

One of Jenks's heroes was Lord Nelson. Each year on 21 October she would say, 'Today is a special day. Who can tell me what day it is?' and we would wave our hands and reply, 'It's Trafalgar Day!' This for some reason still rated a star on our calendar, although the battle had taken place in 1805 in another hemisphere. I can understand why Guy Fawkes Night hung in there – 'Please to remember the Fifth of November, Gunpowder, Treason and Plot' – the excuse for fireworks was sufficient reason. But the Trafalgar story was also told each year and it had certain intriguing details, such as Lord Nelson losing an eye in one battle and an arm in another, and then dying heroically in Hardy's arms on the deck of HMS 'Victory'. In Jenks's view the high point of the drama was the famous signal Nelson sent to the fleet. On 21 October 1805 this message was conveyed by flags, but in our classroom it appeared in beautiful copperplate across the blackboard:

England expects that every man will do his duty.

Nelson's message, of course, was seen to be entirely appropriate again by 1940 although the enemy had changed.

Place names offered historical clues. Of all the destination signs on the front and back of trams, one stood out as exotic – SEBASTOPOL. This was not a tram which we ever caught, for the suburb of Sebastopol was a long way down Drummond Street South, on the rural edge of town. Yet the name intrigued and we children called it Sebass or Sebba-stopple. But no imaginative teacher opened that door to the Crimean War or pointed to other place names like Raglan Street, Balaclava Street or Cardigan and explained the connection. By some form of osmosis we learnt that Sebastopol was in the Crimea, and

Florence Nightingale was held up as a role model from time to time (nursing being one of the few professions available to girls then). English Literature also came to the rescue, for nearly every poetry anthology in later years contained 'The Charge of the Light Brigade' by Lord Tennyson, so we gleaned what little we knew about the brave British soldiers and their hopelessly incompetent commanders (including Lords Cardigan and Raglan) from the galloping rhythms of the poem which described that stirring event at Balaclava. It took place at almost the same time as the gold rush and obviously inspired the namers of streets and localities in our colony.

As our own war cranked up in the 1940s, the original Sebastopol in Russia was sometimes in the news once more. We wore cardigans and garments with raglan sleeves (and still do). We began knitting balaclavas for the troops (and indeed they are still in vogue for armed holdups). Knitting provides an apt metaphor for all these historical threads which are woven into our lives and language, and which we often overlook.

KINGS AND QUEENS

The idea of monarchy was deeply embedded. I took it in at my mother's knee as she read the poems of A.A. Milne.

> They're changing guard at Buckingham Palace
> Christopher Robin went down with Alice.
> Alice is marrying one of the guard.
> 'A soldier's life is terribly hard,' said Alice.

Fairy tales about wicked queens, charming princes and turreted castles reinforced the whole notion, as did religious imagery and metaphor, which were rich in crowns, thrones and kingdoms.

It was but a step from all this to the funeral of King George V early in 1936. We were still in Newcastle when it took place and, being only five, I wouldn't have seen film of the event, but I still hold the pictures of it clearly in my memory. A special edition of *The Illustrated London News* came into the family's possession and for months, perhaps years, afterwards I would gaze at the photographs and paintings of the royal lying-in-state and the funeral – wintry London, Westminster Abbey, huge crowds in the streets, Queen Mary and the royal ladies veiled in black; above all, the coffin on its catafalque in the Great Hall of the Palace of Westminster, at the corners four tall candles and four officers from the Brigade of Guards, heads bowed under their plumed helmets and drawn swords reversed, while through the gloom filed an endless stream of people, paying homage. On the last night of the five-day vigil, the King's four sons replaced the Guards and kept watch over their father's bier. I was so relieved that there were four of them, just the right number! Then the funeral procession – the coffin wrapped in a flag and drawn on a gun carriage, the four princes walking behind, and after them other kings, princes and dukes.

Before the word 'centenary' had embedded its Latin roots in my vocabulary, 'abdication' and 'coronation' were already planted there. They were closely associated with our stamp album where, among the giant kangaroos sitting on top of Australia and the bearded face of George V staring out of an oval frame, there suddenly appeared several mint sets of English stamps bearing an austere profile of handsome King Edward. He was clean-shaven. The word 'coronation' was floating about, but by the time we reached Ballarat the word 'abdication' was being whispered. What did it mean? Why did the adults seem shaken and confused? There was a lot of tut-tutting and listening to news broadcasts on the enormous wireless in the dining room. Then somebody told me that those English stamps would be 'really valuable now'. In the shops the face of Edward on all the coronation mugs and souvenirs somehow turned into another face – quite a similar face. The coronation happened, not to Edward VIII but to George VI who, unlike Edward, had two small daughters and a queen and a good many dogs, and was therefore more interesting, I felt.

The coronation took place on Father's birthday, 12 May 1937. More magazines and pictures arrived to enlighten us about this great event, and the central images were of crown, orb, sceptre, robes and the golden coach. The line between reality and fairy tale became even more blurred. There was a huge bonfire at the Boys' Grammar School which, I think, must have been to mark the new reign, although bonfires were an annual event on Empire Day, 24 May and the two occasions could have been merged.

King George V among his colonial fauna in the stamp album

The two little princesses, Elizabeth and Margaret Rose, became so familiar that they were almost like our very own cousins. We were given a book, *The Little Princesses and their Dogs*, which showed this happy family playing with their corgis on the lawn or looking through the windows of their human-sized dolls' house. The girls were neatly dressed in skirts and jumpers and hair ribbons just like those we wore. In this context royalty was very easy to accept. In those days it was, in fact, a brilliant blend of the fairy tale and the ordinary.

EMPIRE

My parents were both born in Queen Victoria's reign. The old Queen had been dead for only twenty-nine years when I was born, and those Empire Day bonfires were still being fired up annually on her birthday. Ballarat was in fact a Victorian city in every sense and the old Queen's statue, erected in 1900 to mark her Diamond Jubilee (1897), was one of the imposing sights of Sturt Street. There she stood, robed, crowned, laden with orb and sceptre, and gazing forth imperiously over her colonial realms, in this case towards her humble and loyal volcano, Mount Warrenheip. Our particular state of the realm was called Victoria. We went to a school called Queen's. The main entrance to Ballarat was along Victoria Street. The Alfred Hall had been built and named to commemorate the visit of her son, Prince Alfred, in 1867. Craig's Royal Hotel had accommodated the Prince on that occasion and carried the royal favour ever since. There was another unexpected bonus from that royal visit – the Alfred Bells in the Town Hall tower. A citizen of Ballarat, the dastardly H.J. O'Farrell, had made a shocking but luckily unsuccessful attempt to assassinate the Prince in Sydney, and this beautiful peal of bells was hung to commemorate not so much the attempt as the royal recovery. These pealing bells brought the closed-down city to life on Sunday mornings as we drove past to the Cathedral, and we were proud to learn that only two or three other cities in the whole world had town hall bells.

We still joke about the pink or red countries on the map of the world in those days, evidence of the spread and might of the British Empire, but at the time it was with a welcome sense of security that one observed this rash of pinkness. It was no joke then, especially in a remote and underpopulated land like ours; we needed to belong to something grander. The colonies might have provided most of life's raw materials, but British manufactures were considered the best in the world. 'Made in England' was the hallmark of top quality and reliability. 'Made in Japan' meant cheap imitation, shoddiness, goods to be avoided. There were endless streams of shipping to and fro through the Suez Canal or round the Cape, cargo boats and P&O or Orient liners carrying the Empire builders to their various outposts in the colonies and some of the more fortunate colonials 'home' to see how things were done properly. London was the centre of our universe.

In our family, as in many others, the ties with Britain were strong. Both my grandfathers were from the British Isles, one from England, the other from Ireland. The two grandmothers were born here, but their parents, with one exception, were migrants from England and Ireland. My father's sister was married to an English musician, living in London. My mother's sister was married to an English army officer, living in Essex, so most of our aunts and uncles were 'over there'. Letters from the two aunts were a regular event, and there was general amazement when the first airmails began to deliver flimsy blue envelopes in the space of just over a week.

Father (and all of us) belonged to the Church of England, and the head of that was the Archbishop of Canterbury. The flag of Saint George, the patron saint of England, was flown by most Anglican churches. Four out of the five Anglican bishops of Ballarat to that date had been born in England, and so had the Bishop of Newcastle. The latter rejoiced (or not) in the name of Francis de Witt Batty, while one of Father's predecessors in Ballarat was Maxwell Homfray Maxwell Gumbleton. Even their names were exotic (if giggle-making) compared to that of my Australian father, plain old Bill Johnson.

At home we had a large book called something like *Beautiful Britain in Pictures*, a sort of prehistoric coffee-table book. The photographs were in sepia, apart from a coloured frontispiece of a bluebell wood, which was the most beautiful thing I had ever seen. I spent hours poring over these pictures, absorbing the details of Tudor architecture and thatch, cathedral and abbey, village pubs and millennial oaks, moor and fen, crag and torrent. There seemed to be no equivalent volume recording the beauties of Australia, although since then we have overcome that particular aspect of the Cringe.

With all of that weighing down on us, it is no wonder that our school syllabus was rooted in the northern hemisphere and particularly in the British Isles. Their nursery rhymes and games, too, had been transplanted to the antipodes – 'Oranges and Lemons, say the bells of St Clement's' ... we sang at parties, and our rhymes were full of characters

82   Beside the Lake

like the Miller of Dee, Doctor Foster who went to Gloucester, the Grand Old Duke of York, and Dick Whittington, Lord Mayor of London. And, as I have already mentioned, that other great excuse for a bonfire, on 5 November, had come down to us from Guy Fawkes, who had tried to blow up the British Houses of Parliament in 1605.

Even at home we celebrated Guy Fawkes Night annually, as Father produced a packet of sparklers for us to wave about. Sometimes there were a few squibs to explode and a single catherine wheel nailed to a fence for its brief moment of glory. Once only there was a sky-rocket, launched from an empty bottle while we stood back nervously. Then it was all over, so quickly.

1939 – THE WATERSHED

The year of 1939 began badly, and nobody who lived through 13 January, when much of the south-east corner of Australia was ablaze, is likely to forget 'Black Friday'. We were holidaying in Adelaide, visiting grandmother Marmie, and after nearly a week of extraordinary heat the temperature on the thirteenth climbed to 118°F (48°C). As the infernal wind roared down from the north, the Adelaide Hills exploded in flames. The house we were staying in was barely a hundred yards from the beach, but we cowered inside for most of the day with the blinds drawn and the wireless on. It was hardly possible to imagine fire-fighting on such a hellish day, but hundreds of volunteers responded to the desperate radio calls for help. We finally ventured to the beach in the evening, treading gingerly on the sweltering bitumen of the road. The oily sea had black scum floating on its surface, and the sand was dark, too, with the thousands of people gathered like lemmings at the water's edge. Much of Victoria also burned that day, with a terrible death toll. Later, as we drove back to Ballarat through the blackened landscape, the sight of the incinerated houses and townships, reduced to twisted iron and starkly standing chimneys, might almost have been a premonition of things to come.

One day in August, 1939, I left Bishopscourt for school on the morning tram as usual, but I never went back. That afternoon, as I informed Jenks and my classmates in Remove B, I had to find a new way home and, instead of catching a tram, I walked.

In July, Father had taken the unusual step of announcing in a broadcast from the local radio station, 3BA, that Bishopscourt was to be sold and that another house had been acquired. In his statement he was already referring to the 'old' Bishopscourt, and from that moment the house round the lake has always been known, in our family at least, as 'Old Bishopscourt', which is how I shall refer to it from now on.

Old Bishopscourt from the lawns, shortly before demolition, 1939. (CFE)

On that August day when I walked home, feeling like a small explorer, we had left the lakeside and moved to Sturt Street West. None of the hassle of the move was mine, just the excitement. I recall no feelings of regret at leaving the old garden or the scenes of my big game hunts. With the resilience of an eight-year-old I was already looking forward to new delights. The Sturt Street house had nearly an acre of garden with plenty of trees, after all, and the lake – just at the end of Grove Street – would still be within a stone's throw. There was a real tennis court as well, and the new house was two-storied, which meant it had stairs and bedrooms with atticky windows. Best of all, it was only a few minutes' walk from Margaret's house in the same street.

Father and Mother were in many ways sad to be leaving Old Bishopscourt, and at first its gracious attributes seemed to outweigh the inconvenience and inadequacy of the plumbing and heating systems. However, the Ballarat Diocese was in financial straits, and the heavy expenditure of maintaining the place even as it stood was a great burden. Several times, while we lived there, large chunks of plaster ceiling had fallen in, and there was anxiety about the cypress trees after one had crashed to earth.

Bishop Thornton had lived in the house for only three years into the 1880s when he claimed that it was unsuitable. He wanted to build a new Bishopscourt, but was prevented by his Council. The old place continued to house bishops for a further sixty years. John Spooner, in his history of the Ballarat Diocese, wrote, '... it is difficult to understand why Bishop Thornton found it inappropriate. Various photos show it to have been a magnificent structure ... If it were still standing it would be considered a treasured part of the national heritage.' (The Golden See, p.199.)

Looking back now, it is only too easy to regard the sale and demolition of Old Bishopscourt as regrettable, almost an act of vandalism. Even in 1939 there were suggestions that the grounds, at least, should be purchased by the City Council and preserved as parkland, but no-one had quite that much vision, or money. I don't know whether the citizens of Ballarat regretted the loss of the old place; very few people now remember it. My parents engaged a water-colourist from the School of Mines to paint the old house, and they also had some photographs taken before we departed, although by then part of the garden had already been cleared of trees.

The estate was sold for subdivision into forty building blocks and it pleased Father that forty families, rather than just one, were subsequently able to live in that agreeable spot. The area today is occupied by the houses on St Aidan's Drive, Lindisfarne Avenue and The Boulevarde. It is fitting to have the English Saint Aidan and his holy island of Lindisfarne, Northumbria, so remembered on this land, once the site of St Aidan's College, but I daresay the simple Aidan would have had little use for boulevardes. What a pity that the municipal imagination did not stretch just a little further to another saintly street name. Saint Cuthbert, Aidan's successor as Bishop of Lindisfarne in 685 AD, would have been a likely candidate. Father's first parish had been St Cuthbert's in Adelaide, and he chose St Cuthbert's cross as the model for his own pectoral cross. Besides, St Cuthbert loved ducks – the eider duck was his emblem – so a street named for him beside Lake Wendouree would have been an happy memorial.

Out of all this destruction came one significant piece of preservation. The whole transaction made it just possible, financially, to buy the new house and also to rebuild the chapel, exactly as it was, on the new site – so not everything was lost. In addition to the chapel and the furniture, we took with us Dear Tip's tombstone, the urns from the front steps and the copper name-plates from the gates, a small scarlet oak as a memento of the garden, and the carpets from the drawing room, which served us for another fifteen years. Two swing doors inside the front entrance at Old Bishopscourt had contained stained glass panels depicting Ballarat's coat-of-arms, and these panels were placed in the two doors of Father's new study. And the Warden's House from St Aidan's College, being weatherboard, was sold and relocated in a nearby street.

But I have often wondered what happened to the cast-iron gates, the weathercock on the tower and the tiles in the entrance hall, not to mention the white marble mantelpieces from the drawing room. It is only too easy to imagine the common fate of the Cedar of Lebanon, the white wisteria and all the venerable trees. The day after we had moved out, Scruse returned to the old house to collect the few remaining items of garden furniture. He found that these had been spirited away and that the fountain had been smashed to pieces. The end of an era had come, there was no doubt at all.

Within a week or so of the move, on 3 September, 1939, war was declared and Old Bishopscourt, standing as it did as a relic of the gracious days of Victorian and Edwardian splendour, could not have passed into oblivion at a more telling moment.

I was two months short of my ninth birthday.

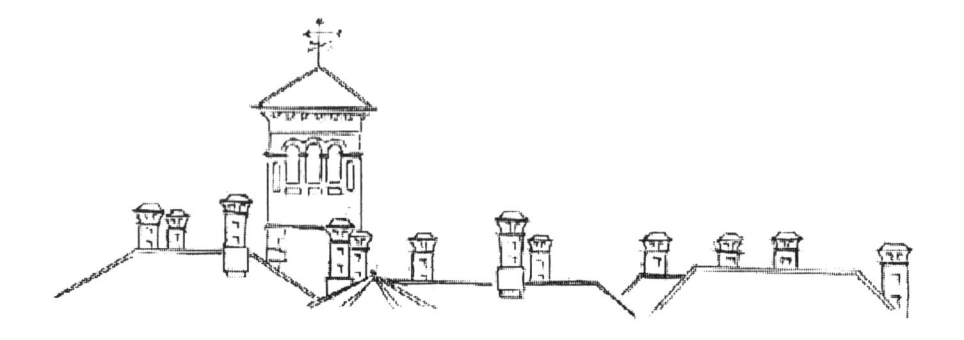

Part Two   1939-45

WAR

Transplanted to Sturt Street

THE NEW HOUSE

We just had time to shake down in the 'new' house before the war broke out. It was actually not new, but second-hand, having been built for a local doctor and his family some twenty years earlier, but Father described it as 'a dignified, spacious house with the same amount of accommodation as the Old Bishopscourt, but modern and in a perfect state of repair'. In other words, the reason for our move had nothing to do with the daunting size of the old place. This was another very large house, with over twenty rooms as well as numerous outbuildings and sheds. But it was more compact in that it was two-storied and not rambling round a courtyard, and certainly the grounds were only a fraction of the size of the old garden, although still close to an acre in extent.

Father was right in another respect. The house at 1416 Sturt Street was solidly built of brick, rendered in grey roughcast, with dark brown paintwork. Everything from the slate roof to the red cement-paved verandahs was of top quality. The foundations, it was said, were impressively deep and set on a bed of old railway lines from the mines.

The first drama was the transplanting of the chapel from one property to the other. There was a small, hedged-in garden at the rear corner of the new house, where it was found the chapel would just fit, although it would have to lie north and south instead of the traditional east and west, and two mulberry trees would have to be sacrificed. I was aghast – the only other mulberry tree that I knew of in the whole world grew in the out-of-bounds Pringles behind school. Now, suddenly, there were two of these treasures growing at our own back door, a source of endless silkworm fodder for me and all the other silkworm farmers at school, and they were going to be chopped down almost before I could harvest a single bunch of leaves! But the chapel wouldn't fit anywhere else, so the builders moved in and the mulberry trees moved out.

The building operations soon distracted me from the starving silkworms. This was amazing, to knock down a chapel and put it up again in a quite different place, brick by brick. Margaret was now close at hand and often came to play, and she and I followed the whole process with deep interest, especially as the master builder had a handsome son, who wore his hat at a rakish angle and winked at us frequently. Secretly, we nicknamed him 'Cockeye' because of his hat-angle. As the building neared completion, we exchanged cakes of chocolate with Cockeye: he gave us each a cake of Honey & Almond Milk, while for him we selected Club Chocolate for Men, paying for it with our saved-up pocket money.

In due course the chapel walls and roof were finished and the panelling and woodwork, the bright coats-of-arms, the staircase, the organ gallery and the wheezing harmonium were all fitted into place just as before. Everything was freshly painted and polished and deep blue carpet runners were laid on the floor, so in the end it looked better than ever. Outside, there were marked changes. Not only were the brick walls coated in grey roughcast to match the house, but in addition the sides which had been my hitting walls were now wedged tight against the fence or buildings, so tennis practice was stalled for the moment.

Another very large house. The new Bishopscourt in 1939. My bedroom at the far right, top. The acoustically brilliant white bathroom is above the front porch. (CFE)

90 Beside the Lake

The belfry was set up as the centrepiece of a small lawn on the west side of the chapel, at the back of the house. This was to become a favoured spot, as it was sheltered and private. Mother espaliéred apple and pear trees against the chapel walls, a red rose climbed over a trellis at one end and certain treasured plants grew in beds around the edges. (An eastern spinebill adopted this garden as his nectar stop-over.) The belfry was, as ever, used for climbing or tying things to or leaning against, and the bell-rope still dangled invitingly. Several years later I annexed the belfry's bottom story and converted it into a pigeon house. After the pigeons had departed to the cooking pot, the wire netting was removed and the highly fertilised soil at the bottom thereafter grew outrageous displays of cinerarias.

Rear view of the house. Chapel and belfry to the left, with nursery in centre and kitchen wing to the right. Photo taken after we had left. Mother's special garden around the belfry had been 'let go'. (BC 18.1.64)

MY BEDROOM

Of my various childhood bedrooms, this new one was the first I remember in any detail. It was at the back corner of the house, upstairs, and had sloping attic ceilings and a view over Grove Street and the neighbouring houses. In due course it was given a coat of pale blue Kalsomine. Mother made me a candlewick bedspread and Father constructed bookshelves, but the room was dominated by two large and rather 'holy' paintings by Margaret Tarrant. One of these I liked especially, as it featured the Christ child with a lot of quite normal looking animals. The other was a nativity scene, triptych style, with a deep blue night sky and the star above the stable, while the side panels were occupied by large angels with sumptuous wings. I accepted angels as part of the scheme of things, like the royal family. They appeared frequently in pictures and in most respects they looked like humans – except for their wings. As we were surrounded by other largish winged creatures (especially the white swans), wings on angels seemed quite unremarkable and I often wished to be able to stroke one. They were lucky to have arms as well, I felt, and it would have been interesting to observe an angel 'taking off'.

I don't think my bedroom was ever wildly untidy, because I didn't have many clothes or possessions to strew about, although I once kept a dead sparrow hawk in the wardrobe for about a week, and a shrivelled seahorse on the shelf for a good deal longer. I spent a lot of time rearranging my Noah's Ark procession of miniature animals, collections of natural objects like birds' eggs and feathers, and keeping the books straight in the shelves.

STAIRS

It was exciting to be moving into a two-storied house, to be able to live on two levels and to look out over other people's rooftops and yards or into the upper branches of trees. But the main advantage of such a house lay in its stairs. To most adults, stairs are a bore and often a burden, but to children they are an adventure playground, and in the new house we had two sets. The back stairs, narrow, noisy, linoleumed, clattered down from the children's bedrooms to the kitchen region. The front stairs, broad, polished, carpeted, quietly connected the main bedrooms to the front hall and the drawing room.

Over the following years we discovered dozens of ways of going up and down stairs, starting with the routine two-or-three-at-a-time and sliding down the banisters. We learned to haul ourselves up the banisters or to mountaineer straight up the outside of the staircase. Sometimes we slid down the shiny lino on a large pillow, bumping violently, or jumped eight steps from the top onto a mattress placed on the halfway landing. From the top of the back stairs we played fishing games or bombed selected passers-by below with cushions suspended on strings. The midway landing of the front stairs, which looked out over the big hall, made an excellent poop deck or bridge, and enthralling maritime dramas could be enacted there by flinging ropes or lifebelts or harpoons over the side, while fierce battles were fought with whales or sharks which thrashed about among the tables and chairs below.

The top flight of the front stairs was ideal for viewing the arrival of visitors. When there was to be an evening gathering, Elizabeth and I would wrap ourselves into cocoons of blankets and pillows and lie up there in the dark watching the guests being greeted at the front door. As the throng moved out of sight towards the drawing room, we eased our cocoons further and further down the top flight until, bright-eyed and giggly, we were discovered and packed off to bed.

DESIGN FOR LIVING

Although not a single room faced sunny north, in every other respect this house had been carefully designed. So had the grounds and outbuildings. The whole plan assumed the presence of domestic staff and we moved in with resident cook (Lilian), housemaid (Thelma) and nurse. By then, Jean had returned to Adelaide and her place was taken during the next two or three years first by 'Nursie' Alexander and then by 'Nursie' Brown. Scruse continued as the gardener.

While this regime lasted, almost every room in the house was in regular use. The design also seemed to assume that 'children should be seen and not heard ... and seen only sometimes'. Upstairs our small bedrooms were segregated from the important bedrooms by a heavy swing door. We had our own bathroom and we descended by the back stairs to a self-contained 'nursery' which was separate from the main house. The kitchen wing was the domain of the domestic staff – there were two bedrooms and a bathroom downstairs, for cook and housemaid, while the nurse slept upstairs among the children. These arrangements had been carefully thought out, mainly for the benefit of master, mistress and guests, but they depended for their success on a very rigid domestic routine.

CRACKS IN THE DESIGN

Close to the chapel was a big square room, quite separate from the house but connected by a covered way. This was the nursery. Everything about it was carefully planned; its walls were panelled up beyond scribbling height; its windows were high and inaccessible; it had a hefty cupboard for toys, a hand-basin for cleanliness, and a large open fireplace, well screened. All it needed was a blazing fire and a built-in nanny to bring it to life. The little adjoining mulberry garden must have once enhanced it greatly, but now the chapel wall loomed darkly alongside. At times we played in the nursery, especially at first when there was a nurse to supervise us, and being isolated from the house it was a good spot for making messes and for the puppet theatre which we later built. But on the whole, the nursery was a failure. It was usually cold and dark, because the fire was rarely lit, and being independent Australian children we were not partial to the strict Nanny regime of the English tradition. In later days the nursery was sometimes used as an emergency bedroom.

Also set apart from the house was the ironing-room. Being close to both laundry and clothes-lines it was well placed, provided that there was an ironing lady or a laundress to go with it. It also had a large open fireplace, probably designed to air the clothes rather than to comfort the ironing lady. Mother found, when she became the ironing lady, that she couldn't hear the telephone or the doorbell from the ironing room, which simply proved that a housemaid was needed as well.

So, there were already two large open fireplaces before we have even entered the house, simply confirming that the Ballarat winter was a central fact of life. Inside the house there were nine more fireplaces and the majestic range in the kitchen, but we moved into this splendid 'modern' house with added glee, for there was a central heating system as well! The placement of the radiators for this system was most unjust. The front, public end of the house and the main bedrooms upstairs had both radiators and fireplaces. The kitchen wing had no radiators, but it did have the range and fireplaces in the two maids' bedrooms. The minor bedrooms upstairs, where the children slept, had no heating at all!

The centre of operations for the heating system was in the cellar – for yes, we were confronted by another cellar. One approached this cavern down a steep, clattery wooden staircase in the central passage of the house. A handsome wooden balustrade and a gate prevented careless by-passers in the passage from falling into the stairwell, but did nothing to discourage the draughts and vapours from rising out of it, and the cellar itself, like most other excavations on the Ballarat plateau, filled steadily with icy water. Having learned by experience at Old Bishopscourt, we searched at once for a siphon tap. Sure enough, this device was again on the far side of the cavern, near the ceiling, but nobody had to swim to it for it was accessible from ground level outside through a small window. Admittedly one had almost to lie down to turn it on, but it was efficient and siphoned away lustily, making sounds like a giant bath emptying just below the dining-room.

In one corner of the cellar sat the furnace, brooding in the shadows like an outsized Dalek. This was the source and fount of all the hot water gurgling in the radiators above. Mounds of coke lay on the gritty floor around it, having been supplied through the top window, and there was no doubt that the heating system worked. The question was, however, who was going to be the boiler attendant? It was not a job for the cook or the nurse, and while a housemaid cleaned out fireplaces as part of her duties, she could not be expected to hump bags of coke or buckets of ash and clinkers, or to shovel fuel at regular intervals. The only person who could deal with the boiler was Scruse, and this he did for a very short time when we first moved in. For that brief period of bliss we basked in tropical warmth, but in the meantime two things happened – my parents discovered the furnace's insatiable appetite for expensive coke, and the Second World War broke out. Scruse left us to 'do his bit' for the War Effort and the furnace went out for ever, while we tried to forget all about central heating. Sometimes Elizabeth or I would put on gumboots and descend the clattery stairs to paddle in the icy flood, but on the whole the cellar was ignored.

There was, in any case, another boiler to contend with – the hot water boiler in the laundry. One could exist in Ballarat without central heating, but not without hot water. The laundry was a tiny room at the end of the kitchen wing, opening on to the back porch. Into it were crowded a gas copper, three cement troughs, the trusty washing machine, a large hot water storage tank on top of a cupboard, and the boiler. Like its relative in the cellar, it sat sullenly in the corner surrounded by shovels, brushes, pokers, buckets of coke, little piles of ash, dust, grit and clinkers. As a combination, coke-boiler room and laundry left almost everything to be desired. However, unlike the range at Old Bishopscourt, this boiler, when it felt like it, produced cascades of gloriously hot water, which sometimes boiled in the pipes, causing the walls to shudder and explosions of brown steam to shoot from the bathroom taps. But it was a temperamental brute and needed tactful handling. As soon as we had no boiler attendant, this role was taken on by Father, but when he was away or too busy we all took turns to poke and stoke, to lug in coke and carry out ashes, and to mutter threats and incantations in the hope that the boiler would not sullenly expire overnight. It frequently did, nonetheless.

There were three bathrooms: the White, the Green and the Maids'. Each bathroom had its own toilet and there was a fourth outside for the gardener. The White bathroom was the largest, and close to the master bedroom at the top floor front of the house. Under its linoleum there was a leaden floor curved up at the edges like a square dish, presumably to save the entrance hall below from untimely overflows. The bow window alcove was shelved in at table height, and on this platform sat a gas-ring and kettle. Other accessories quickly appeared: Mother's hair-curling tongs (heated over the gas), a mirror on a stand, a loud-speaker for the wireless, a fully equipped tea-tray, Father's shaving gear, and so on. It was strictly our parents' retreat in the mornings, and as we shouted farewell through the closed door before leaving for school, the noises issuing forth were an interesting blend of swirling water, the hissing kettle, the ABC News and the clink of tea cups. At night, Elizabeth and I liked wallowing in there to warm up before bed; and we discovered that the White bathroom was both acoustically flattering and sufficiently remote from the rest of the house for a good sing. 'The Holy City' sounded particularly stirring in the White bathroom. Richard Crooks was always rendering it on the ABC's Hospital Half Hour at breakfast time, so one picked up the words (and such words! ... 'Methought the voice of angels from heaven in answer rang ...'). I suppose the neighbours and passers by, on hearing voices soaring up to 'Hos-ANN-uh in the hi-YEST', simply assumed that the inmates of Bishopscourt were given to outbursts of religious fervour, although I doubt that they would have bethought ours to be the voices of angels.

The Green bathroom was at the top back, right beside my bedroom. It was a recent addition to the house and was 'modern' in the extreme, with light green porcelain and tiles and a smart glass shower screen. It was so compact that one could reach the towel rail from the bath. This was the bathroom for guests, but the children and the nurse also used it. The Maids' bathroom was at the end of the kitchen wing, downstairs, and in winter it had one clear advantage over the other two – its cosy proximity to the boiler in the laundry. It had a chilly green cement floor and a strange sunken bath whose rim was only a few inches above floor level. It was back-breaking to clean.

That corner of the kitchen wing also contained an annexe for brooms and cleaning materials, a walk-in larder with a fly-proof safe and many shelves, and a maid's bedroom. A second maid's bedroom lay on the far side of the kitchen. The kitchen itself was much brighter than the previous one, but not much more up-to-date. Some of the furniture had come with us and again there was a black range and a gas stove. Half of the room was the cooking area; the rest was divided into the washing-up alcove and a dark china pantry, each with a sink. From the kitchen, a short passage led past the foot of the back stairs and then on to the dining-room and the front of the house. Carpets began at that point.

On the wall of that short passage there was a telephone. It must have been sited there to discourage long conversations, as it was right at the foot of the stairs, in the busy passageway between kitchen and dining-room. There was nowhere to sit, and draughts whistled from several directions. This phone had a daffodil-shaped mouthpiece on an adjustable neck; it also had two ear pieces, and as there was another phone on the same line in the study, three people could listen in at any one time (not always an advantage!). Father's study phone was an enormous, black, very 'modern' handset model, like the sort one saw in Hollywood films, but not so modern as to have a dial – we lifted the receiver and waited for the operator to say 'Number please'. Of course we all preferred to use that phone, if Father was out, especially as it was beside a huge armchair and the fire. High on the wall of the back passage was a box of numbered bells which summoned the housemaid to various parts of the house. These were soon to be disconnected, but the bell-pushes remained in the reception rooms and the main bedrooms.

And so, cracks were already appearing in the carefully planned infrastructure not long after we moved in, and for reasons which the architect could not have foreseen the rigid domestic regime was soon to collapse. It is enlightening now to look at what happened as the principle of segregation broke down under wartime conditions. As cook, housemaid, Scruse and then nurse all left, as the household dwindled to just ourselves, there were suddenly empty rooms. The entire building became our kingdom and there was a sense of liberation we had never known before. We became free range children.

FREE-RANGE KIDS

In general, the features of the new house which appealed to us as children would have been out-of-bounds in stricter times. Such a house provided wonderful opportunities for imaginative games. These hardly ever took place in the well-planned nursery, where the planning was directed towards boring things like safety, cleanliness and soundproofing: they took place in enticing private corners like dark alcoves, large cupboards and remote regions of the back yard, or challenging structures such as the stairs or roofs. Below the bedroom windows overlooking Grove Street ran the roof of the verandahs, and when Elizabeth had grown a little bigger she sometimes climbed out and capered about on the steeply sloping slates. Mother, indoors, never knew.

It was a brilliant house for hide-and-seek, offering endless places of concealment in the cellar or the nursery, in wardrobes, wood-boxes and tall, wicker laundry baskets, behind couches, under tables, or smothered beneath Father's robes in the hall cupboard.

Just off the master bedroom there was a tiny balcony with wire safety guards on top of its cement walls. In the summer I would be allowed to put a stretcher out there if I felt the urge to 'sleep out'. It was very exhilarating, peering up at the stars, almost drowning in the waves of fresh air, and hoping that the luridly striped caterpillars on the rampant Virginia creeper wouldn't wriggle in to seek refuge in my bed. This balcony was also good for parachute games, as it was one of the few places on the top floor with a clear drop to the ground. We made parachutes out of string, corks (for the body) and Father's white handkerchiefs, and dropped them over the parapet. Usually the corks were too light and the wind blew the parachutes off course to ruination in the rose bushes.

The handkerchiefs came from a drawer in Father's dressing room, and in a nearby cupboard could be found the remnant of his uniform from the First AIF. He had been a chaplain with the 13th Light Horse, and while the khaki cap and coat and the shining belt were interesting, the shaped leather leggings were the real prize. We would stagger about in them as though in splints. In Mother's wardrobe was her 'fur' – a bushy animal which lay round her shoulders biting its own tail. It had beady glass eyes and an odd, musky smell. We could also ransack her cupboards for shoes and hats to parade about in.

Seclusion and space were the great advantages of this house. Father enjoyed these in his ground-floor study, which had once been the doctor's surgery and waiting room, with an outside entrance. Father had the two rooms converted into one long, cosy sanctum, heated by an Esse coke stove and lined with wall-to-wall carpet and floor-to-ceiling bookshelves. The doctor's hand basin, with its strange taps, had been left in place. Father had two huge desks. He worked at the one near the window, while on the other one, by the stove and a vast mulberry-red armchair, sat the Hollywood telephone. The hundreds of books lining the study were nearly all works on abstruse subjects such as the Nature of the Trinity or the Question of Original Sin, so they weren't of much use to us children beyond suggesting that reading was an important part of life. But there were three books which, to me, were worth all the rest – Pears' Cyclopaedia, an atlas and Webster's back-breaking dictionary.

After the final nurse had departed, the bedroom next to mine became 'spare'. It housed a large roll-top Cutler desk, full of drawers and pigeon-holes, and I often went in there to draw and scribble, with the door firmly closed against intruders.

The front hall could be closed off from the rear of the house by another swing door. Margaret and I spent much time under the front stairs, for we felt certain that if the house had a secret passage or a hidden room, here was where it lay – behind the dark panelling in this alcove. Equipped with table knives and feverish imaginations, we spent many an hour probing and prising and tapping the panels, investigating by torchlight strange markings on the woodwork, and gradually weaving together a tale of mystery and terror which involved a limping ghost whose shuffling steps could be heard in the house by night. This gave me the chance to tell Margaret that I had heard him walk abroad, even to the very threshold of my bedroom – but no further. We were then at the age when the tower at Old Bishopscourt would have yielded up its phantoms. Margaret was the ideal companion for a tower, but it was too late.

On the other side of the hall, a broad lead-light window faced onto the front garden. It had brown velvet curtains which drew right across, and a generous, polished wooden sill of about thirty centimetres deep by two metres across. Below it sat a heavy old couch. It didn't take us long to recognise the theatrical potential of this set-up, for there was room at each side for one of us to hide behind the curtain and from there to step out onto the narrow, slippery stage. It didn't allow much elbow room for fierce sword-play or even moderate by-play, but we were fairly small and skinny and, besides, a large part of the fun lay in falling off the stage onto the couch in the orchestra pit below. Mother was long-suffering about these antics, provided that we first removed her brass ornaments from the window sill and the shoes from our feet, and didn't make too much noise and didn't bounce too violently on the springs and didn't break the window. We did our best to obey these instructions; we took our shoes off, but left the socks on as they were slippery and led to more frequent accidents. The swing door ensured that these theatricals were strictly private: they were also quite impromptu. Our favourite act was to impersonate the currently popular screen idols Jeanette Macdonald and Nelson Eddy, who appeared in romantic film musicals. We would surge onto the stage to sing a passionate duet, such as 'My Hero' from 'The Chocolate Soldier', at the top of our lungs. As the climax and top notes of the song approached, disaster would strike – either hero or heroine would fall headlong from the stage with a strangled cry and need rescuing by the surviving partner, or some personal misfortune would occur, such as the elastic in the hero's pants giving way, and the whole act would break up in feigned confusion and gales of laughter. None of this would have taken place without that inviting window ledge and the seclusion provided by a large house. One of the greatest privileges of my childhood was that of space, both physical and psychological.

Mother in the sitting room, seated below the water colour of Old Bishopscourt.

Holy Days

SUNDAYS

The Bishop's family pew was at the very back of the Cathedral, a step above the rest of the congregation and matched by the Vicar's pew on the other side of the west door. Although the bishop's throne was in the Cathedral, the responsibility for that church and its flock lay with the vicar/dean.

I liked sitting at the back because it gave a good overall view of proceedings, with nobody behind us to observe minor misdemeanours (such as dropping one's collection) when they occurred. We could even have fainted, as people sometimes did in church, and been borne away through the west door without arousing much notice.

After Newcastle Cathedral, which was a considerable pile, Christ Church Cathedral in Ballarat was a modest building, more like a large parish church. It was dedicated in 1857, with later additions. The foundation stone for a much grander edifice, with a soaring spire, was laid in 1888, but plans never reached fruition except for the crypt, which became the chapter house. The stonework and solidity of that undercroft made us yearn for the completed whole on the edge of the escarpment; seen on the approach from Melbourne, it would have modestly combined the position of a Durham Cathedral with the spire of a Salisbury. Shortage of funds scuttled the whole enterprise.

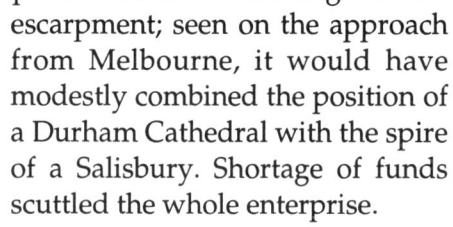

What might have been – the design for the cathedral which was never completed.

In tIn the south wall beside us was a stained glass version of Holman Hunt's painting 'The Light of the World'. Its meaning was explained to us; the door was the entry to the human soul, bolted and barred against Christ and offering no outer handle. I noted the door, but found the vegetation more interesting – what looked like nettles and blackberries and creeping ivy – not realising that they also were rich in weedy symbolism. The nocturnal gloom of that window was illuminated by the bright Australian daylight during morning services, but at night, when Christ's lantern should have shone forth most brilliantly, it vanished into darkness. Holman Hunt's symbolism was not wholly effective in stained glass!

As we drove down Sturt Street on Sunday mornings, the town belonged to the churchgoers. The trams slept in, the shops were firmly closed, the city was at rest. Sometimes the Town Hall bells rang a few peals (but not, I think, in wartime), and crocodiles of school boarders shepherded by watchful teachers were swallowed in at various church porches, along with scattered pedestrians. We did not always go to the Cathedral; Father, when he was in Ballarat for the weekend, usually preached at services in two or three different churches and we would accompany him to one of them. When he was away in the country we would walk down to St Peter's in Sturt Street, whose peal of bells rang out from its bluestone tower at well-defined hours of the day. Florrie did not come to us on weekends, so we looked after ourselves and the chooks. Everything was arranged around Father's comings and goings and Sundays could be quite busy.

No doubt remembering his own high-spirited youth, Father considered it enough for us to attend church once on Sundays, after which we were reasonably free, provided we didn't do anything rowdy outside. In other words, we were not subjected to the repressive sabbath regime which some of our generation still endured. Looking back, it seems that Father's policy about our religious upbringing at home was almost one of laisser faire, by which I mean non-interference rather than indifference. Apart from family prayers round the fire sometimes, there was no heavy emphasis on religion at home. It didn't need to be emphasised – we were surrounded by it.

We were not sent to Sunday school, but there was regular religious instruction at school, which at some stage included learning the Catechism and the Ten Commandments. When we left Jenks in Remove, Divinity (also known as Scripture) was usually taken by the school chaplain, whoever it happened to be. In the middle forms we studied the Acts of the Apostles, while later we tried to understand when the chaplain expounded the Creed, or various doctrines, but much of the time this was way over my head. Those schooled in theology are not necessarily on the same wavelength as children – or many adults. I think Father recognised this, for his sermons were usually fairly simple and anecdotal. I now think that a straightforward history of the Jewish people, based on the Bible, could have been a much more rewarding study at school, especially as I had already found the stories in Exodus so gripping.

We were usually the first to arrive in church, for Father needed time to carry his case of robes to the vestry, attire himself and talk to the vicar. As we sat waiting, I found various things to examine no matter which church we were in. There were memorial tablets and First World War rolls of honour, often listing two or more names from one family. When the psalm and hymn numbers were posted on the board I would find them in *Hymns Ancient & Modern* and the *Book of Common Prayer*, both of which contained other sorts of intriguing reading matter, such as lists of hymn tunes with surprising names like Capetown, Redhead, Martyrdom and St Bees (was he the one with the knees?). I would pore over the Table of Kindred & Affinity and wonder how many women would ever get the chance to marry their husbands' mothers' fathers, even if they wanted to! Then there was the Table to Find Easter Day, which sounded like a magic spell or one of Jenks's mental teasers '... To find the Golden Number, or Prime, add One to the Year of our Lord, and then divide by 19; the Remainder, if any, is the Golden Number ...' Oh dear, the other rule was easier – 'the first Sunday after the first full moon after the 21st of March' – but that depended on knowing when the 'Paschal full moon' occurred (that rich word 'Paschal' reminded me of a well-known brand of toffee). There was also the service of Baptism for 'Such as are of Riper Years', making these persons sound like rosy apples.

It was wise to take stock of the kneeler situation and to be prepared for those pews which were not anchored and thus likely to scoot away from you if you leaned against them while kneeling. I felt a little superior to Presbyterians when I heard that they didn't kneel in church, but slightly envious as well. Of what went on in churches of other denominations I was almost totally ignorant, and I didn't enter any of them until after I had left school. Yet Father was on good terms with his non-conformist and Roman Catholic counterparts in the town, particularly with Dr Button of St Andrew's Kirk.

Our parentage did not guarantee us against getting the giggles in church, or at concerts. At certain stages of our lives, Mother had to sit between us or devise other means of separating us so as to lessen the possibility of an infectious snort spreading through the ranks. It was largely a nervous affliction and usually triggered by one of those minor mishaps which take on major dimensions in a hushed building – a blurt on the organ, a hiccup, or a sudden skid on a wayward kneeler. In any case, Father had a fund of church-mishap stories which made us acutely aware of the possibilities, although we never witnessed anything like the scene in his favourite anecdote about a clergyman who preached with such fervour that his dentures flew out of his mouth and were fielded smartly at short leg by a choirboy, who returned them to the pulpit with the loud and unnecessary remark, 'Your teeth, sir!' Yet, unpredictable things were apt to happen in isolated country churches, such as the arrival of a cow in the back porch and her engaging 'Moo-oo' through the west doorway during the responses.

The worst disaster befell us in the small church at Natimuk. Just as the clergy were processing down the aisle, Elizabeth, from her front pew position, managed to overturn a tall pedestal and send its crowning floral arrangement crashing in ruins to the floor. This was far too awful for giggles. I grew hot all over and assaulted Elizabeth with my elbow for bringing such shame upon us. The procession did not waver and the situation was saved by a capable lady who bundled the wreckage through a side door into the vestry, discreetly mopped up the flood and managed to regain her seat in time to sing 'Amen' to the processional hymn. She had probably spent hours arranging the flowers in the first place, poor thing.

Very occasionally, when Father had no Sunday engagements or when we had visitors to stay, we would sometimes have a private service in the chapel at Bishopscourt. This had advantages – being within ten paces of home, having no sermon, and not having to wear hats. We didn't have many 'good' clothes and I grew out of mine rather rapidly, so those we wore to church were usually uncomfortable and, I felt sure, unflattering, especially the horrible hats (anchored under the chin with elastic). But despite these advantages in chapel-going, I missed the atmosphere of a full church and especially the music.

The orders of service which were followed in the Prayer Book became deeply ingrained. Those mysterious words like 'vouchsafe', 'endue', 'succour', 'unfeignedly' were interspersed with passages of perfect clarity, such as 'meekly kneeling upon your knees' and 'all perils and dangers of this night', and with lovely metaphors – 'Pour upon them the continual dew of thy blessing'. The rolling rhythms of the collects sank in through repetition – 'O God, from whom all holy desires, all good counsels, and all just works do proceed, give unto us that peace which the world cannot give ...' This language and that of the Authorised Version of the Bible was magnificently suited to being read aloud.

I was attracted too by the straightforward language and natural imagery of the psalms: 'In his hand are all the corners of the earth: and the strength of the hills is his also. The sea is his, and he made it: and his hands prepared the dry land ...' (*Venite* 4-5). In those days when its long catalogue of creation was still sung occasionally at Morning Prayer, the *Benedicite, Omnia Opera* greatly stirred my imagination, especially such verses as 'O ye Whales, and all that move in the Waters, bless ye the Lord: praise him and magnify him for ever.' Is that what whales were doing when they 'blew'? Predictably, this canticle was abandoned in favour of the brisker ones.

HYMNS

These appealed to me above all. Unlike the liturgy and the Bible, hymns were hardly ever explained or analysed in sermons or Divinity lessons; they just happened, several times during the Sunday service and every morning in school assemblies. We knew some hymns better than the poems we read, for we sang them over and over again and memory was reinforced by the tunes. Being Anglicans, we relied on *Hymns Ancient & Modern* at both church and school and so knew nothing of the more rollicking style of Sankey's *Sacred Songs*, for example.

I was always anxious to know which hymns were 'on', as I much preferred those of a martial or cheerful style. Hymns concerned with (spiritual) fights and battle cries were, I felt, much better for you than cringing hymns about sin and guilt like 'Rock of Ages' – and yet the latter were sung fervently and often. In later life I discovered Noel Coward's song about Uncle Harry, the missionary, in which 'Great Aunt Maud was eaten up [by cannibals] while singing Rock of Ages.' The cannibals seemed to be on my side. The 'Christian up and smite them' approach was to be preferred, I decided.

Parodies were fairly common, and being not very pious we enjoyed the perennial jokes about shepherds washing their socks, the highly-flavoured lady and the child she-bear, not to mention 'Just as I am without one flea', but on the whole parodies and misunderstandings were fringe matters and made less impact than other things.

My vocabulary was extended not merely by 'hosannas' and 'hallelujahs' but also by 'daysprings', 'harbingers', 'cherubim' and 'seraphim', and by piles of thundering Latinisms of the 'consubstantial', 'coeternal' or 'ineffably sublime' variety. Hymn writers had devised many ways of expressing the inexpressible, a catalogue of rolling phrases to convey notions of infinity, divinity and eternity: 'which wert and art and ever more shall be' or 'till moons shall wax and wane no more'. Oceans and tides supplied images of power and extent: 'singing in chorus from ocean to ocean', or 'His kingdom stretch from shore to shore', or, very thrilling when roared out by a full church (to the tune mysteriously called 'Moscow'):

Boundless as ocean's tide/ Rolling in fullest pride
Through the earth far and wide/ Let there be light.

This expression of the eternal verities through natural imagery was one reason for the attraction of such hymns, with their balanced references to sun and moon, day and night, light and darkness, height and depth, milk and honey, icy mountains and coral strands (and sunny fountains). They gained added grandeur from the symbols of majesty – thrones, crowns and sceptres. Often the imaginative power of this language was very real: 'How the troops of Midian/ Prowl and prowl around ...' (I imagined wolves and black panthers); '... all Thy saints adore thee/ Casting down their golden crowns around the glassy sea ...' (I thought what a clatter there must have been and what a dazzling brightness).

Singing those hymns so often helped me to develop a rhythmic sense, an awareness of variety in verse form and metre, a familiarity with Latinisms, and the ability to cope with contracted syntax and the piling up of ideas. When it came to their music, some tunes could only be described as dreary; they made me sigh and want to give up religion at once. Father had an endearing habit of cutting hymns short if he felt they were defeating the congregation. Seizing a moment while the organist was twiddling with stops, he would command the congregation in ringing tones to 'omit verses seven and eight!'. (This habit was not endearing, of course, to choir and organist if they had prepared a descant for one of those verses!) This sort of pruning was never necessary with the great hymns, those with rousing tunes which swept the congregation along and gave no opportunity for wailing or dragging behind. In amongst the dreary tunes were more than enough noble ones. Haydn, Mendelssohn, Handel, Vaughan Williams, Parry, S.S. Wesley, and J. Bacchus Dykes were all there, along with brooding Welsh melodies and Bach chorales, instilling in us a feeling for harmony and musical colour, and a soaring of the spirit.

Upheaval

WE ARE AT WAR WITH GERMANY

By 1939 I was old enough to sense the tremors which were shaking the adult world. The wireless seemed to be on very often to catch news bulletins. Even earlier I can recall hearing reports about the Italian invasion of Ethiopia and the extraordinary names of Haile Selassie and Mussolini. As well the Japanese and Chinese seemed to be fighting. Then, only a week or so after we had moved into New Bishopscourt, I arrived home from school one day to be told in awed tones by Thelma, the housemaid, that war had been declared. I remember exactly where I was when she made this announcement – on the window seat of the sitting room – and although I wasn't sure what I was supposed to feel about the matter, I took my cue from her and said 'Gosh!' – a word we were encouraged not to use.

On that very day the Adelaide Express deposited my grandmother, an aunt and two uncles at the railway station. Marmie and Uncle Hal had come from Adelaide, while Aunt Doris and Uncle Clive were visiting from London and their arrival in Ballarat was to be the occasion of a family reunion. However, the excitement was overshadowed by the grave news, by the sober voices of Mr Chamberlain and Mr Menzies telling us the worst. Aunt Doris and Uncle Clive were already wondering what to do for the best. (In the event they stayed in Australia until 1945.)

After the initial shock of the declaration, being at war made very little difference to us at first, although it was to be the great watershed of our lives. I had no brothers or even a young uncle to vanish into the armed forces. Father belonged to the First World War generation and he was now in a 'reserved occupation'. The war reached us most nearly through the letters of our other aunt, Mother's sister, who lived in Essex, just inland from Britain's east coast on the North Sea. She used the amazing airmails to speed the news of those jittery days, and when one of her blue letters arrived everything at Bishopscourt stopped while Mother read it. Aunt Dorothy described the weird details of daily life during the 'phoney' war and later during the Battle of Britain – getting lost in the blackout, filling sandbags in the back garden, seeing the evacuees off on trains to Wales and the West Country, the homeless sleeping in barns and washing themselves under garden taps before setting off to 'work as usual' in the morning, people burying the family silver 'just in case' and making plans to move further inland should the invasion come.

> *I sometimes look wildly round & wonder what I really would take if we had to evacuate at short notice — & I feel thankful I haven't a cat & a parrot !!!*

Letter from Aunt Dorothy (LDT) 1939

At school, Current Affairs became a new and solemn subject. Sixth-formers, equipped with large maps and a long pointer, addressed school assemblies on the progress of events in Europe. (Seated on the stage beside the map was Miss Krome, whose father, Otto Krome, was German, but that never occurred to me at the time. Miss Krome was one of us.) We learnt about the Siegfried Line and the Maginot Line, the two opposing lines of fortifications along the French/German border. The French Maginot Line, we were assured, was impregnable and as the phoney war drifted eerily on into 1940 we joined in singing the world-wide taunt:

> We're going to hang out our washing on the Siegfried Line,
> Have you any dirty washing, Mother dear?

But, as Hitler began his wildfire conquest of Europe and the bombing of Britain, we stopped singing this song. The newspaper maps showed threatening black arrows pincering their way towards Paris and Dunkirk. The Maginot Line was useless and forgotten.

Jenks must have conducted lessons on current affairs even in the lowly Remove, for I remember surprising her by being able to name various strategic towns in North Africa during the early battles there with the Italians.

Father took out a subscription to *The Illustrated London News* (which piled up in the sitting room throughout the war) and he also bought a booklet about the evacuation of the British Expeditionary Force across the Channel from Dunkirk. I was entranced by the photographs of this event. Like many of the episodes of the Second World War, Dunkirk had great imaginative impact; this had little to do with the subsequent embroidery of *The Snow Goose* or the film *Mrs Miniver*, although these showed that it was the stuff from which legends are made. Dunkirk was more like a chapter from classical epic than a routine military operation, and even at the age of nine and 12 000 miles away I felt the imaginative power of it in that little book of photographs.

The 'little ships', crammed with troops, escape across the English Channel from Dunkirk.

An even earlier episode, in December 1939, had likewise mesmerised me. This was the naval action off the River Plate (Uruguay) in which the German pocket battleship 'Admiral Graf Spee' was driven to scuttle herself in Montevideo Harbour. This was a morale-boosting battle because it was one of the few that 'our side' won in those early days, and, as later events confirmed, naval battles tended to be the most interesting, because the protagonists were easily distinguishable and the action was slow enough to follow. Many of the great films of the

Second World War were about naval engagements. In due course, the Battle of the River Plate was set out before us in *The Illustrated London News* like an outsize game of chess. It was a sea-hunt in the tradition of Drake or Nelson, with the smaller British ships closing in on the prey and holding her captive in the harbour. Having given orders for his battleship to be scuttled and seen them carried out, the German commander, Captain Lansdorf, shot himself. My interest in this episode had little to do with the immediate excitement of the battle, for wireless and newspaper reports were sketchy and we had none of the instant-replay thrills of television to stir us up. We had to wait many weeks before *The Illustrated London News* reached us (by sea) with its account of the battle, but then it presented us with the entire engagement, enshrined in map and print and picture, and already securely placed in its historical context. In this way the events of the war reached us as a series of completed chapters in which the historical logic was clear to see.

Other things emerged from the Battle of the River Plate. Attitudes and prejudices began to harden: the allied ships bore names like 'Ajax' and 'Achilles', classical and heroic. German warships, pocket battleships and U-boats in particular, were seen as sinister, fast and predatory, with unpleasant names like 'Scharnhorst', 'Gneisenau', and 'U-13'. It became commonplace to describe German speech as 'guttural' (a suggestive word, indeed), and names like 'Gneisenau' seemed to confirm this. So did Winston Churchill, who always made a point of pronouncing Nazi as 'Narzee'.

I also learnt another new word and notion from this battle – to 'scuttle', the strange procedure of sinking your own ship so that the enemy couldn't have it. Our vocabularies expanded steadily and along polyglot lines as the war progressed; we talked easily about propaganda, refugees, evacuees, Quislings, the Blitzkrieg, incendiaries, swastikas, Il Duce, the Gestapo, the Luftwaffe, austerity, and so forth.

In 1940, as Hitler's armies approached Paris, we were set to learn 'La Marseillaise' at school so that we could sing it in assembly, as though to give fresh heart to the crumbling French forces. At our age this was a stern introduction to a foreign tongue, but 'L'étandard sanglant est levé' is certainly a more interesting notion than 'la plume de ma tante', and there was something irresistible about 'Aux armes, citoyens! Formez vos bataillons!', so we committed this resounding battle-cry to memory along with its thrilling tune and sang it with gusto, but even at nine years old I felt it to be futile. The French armies did not respond to our call, and Hitler marched into Paris. Later on, the hymn 'God the all-terrible!

Upheaval 111

King, who ordainest/Great winds thy clarions, the lightnings thy sword ...', whose tune had Czarist associations, was added to our morning repertoire, this time in support of our new (non-Czarist) Russian allies – and with rather more success.

LDT 1940

> Colchester
> Essex.
> June. 16th '40 -
>
> My own darling Dyon,
> Another week has gone by, & brought with it the entry of Italy into the war, & the fall of Paris.
> Events are so stupendous that one begins to lose all sense of proportion.
> My heart aches for the French people leaving their homes, & knowing that their capital is in the hands of the invaders.
> I wonder if you listened to the Queen broadcasting to the women of France last night – a most touching message.

On the newspaper maps the black pincers began to claw into the Mediterranean, Greece, Crete and Libya and across North Africa, and towards Russia. The shapes of Europe and the Mediterranean became very familiar to me and my knowledge of the world grew with the spreading conflict. The war was a vast and living geography lesson, filled with action and drama. The missionary world of Greenland's icy mountains and India's coral strand was gradually replaced by a litany of names with a rhythm and mystique of their own – Benghazi and Bardia, Sidi Barrani and Mersa Matruh, Tobruk and El Alamein. There seemed to be no sign of 'Afric's sunny fountains' in the North African desert.

At a simple level I could make out the reasoning behind military strategy. All that battling in the North African desert was to prevent Hitler from capturing the Suez Canal and the Gulf oilfields, it seemed. Oil was a vital ingredient in the war. Ports, bridgeheads, railways, food and water supplies were all of 'strategic' importance. After early successes against the Italian armies in North Africa, the Allies captured thousands of prisoners. *The Illustrated London News* showed photographs of endless columns of these men trudging through the sand. I wondered where they would all be put and how they would be fed? Would someone take down their names and addresses and let their families know where they were? Casualty lists began to appear in our own papers, including the names of POWs.

As an impressionable child I was absorbing the stuff of history and geography without realising it. Heroes were not football stars or pop singers, but massive figures of destiny. Their features stared forth from the swap cards in sweet packets – the sombre, determined faces of Churchill, Roosevelt, de Gaulle and General Smuts, of Monty and Wavell and Mountbatten – all associated in my mind with the taste of licorice. I drew caricatures of Hitler, Goering, Himmler and Mussolini, or pictures of aerial dogfights filled with plummeting, smoking Messerschmidts and triumphant, soaring Spitfires. (I didn't attempt to sketch those unnerving aerial terrorists, the Stuka dive bombers, which films and newsreels presented to us in all their screaming horror.) Union Jacks and Swastikas adorned my blotters. 'Battleships & Cruisers' was a favourite game under the desk. We lived through 'Turning Points in History' – Dunkirk, the Battle of Britain, the Siege of Tobruk – and by the time *The Illustrated London News* had reached us, these turning points could be seen for what they were in the scheme of things.

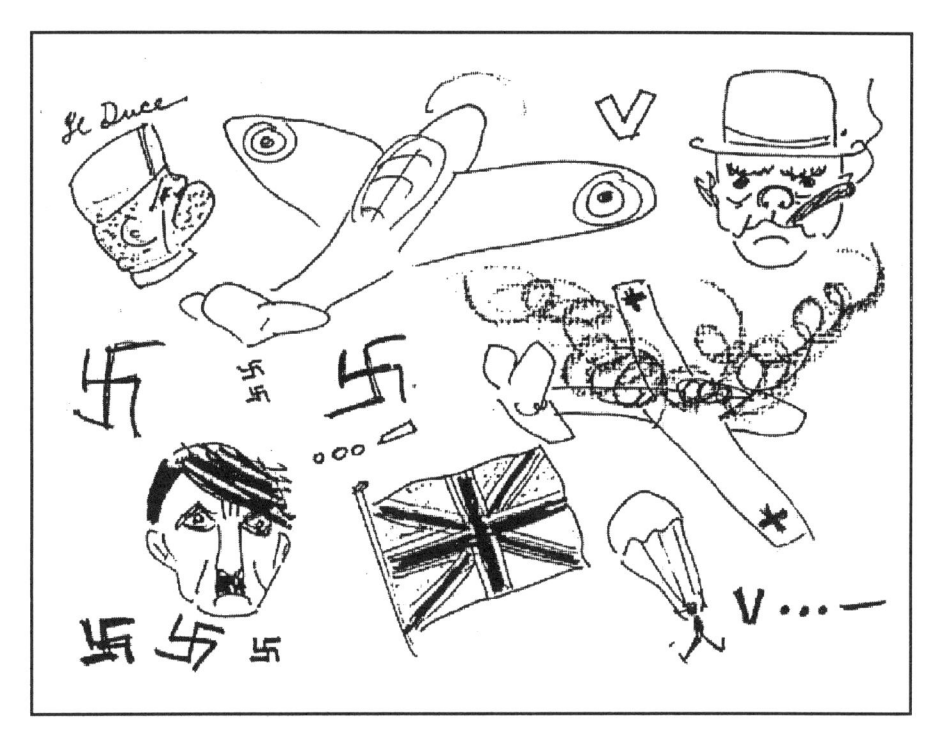

Wartime doodles recollected

Relatively speaking, there was something almost romantic about the Second World War, at least from the viewpoint of a child who was safely distanced from the real horrors. There seemed to be no doubts about the morality of our cause, and to a small onlooker the war was like a gigantic and very serious game of goodies versus baddies played out in an endless variety of scenarios – the stealthy and deadly manoeuvres between U-boats and Atlantic convoys; the London Blitz and the indomitable Cockneys; bombs on Buckingham Palace; the fire bombing of Coventry and its cathedral; the sinking of the 'Bismarck'. At the time of the Battle of Britain, Elizabeth and I, girls though we were, were given specially made 'Air Force uniforms' to dress up in.

Despite the increasing mechanisation of warfare it was still possible to recognise individual human beings and exploits on this vast arena – the 'Few', Rats of Tobruk, Dam-busters. Our view of things was of course influenced by the films we saw, but these generally appeared long after the event, and they were sanitised and censored. The accumulated violence and close-up horror of today's television newscasts were missing. My first impressions were formed by the press and the wireless.

THE WIRELESS

The wireless came into its own during the war. Mother recalled fêtes in the 1920s at which the chief attraction was the 'wireless set'. One paid threepence for admission to a tent to listen to one of these magic boxes emitting static and crackles over a dimly heard voice. My parents bought their first wireless in Newcastle when many people still had deep suspicions about this new-fangled device. Bishop Batty refused even to listen to ours, apparently, until Mother told him he could hear the chimes of Big Ben over the air waves. The Bishop, being English to his boot-straps, was instantly converted and acquired a set in no time. Our wireless came with us to Ballarat, and at Old Bishopscourt it sat in the dining-room and was hooked up to a very tall aerial mast planted on the edge of the front lawn.

It was at New Bishopscourt, after the war broke out, that we became compulsive (or enforced) listeners to the wireless, as Father was determined to hear every possible news broadcast from the 7.45 am session to the late night service crackling dimly from London. Our set was a large console affair, established permanently beside the fireplace in the front sitting-room and again hooked up to the giant aerial (which had somehow been brought from the old house) so that we could pick up transmissions from Melbourne more clearly. If you wanted to listen to the wireless, therefore, you had to stay put in the sitting-room. If there was no fire burning in there, or if you wanted to be doing something else at the same time, this was most inconvenient. In winter I sometimes shivered in the sitting-room to hear the ABC Children's Session at 5.30 pm. The dusk gathered outside, there was no fire within and, as I crouched there in the semi-dark, a sort of black emptiness or panic would engulf me, no matter how cheerfully the program bubbled along beside me. I would have to flee in search of light and warmth.

Father, who had an inventive, Heath Robinson turn of mind, quickly realised that wirelesses needed to be portable, especially in a large

From a 1941 advertisement

ASTOR
releases a
brilliant range
of Mantles

house, so he purchased two moveable speakers and miles of flex and very soon had Bishopscourt wired up for listening in all the vital rooms – his study, the kitchen, the dining room, a couple of bedrooms and the White bathroom. Any other spot could be served with the addition of further yards of extension cord. All we then had to do was to switch on the main wireless in the sitting-room – which, after it had warmed up could then be muffled by turning off another switch within its bowels – and then plug in a portable speaker wherever it was needed. Thus we were able to listen to the news during meals, while washing up, in the bath or in bed or while cleaning the car or weeding the garden. There was no escaping it.

I became rather sick of the news, but it all sank in nevertheless. The war unfolded at regular hours of the day, battle by battle, and the names of strange foreign places became as familiar as my breakfast porridge – Smolensk, Murmansk, Scapa Flow, Tripoli, Casablanca. The chimes of Big Ben and the brave, unflurried BBC voices announcing 'This is London' over the rather wobbly air waves, were an everyday part of childhood. We were sustained by Churchill's growling rhetoric and Beethoven's Fifth Symphony – V for Victory, dit dit dit DA! I wonder how many other children were inspired by Beethoven, as I was, to learn the Morse Code?

THE DOMESTIC REVOLUTION

During its first two years the war had a considerable imaginative effect, but in practical terms it was still fairly remote from our daily lives. The most immediate and drastic change on the home front at Bishopscourt was the departure of our domestic staff to be drafted into war work. It was decreed that from the start of 1943 no household could employ a servant for more than twenty-four hours a week, without a permit, but most of our staff had departed long before that.

This fact of wartime was to have a revolutionary effect on society, as women and girls who had been cooks, housemaids and nursemaids found themselves in the services, driving trucks, harvesting, operating lathes, running businesses and so on. Mother had been fortunate to have help in the house for so long.

Never again were we to have staff living in, but we were not left without help of any sort. Scruse was replaced by Stan, who arrived once

Letter to Margaret (LM) 1943

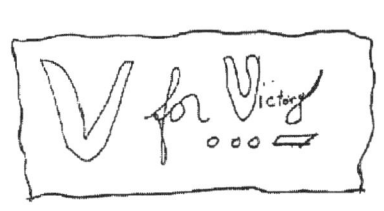

a week on his motorbike to mow the lawns and tidy the paths, and to fill the wood boxes. Stan had been gassed in the First World War and had a bad cough. Mother no longer had her uniformed chauffeur – another of the pretensions swept away by the war. Like everyone else, she used the tram.

After advertising, my parents also found Florrie, who was destined to be our daily cook – and much more – for the next thirteen years. She arrived on her impressive bicycle soon after seven each week morning and departed after lunch. She must therefore have overstepped the twenty-four hour rule, but this fact didn't ever percolate through to Canberra. The new arrangements meant that the kitchen wing was ours at weekends and in the evenings.

Austerity measures began to bite harder and it became necessary to rationalise living patterns at Bishopscourt, especially in the cold weather. The central heating had been abandoned, anyway, and as the war progressed we gravitated more and more to those rooms which were most easily heated, and especially to the kitchen where the range could perform many functions at once: while it cooked the dinner, it could also render down fat, air the washing, dry the shoes and warm us.

It was a nice irony that, as the domestic staff left us, we moved into their quarters in search of warmth and comfort. The kitchen became the social centre of the house – the ironing came into it from the backyard ironing room; a loud-speaker hung on a hook by the door; before school we cooked our breakfast eggs on the range and after school we thrust our frozen feet into the oven; we raided the larder at bedtime; we watched Florrie making jam and Mother bottling fruit; we children, too, learned to cook.

The main reception rooms were used less and less, and in the end the servant's room below the back stairs was converted into a tiny living room. It had a fire-place and was quickly warmed, it was easily blacked-out, and it was next to the kitchen. It was also very small – about fourteen feet by eight – and it became known affectionately as 'The Pughole'. I always assumed that this referred to its cramped, dog-kennel-like dimensions, but a search in the *Oxford English Dictionary* has revealed that in nineteenth century servants' parlance, a 'pug' was an upper servant in a large establishment, and that the Pug's Hole or Pug's Parlour was the housekeeper's room. The term must have been familiar to our parents, who named the room for its previous function.

Chooks, and Much Else, in the Backyard

FLORRIE

Florrie was middle-aged and solid, with grey hair neatly confined in a hair-net and herself neatly garbed in a pale green, starched overall. She was not a 'motherly' person, but she commanded respect and wouldn't put up with any nonsense. She arrived before breakfast each day, having pushed several miles from home on her bicycle, whatever the weather, and collected the day's meat from the butcher on the way. After donning her overall, she then lit the range (except in summer) and, during the morning, she cooked a hot midday dinner for us all, kept the cake and biscuit supply up to the mark, made jams and preserves, scrubbed the kitchen floors and tables, and still found time to run a small farm outside.

When she first arrived at Bishopscourt she took stock of the estate, and before we knew what was happening our back garden had gone into production. It all began with vegetables. Alongside the tennis court there was already a wide strip of garden which was evidently designed to be productive, as there were fruit trees growing there. Florrie took one look and, after asking permission, seized a spade. Bit by bit that whole area of garden came under her spell. Whenever there was a lull in the kitchen, she would sally forth to dig or plant or prune, or to harvest something for lunch. Even the horse chestnut tree, which occupied some of this precious ground, bowed before the onslaught; it was grubbed out in favour of the vegetables. (This time I lost my conker supply!)

Then someone presented Elizabeth with some bantams – several brown, speckled hens and one pompous little rooster with spurred and feathered legs, who shone in his fowlyard like a golden sun. A run was created for the bantams near the woodshed. Florrie knew all about keeping chooks. As we were now committed to a supply of food and grain for the bantams, she reasoned, it seemed silly not to have some real hens as well, especially as there was already a vacant fowlyard right at the end of the property, going to waste. And if we wanted decent vegetables, we needed manure. Thus, in no time, Florrie had acquired some of her favourite breed, Rhode Island Reds. Strips and corners of the land around the tennis court which were not already under crops were gradually colonised by Florrie's poultry empire. Muscovy ducks were a later addition.

Elizabeth and I learnt many practical skills from Florrie, without any sense of being 'taught'. We simply watched and then helped her. Growing things, digging, carpentry, chopping wood, care of livestock, cooking were all picked up as part of everyday survival. To Florrie, and to most people then, 'organic' gardening was the normal state of affairs, not the mystic rite which it has nowadays become. There was always the steady supply of fowl litter, as well as cow pats in the paddock next door, and we tidied the street by shovelling horse manure into a

Elizabeth making hay in the paddock.

Florrie on the tennis court, inspecting the duck yard. Taken by Elizabeth on her 'Box Brownie' camera.

kerosene tin – if we managed to beat the neighbours to it. And Ballarat, with all its deciduous trees, must have had the richest supply of leaf mould in Australia, all rotting gently in the damp climate. Florrie dug over her vegetable beds with great science and vigour, trenching all this organic wealth into the soil, together with any weeds which were not reserved for the livestock. Milk thistles and chickweed were served up as 'green stuff' to the hens. 'Shellbacks' (Florrie's name for snails) were hunted ruthlessly and thrown to the ducks, while earwigs were trapped in rolls of newspaper and scattered to the chooks.

When I was about eleven I was allowed to have a vegetable garden of my own in a spare piece of ground near the bantams. It already boasted a small Jonathan apple espaliered against the trellis beside it, with a maiden crop of four fruit. How these ever survived I don't know, so much did I feel, measure and polish them each day. The vegetables suffered from my attentions, too. Root crops were particularly trying, and many of them were pulled right out as I tried to discover how much they had grown.

Florrie's garden was a different matter. Barrowloads of tomatoes and bucketsful of peas were harvested. In January when we went on holiday, sacks of peas and beans went with us and once, I believe, Florrie sent more sackloads after us by rail. The scarlet runner beans hauled themselves up the twelve-foot tennis court fence and were picked from a step ladder. Pumpkins and marrows had to be restrained from rambling off along Grove Street. There were apples, pears, plums and berry fruits. Country expeditions brought in blackberries and mushrooms. As much as possible was stored and put down for the winter. Bunches of brown onions were strung up in the shed; the highest pantry shelves were laden with pumpkins, while sacks of potatoes were stowed in dark corners. Eggs were smeared with greasy Ke-Peg preservative, the shelves filled up with jams, and regular fruit bottling sessions took place using the Fowler's Vacola sterilising set.

There was so much information to be gained by watching and doing. From very close observation, we knew that the hen with the floppy comb laid fat, brown eggs, whereas the speckled hen's eggs were paler and pointed. Peering at vegetable crops, I caught moments of metamorphosis, as the fading broad bean flowers merged into tiny pods or the green bulge behind the pumpkin flower began to swell. After a bit of practice at observing new seedlings poking through the soil, there was never any mistaking a newborn carrot for a turnip, or either for a weed – perhaps the most valuable lesson any gardener can learn. Florrie was forever doing something worth staring at – plucking ducks, trenching the garden beds, pruning the Five Crown apple tree, dosing a sick chook, digging the potato crop. The potato harvest was perhaps the nearest I ever came to experiencing gold fever, for one never knew what treasure the next turn of the fork would unearth. To find a noble spud impaled on the fork was nearly as bad as being stabbed through the middle oneself.

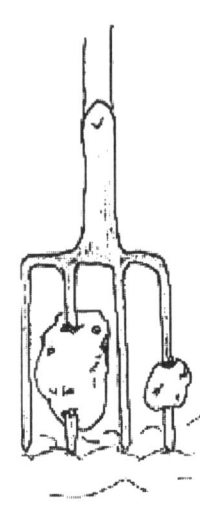

Feeding the chooks was a daily ritual. When Florrie was absent at weekends, Elizabeth or I carried out this chore, and when she was there she expected us to help her. On the stove, she kept two large old saucepans into which were tossed scraps and slops and peelings, which gave rise to a rare aroma as the brew simmered on hour by hour. Next morning this hot brew was mixed with bran and pollard in an old wash-up dish with a giant wooden spoon, and we then staggered out in hessian aprons and gumboots to serve breakfast, steaming hot, to the poultry. On bright, fine mornings this was pleasant enough, but more often the mornings were soaking wet and the yards covered in mud; blue fingers ached and noses drizzled as we slopped about with dirty water pots and struggled with frozen taps. But in return for those warm breakfasts we received glorious eggs, regular meals of roast chicken or duck, and manure.

As well, we lived with the sounds of a contented fowlyard, among the most amiable of nature's noises – those various sounds of inward contemplation ('I do believe I'm going to lay an egg'), and later of cackling triumph, sounds of gossip and hysterics and outrage, of clucking motherly encouragement and of fatherly pride. Sometimes, however, shrieks and squalls of alarm would bring us running. Once a dog invaded the ducks' yard and committed wholesale massacre before anyone could save them. Elizabeth led Father to the gruesome scene. 'Look!' she shouted. 'Won't God be wild!' Well, Florrie's wrath was majestic all right, but God gave no sign.

Taking our cue from Florrie, we never became sentimental about the chooks. She usually had several candidates in mind for the pot and when the condemned were brought to the chopping block in the woodshed, Elizabeth and I would watch as Florrie expertly wielded the axe. She gave us the chance to be executioners sometimes, although I didn't enjoy that much. After the blood-letting, the corpses were taken to the kitchen for plucking and cleaning. The worst part of that was the smell of wet feathers as the bodies were doused with boiling water to ease the plucking. Under Florrie's instruction, we learned the tricks and hazards of cleaning out the innards, how to hook two fingers around the gizzard and steadily pull, trying very hard not to rupture anything because of the pong. We learned which bits to keep for soup and which bits the cat would relish, how to peel the gritty lining from the gizzard, how to screw the tendons from the drumsticks and to peel the scales from the feet. This was kitchen sink biology.

Practical genetics was a backyard subject, for it was out there that Florrie set her broody hens. Before the hens went clucky, clutches of suitable eggs had to be assembled and the pantry shelf became a kind of selective breeding laboratory. Eggs which were known to come from champion layers or hens with superior intellects and decent habits were marked with dates and squiggles to denote their origin, and these were held ready to be sat upon. The nesting parlours were wooden fruit cases stood on end, with straw in the bottom and a sack hanging over the front. They looked like a row of confessionals in the corner of the shed. Hatching took about three weeks for hens' and four weeks for ducks' eggs, and most birds stuck to the task, sitting there in the dark in a state of sozzled, fluffy stupor. Each day the sitter was lifted out for a feed and to stretch her legs and do her 'jobs'; we had to watch that she didn't get carried away by the joys of the dustbath and allow her eggs to get cold.

Marks appeared on the kitchen calendar to denote Hatchings, which were deeply exciting. Elizabeth and I would be up early to accompany Florrie to the shed for the ceremonial unveiling of the nest. Often we were disappointed for the nest was still full of eggs, chipping and cracking certainly, but still eggs. But eventually the hen would be lifted up to reveal a seething mass of chicks or ducklings beneath, all bright-eyed, dry and fluffy. It was always worth the long wait. We would carefully extract the discarded shells, count the little heads and hold our breaths as the beaming hen climbed back on to them, inserting her great knobbly feet amongst the frail, fluffy blobs and then shimmering herself down over them like a feathered tea-cosy.

Florrie increasingly favoured the bantam hens for hatching, for as well as having dainty feet they were devoted and reliable mothers with few hang-ups. Their only deficiency was their size. They could barely cover six large hens' eggs, and as the chickens grew bigger the problem of tucking in the family at night grew with them. Nevertheless, the gallant bantams raised clutch after clutch of hefty Rhode Island chickens – then Florrie decided to confront them with ducks' eggs. The bantams took up the challenge, undaunted by the giant eggs, the extra week of incubation, or by webbed feet, quacking and being abandoned by their broods in favour of a muddy pond. The tiny hen would settle down each night in the midst of her heap of dirty, adolescent ducks, doing her best to spread her little wings over the mountainous family.

PETS

With all this burgeoning of livestock, it wasn't long before pets began to accumulate. My first feathered pet was Joey, an Eastern Rosella. I saw him in a pet shop, looking rather dismal in a cramped cage, and I conned Mother into buying him as an act of mercy. We took him home on the tram in a shoe box and made a big roomy cage for him out of a roll of cyclone wire and netting. Joey was a pre-owned parrot and quite tame, although given to biting. His chief accomplishment, apart from being beautiful, was his ability to whistle 'The Quaker's Wife', although he had a maddening way of not finishing the last line. He was also a master of the wolf whistle.

Cocky, a galah, arrived a bit later from the Wimmera. He had fallen out of his nest as a baby and been reared by hand, then given to Father to bring home to me. Cocky smiled and twinkled; he bobbed up and down on his perch and screeched to welcome us home, and he enjoyed riding round the garden on my shoulder without attempting to escape or to do more than softly nibble my ear. It was a dreadful day when Cocky was killed by a marauding dog. Beheaded chooks and drowned kittens were one thing, but Cocky's was the first death which caused me to howl.

Compared to the two bird comedians, who lived on either side of the belfry on the little back lawn, the pigeons I kept for a short time were very dreary birds, interested only in reproducing themselves at regular intervals. However, Florrie had a penchant for canaries and a lot of luck in discovering escaped canaries in the garden and hunting them down with the hose. Standing out from the ironing-room there was a pergola, and it was a simple matter to convert this into a fine roomy aviary, with access through the ironing-room windows. The canaries evidently approved of this residence, for they raised many children in it and most of the time sang themselves silly. That part of the estate was rather theatrical, what with Joey whistling 'The Quaker's Wife', Cocky shrieking at his own jokes, and the canaries carrying on like a Welsh eisteddfod.

My very first pet was Popeye, an ordinary tabby kitten who grew into an ordinary tabby cat with a bad temper. She quickly bonded with me, and spent much time draped about my neck like a fur stole, or waiting at the gate for my return from school, or asleep in my bed. Last thing at night, the parents would include 'putting the cat out' among their final duties. Popeye would be hauled out of her cosy nest between my feet, carried downstairs and ejected into the darkness. While her persecutor was locking the door and climbing back upstairs, Popeye sped to the side of the house, swarmed up the tall palm tree, leapt through my window and burrowed into her nest again. Everyone then spent an undisturbed night.

LM 1944

Popeye

Before she was very old, however, Popeye was the cause of one splendidly disturbed night. As luck would have it, Margaret was staying with us and she and I were sleeping in the same room, she (as guest) in the bed, I on a mattress on the floor, Popeye between my feet as usual. In the small hours I awoke, aware of some momentous happening which seemed to be going on all round me. There were squeaks and grunts, tumult in the bottom of the bed, and Popeye was storming dementedly about the floor, purring like a two-stroke engine. I switched on the torch. There was a bundle of fur on the floor, and a second near the pillow on the other side; I lifted up the blankets – down near my feet was a third! KITTENS! Popeye, being a novice at all this, was in a dither, wondering how to assemble her new family together in one place. I scrambled out of the labour ward and shook Margaret furiously. 'Quick!' I hissed, 'Popeye's having kittens in my bed!' This was wonderfully exciting, even better than a midnight feast, for it was totally unexpected. We turned on the light and surveyed the scene. The bottom of my bed was a disaster zone, so we picked up the stragglers and put them all in a squirming heap in the middle of it. The time to call in an expert seemed to have come, so I padded along the passage.

'Mummy, are you awake? Popeye's having kittens in my bed!' I announced happily. What joyous news to receive at three in the morning – yet such tidings are all part of the parental lot and no more challenging, I daresay, than 'I've got earache,' or 'I've just been sick on the eiderdown'. Mother rose to the occasion and even managed to show some sympathy towards Popeye, who had not finished her night's work yet. She and her babies were removed in a carton and shut in the ironing-room, while my bed was rehabilitated and we all tried to settle down, but Margaret and I were tip-toeing towards the ironing-room soon after dawn. Popeye lay purring and dribbling in a stupor of maternal ecstasy, while around her writhed and mewled five bundles of tabby fur. Five kittens! They were blind and ugly, with silly little ears, but to us the whole affair was electrifying.

It now seems incredible that no-one had noticed Popeye's barrel shape and given warning of the happy event, and also that in subsequent years she was never de-sexed. After that first litter, of course, we were well prepared. Florrie was a fount of information on the subject. 'It takes sixty-three days,' she proclaimed, 'it' being the gestation period for cats, and thereafter we watched for lecherous toms and, at the merest sign of coyness on Popeye's part, we would start counting the days. In among the Hatchings on the kitchen calendar, crosses appeared to signal when Popeye's time was due, and as this time approached the poor creature knew no peace. She was spied on, followed about, flung out of chairs and locked up at night in the 'fernery' on the side verandah. Margaret's mother donated an old dress basket, and in this Popeye usually produced her litters, although sometimes she outwitted us. One litter arrived in Father's study chair by the phone, and another family appeared in an upstairs drawer. Some more, half-grown, were carried singly up the palm tree and into the spare room next to mine, where they set up house in an armchair. Poor Popeye had just completed the final journey across the roof, her jaws full of large, wriggling kitten, when her subterfuge was discovered – and back they all went to the beastly fernery. Another brood were carted into the garden next door, over an eight-foot high fence topped with wobbly trellis and creeper, while yet another family were found floating in the flooded cellar on a plank, like shipwrecked mariners. No wonder Popeye was neurotic and bad tempered – her life was an endless round of motherhood and human interference.

When I was feeling upset or outraged I would retreat to a remote corner of the front garden, taking Popeye with me, and there I would harangue her about the injustice of the world and of my family in particular. She listened, understood and offered smoodges in place of advice.

THE FACTS OF LIFE

At school there was no such thing as sex education. In Form VA (year 10) we were shown, in science lessons, the reproductive organs of a rabbit and a frog, but there was a wall of silence about how these organs actually worked, and nobody dared to ask. In middle school, the systems of human physiology were covered in very satisfying detail, and I felt quite knowledgeable about hair follicles, sebaceous glands, metacarpals, the duodenum, right and left ventricles, and even the urethra, but the organs of sex and reproduction might as well not have existed.

A little earlier, Mother gave me a small booklet which she said I might find 'interesting'. Its title was something like *Growing Up*. Most of this volume was devoted to birds, bees and especially plants, but it slipped into vagueness as it approached the mammals and primates. Pollen was all very well, but I would have preferred a more practical handbook about the plumbing and engineering involved at the human level. Going to an all-girls school and having no brothers were further handicaps, but the chief problem was the prudishness of the time.

We relied on the world of the backyard to fill in some of the informational gaps and at the birds, bees and cats level we children were fairly well placed at Bishopscourt to engage in research. I would watch the hens for ages, hoping to catch the moment of egg laying, but the hens were very unco-operative and obviously preferred not to be perved on. Besides, it was necessary to stand on one's head to see anything and even then there were too many feathers and straws in the way. Tom cats and roosters were less modest about their role in mating, and I often saw them mounting their females and shuddering in a strange way, but again it was difficult to see what actually happened. On a visit to the country, Dorothy was warned that if she ever saw cattle climbing on each other's backs, she was not to ask why.

Hollywood didn't help much, either. The most one could expect from screen lovers was a chaste kiss, usually beside the mouth rather than full on, and certainly nothing like the screen kisses of today which

126   Beside the Lake

suggest that the lovers are trying to eat each other. At a Saturday matinee, any sort of kiss called for jeers of scorn and wolf whistles from the kids in the front stalls. In films even married couples slept in single beds, and if the chaste kisses ever led to anything further (most unlikely) the audience never saw it. In later years, when we were sixteen, Margaret and I announced that we were going to see *Gone With the Wind*, but our mothers first had an anxious telephone conference to decide whether we were old enough. I believe their problem was the scene where Rhett Butler swept Scarlett off her feet and carried her upstairs to the bedroom, even though the filming stopped at the bedroom door! We were more affected by Melanie's childbirth scene, although that was mostly shrouded under the sheets.

Today, television ensures that children of five know more about the facts of (human) life than I did at fifteen. While this lack of information was mystifying, I don't think I cared much at the time. Sex was something that would come later; for the moment there were far too many other things to do and think about.

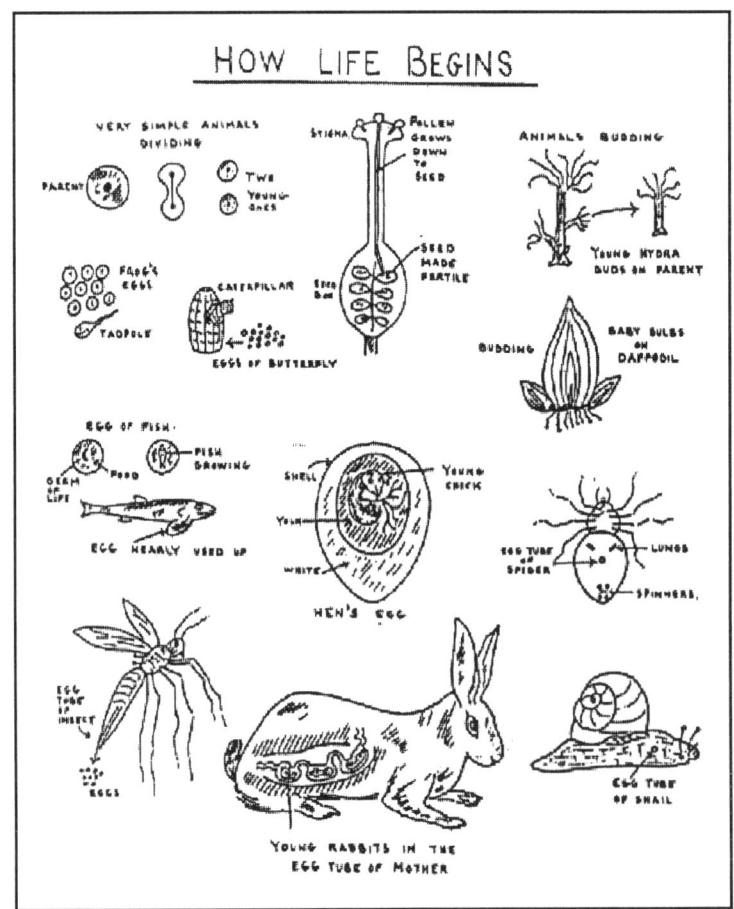

The egg tube of the rabbit was of great interest, but how did the babies get there? From *Living Things for Lively Youngsters*, 1939.

SISTERHOOD

Father was frequently away from home for days or weeks at a time; when he returned he was almost like a stranger learning anew how to fit into this female household of which he was the head. When he was there, however, he and his doings were the focus of the domestic routine. Growing up in a home and a school both of which were run by women and girls was relaxing and often hilarious, but the absence of brothers at home and boys at school was a mixed blessing. It meant that I was fairly ignorant and wary about boys as a species, but it also meant that at home, for example, I didn't have to compete for space at the carpenter's bench or at the chopping block. At school we organised our own games and sports and were responsible for running things in our own way, and we weren't daily distracted by the need to 'preen'. As we grew older, of course, we became very interested in those manly creatures at the boys' schools and were keen to cheer them on at interschool athletics and rowing contests and to make much closer contact with them at senior school dances.

I expect Father would like to have had a son, but I doubt if the presence of a boy would have made much difference to Father's attitude to us. He was quite advanced in believing that girls needed a good education and some sort of career training, rather than being kept at home to wait for 'Mr Right' to appear.

HOUSEWORK

The 'new' Bishopscourt was not exactly a mansion, but its twenty or so rooms, plus passages, staircases and verandahs, all had to be kept reasonably clean – without domestic help. Mother, despite her busy public life, took over many of the domestic chores, and she was lucky to have three well-spaced daughters coming on. We found ourselves learning to do things which in earlier times might have passed us by and I don't recall any feelings of resentment or rebellion over this, except perhaps when it came to the washing up. My favourite jobs were wood chopping and fireplace drill (shades of Doris), polishing the brass and the copper nameplates at the gate, and even scrubbing linoleum floors with sandsoap.

The chapel had to be cleaned from time to time, and it was equal to three rooms in itself. Mother and one of us would arm ourselves with mops and rags and O'Cedar oil, and around the oak panelled stalls we would go, oiling and buffing the woodwork, straightening the red hassocks, then plodding up and down the floor and the staircase and the gallery with the oily mop. The altar brass and the candle snuffer were taken to the pantry to be Brasso-ed, and eventually everything gleamed and smelled richly of well-oiled wood.

On the domestic front Father took up three regular duties – carving the roast, stoking the boiler, which he loathed, and cleaning the shoes, which I think he found rather soothing. Every evening as we sat round the fire in the Pughole, he would round up the family footwear to be dried off and polished. He also bought a cobbler's last, so that he could hammer metal tips on our shoes and glue on synthetic soles in the endless battle against mud and gravel and hopscotch. One domestic ritual which had always belonged to him was that of carving the joint at the dinner table. With Mother at the other end serving the vegetables, it was a relic of the age-old division between hunter and gatherer – although, of course, Father had not killed, fetched or cooked the meat! It would not have occurred to him, or to anyone else, that the man of the family might help with housework in any other ways, especially with such a wealth of womanpower available.

The sum of our electrical appliances was small – the washing machine, iron, vacuum cleaner, a couple of radiators, the wireless, and an electric toaster used only when guests were present. There was still no refrigerator. Most housework was performed, or controlled, by hand rather than by machine, and although slow much of it was open to view, instead of being sealed away in white boxes, and I found it interesting to watch or take part in.

The miracle washing machine had come with us from Newcastle, but it was only one element in an elaborate laundry ritual. Once Mother had become the washerwoman, the washing usually took place on Saturdays and Elizabeth and I often squeezed into the tiny room among the coke buckets and clothes baskets to watch and to help. The gas-fired copper in the corner was filled with cold water, and while it was heating up one of us was given a knife and a cake of Velvet soap to scrape into it. When these soap shavings had melted and the water steamed and frothed, the sheets, towels, table linen and handkerchiefs were rammed in with the furry white copper stick and left to bubble away until the last germ had presumably expired. Meantime, clothing was jerking to and fro in the machine, lathered by a sprinkling of Lux flakes. Gingerly we helped to feed these articles through the machine's electric wringer, first into the rinsing water, then into the second trough (blue-bagged water), and for the third time through the wringer into the basket. We were firmly warned about the evil ways of the wringer and shown how to bash the release lever to free mangled fingers or whatever. Elizabeth's skinny plait once almost fed itself into the rollers, but being very soapy it slithered out before she could be scalped in front of our very eyes. The lesson of wringers was learned for ever.

Hauling the sheets and towels out of the boiling copper was likewise perilous, and we stood well back while Mother raised the steaming linen on the copper stick and fed it through the wringer. The long clotheslines were held up by 'props' in the yard by the woodshed. If the prop slipped or blew over, the snowy linen sagged and scraped along the ground and had to be re-rinsed.

The third laundry trough was reserved for starching. Starch came in hard, white lumps like knobbly macaroni, and one of us prepared the mixture by softening the lumps in cold water and then adding boiling water. Into this slimy fluid were dipped the tablecloths and napkins, traycloths and doilies, and whatever garments needed stiffening. They were then squeezed by hand and hung out to dry into crisp, cardboard shapes. Once dry, they had to be wet again with the sprinkling bottle and rolled into damp sausages until ironing time. When the washing was finished, our hands looked just like the copper stick – white and soggy.

Ironing was an extensive operation, and it is no wonder that both houses included an ironing-room in their original layout. Irons were at best electric, although flat irons (heated on the stove) were still found in houses without power. Electric irons were clumpingly heavy, with creaky wooden handles and a socket at the back into which the flex was plugged in a rather wobbly fashion. The only controls one had over the temperature were the 'spit test' and the 'scorch test'; if the iron sizzled when spat upon it was at least hot enough – if it scorched the white tray cloth it was, alas, too hot. Ironing, therefore, was a hit-or-miss affair and all ironing boards and coverings were branded with the familiar triangular, brown scorch mark. Drip-dry or crease-resistant fabrics were largely unheard of, so almost everything needed pressing, usually after damping down.

For much of the year the house was decorated with wooden clothes-horses laden with airing sheets and towels, in the vicinity of any fire or in front of the kitchen range. As the study was cosy, Father often composed his sermons and wrote his letters festooned about with white drapes. I wondered if that explained the saying about cleanliness being next to godliness?

'OVER-DAINTING'

I invented this term to describe the way some people held their teacups while sipping. The slim, bone-china cup handle would be gripped delicately by thumb and two forefingers, while the little finger described a fan-like curve in mid air, as though dissociating itself from such commonplace matters as food and drink. Sometimes over-dainting occurred at the dinner table, especially when cut-glass finger bowls containing water were provided for guests to dabble in, but this happened only on very high-falutin occasions, never when we children were present.

Over-dainting was much more rife at afternoon tea parties. The afternoon tea ritual was elaborate and the paraphernalia extensive, considering how little the guests actually ate. (From our juvenile point of view, the less they ate the better, as we were waiting in the kitchen like scavenging seagulls at the tip.) The tray-mobile was set up with the silver tea service, cups, saucers and plates, silver spoons and cake forks, plates and dishes doily-ed and piled with scones, sandwiches, asparagus rolls, biscuits, butterfly cakes, sponges, chocolate cakes, eclairs, cream puffs, brandy snaps, nutloaf, fruit cake – not all at once, of course, but four or five of such items to provide a choice. There was just room for the silver hot-water kettle, simmering above its spirit lamp, and for the silver sugar bowl, filled with sugar lumps waiting to be conveyed to the cups by dainty silver tongs. Usually someone had to carry in the three-decker cake stand (known for some reason as the 'curate'), for it wouldn't fit on the tray-mobile.

Preparing the food and setting up the tray were only part of the overture leading up to this performance. As well, the silver had to be polished and the table linen starched and ironed. Ladies in their leisure moments brought out their 'fancy work', embroidered tablecloths or doilies with finely crocheted edges, which all ended up in their own or someone else's linen drawer. The war certainly simplified the ritual, owing to food rationing and people having more important things to do, and fancy work was apt to be put aside in favour of khaki socks; yet the afternoon tea custom was revived in due course, although it was never again to be so pretentious.

For me and Margaret, or Elizabeth, a thrilling game was to infiltrate afternoon tea parties. From the top of the stairs we would watch the ladies arrive, dressed in their best winter suits or summer florals, wearing hats, gloves and solid shoes, and carrying handbags which went 'clunk' when the clasp was closed. The object of the game was to crawl into the drawing room where Mother was dispensing tea, to crouch for some time (without giggling or snorting, but feeling very hot) behind the couch or chairs in which the visitors were sitting, and then to crawl away again. It was important to make sure that Mother saw us, so that she had to keep a serious countenance despite the elevated bottoms heaving about behind her unsuspecting(?) guests. If we were very clever we managed to purloin a biscuit from the lower deck of the tray-mobile, in passing.

In later years, Mother on one occasion entertained the State Governor's wife to afternoon tea. Florrie had left everything prepared in the kitchen and Mother did the rest, but in the heat of the moment she quite forgot refreshments for the two policemen on guard at the front gate. However, Elizabeth, who was mooching about the front garden waiting for things to return to normal, felt sorry for the two constables and piloted them by a back route to the kitchen for a cup of tea and a good sit-down, leaving the Vice-regal party completely unprotected on the forward flank. But the guard was back at the gate, vigilant as ever, in time for the Vice-regal departure, and all was well.

THE BACKYARD

Today's suburban houses are graced with 'outdoor living areas' rather than the humdrum backyard of earlier times. The nearest thing to an outdoor living area at the new Bishopscourt was the tennis court with its attractive little pavilion. The latter had a smooth brick floor and wisteria roaming about its pillars and over its shingle roof. Dorothy had one or two tennis parties soon after we moved in, with white dresses and flannels, cool drinks and cane chairs in the pavilion and mixed doubles on the lawn. I was kept at bay, or at most suffered only as a ball girl.

It was a luxury, this lawn tennis court, a splendid thing to have (like the central heating system) if there was a full-time attendant to go with it. We had no such person after Scruse left. Stan mowed the grass when it looked shaggy, but all the other pamperings which grass courts require were left to us young ones. We had to roll it ourselves and paint on the white lines, using a long wooden stencil device which Father made to help the process along. It was a tedious business, and the white-washed lines barely survived a shower of rain and were shaved off during the next mowing. We didn't mark the lines very often. In fact, a lawn court in Ballarat was something of a folly, given the damp climate, and even in fine weather there were copious dews. Our tennis rackets were very precious and had to be protected from the wet.

However, the tennis court was a wonderful arena for other activities. Father was often heard to say, 'Oh, the energy! Go at once and run five times round the tennis court!' Occasionally he would try to teach us to play cricket with a tennis ball, and the court was just big enough for boomerang throwing and modest kite flying. Father taught us to make kites, too, using crossed sticks, string and brown paper, with lots of glue. Archery was another possibility, with home-made bows and arrows from the pussy willow tree. The tennis net could be wound up and down for high jumping, and a horizontal bar angled across one corner of the high fence was our gym. In summer a big revolving sprinkler played on the grass, and in our thick, woollen bathers we chased the jets of water round and round, gasping and shrieking as they caught us.

When Elizabeth and I were more competent at tennis, Father constructed a hitting wall on the fence in the most remote corner of the tennis court. I painted a line across it for the 'net' and years of strenuous slogging followed. Before this, I had used the garage doors to hit against, so Father's generous action in building a new wall was not entirely altruistic. I think the neighbours across the street might have complained about the thumping. After making do with a cathedral and a chapel, what bliss it was to own a real hitting-wall, a pleasure which most children crave but very few have.

Between the tennis court and the house were all the sheds and the backyard proper. The garage was an ugly corrugated iron building the size of a small cottage. There was space for two cars, although we, like most car-owning families then, had only one. One side of the building was divided between a workshop with carpenter's bench, and a storeroom filled with musty old blinds and lampshades, broken chairs, dusty pictures and the inevitable spare bed ends and wire mattresses which had to be dragged out and bolted together when surplus visitors turned up. Elizabeth and I spent long hours at the carpenter's bench engaged in crude but useful woodwork. Chicken coops were our speciality, another trade we learnt from Florrie. Materials like old fence posts were always to be found in the backyard and wooden packing cases were readily available from the grocer. I revelled in sawing and hammering and chiselling, and could never see why carpentry seemed to be a male preserve while females were fobbed off with hem stitching. Florrie was a competent carpenter, and Mother must have harboured the same rebellious tendencies, for after the war she enrolled for evening woodwork classes at the Ballarat School of Mines.

The backyard of those times was a 'resource centre'. Margaret and I made a seesaw, the only seesaw that I ever actually 'rode', when we found a long, slightly warped plank. It was a matter of moments to straddle it across the saw-horse from the woodshed, and our seesaw was in business. The plank was found to be bristling with ferocious splinters, so we tied cushions to the ends with string, making two comfortable saddles. Weeks of rapture followed. This seesaw was only distantly related to the lumpish brutes of the playground, for it was light and springy and full of high spirits. The ends could be made to wave up and down in unison, like the wings of a great, lazy bird. It slithered and swivelled about on and off the saw-horse. It bucked. It almost smiled. In the end, fatigued by weeks of hard work and eccentric, hilarious exercise, the plank cracked across the middle and was sadly laid to rest, but in its short, gay life it taught us a lot about weights and fulcrums – backyard physics.

One of our more conventional constructions (that is to say, one which adults loudly approved of) was a puppet theatre which we built in the nursery. It was run up out of pieces of backyard timber (I think Father might have helped with the heavy joinery) and old drapes, and it sported a red plush curtain, with a fringe of bobbles, which wound up and down on a blind roller. The heads for the glove puppets were created in the usual way out of papier mâche on clay moulds. In the long run we found that the actual handiwork was much more interesting than the puppet plays which lay at the end of it. After the opening performance, which was badly under-rehearsed, we soon decided that presenting plays to rows of empty seats was a mug's game.

We built cubby houses here and there, and a dugout under the cypress tree behind the garage. The dirt from the foxhole was piled up around three sides and overlaid with planks for a roof. We then retreated into the dank and murky depths with weapons and supplies, and acted out some last ditch stands and Siege-of-Tobruk engagements. One welcome by-product of this excavation was a quantity of brown clay which I used for modelling heads. The most successful of these was a small bust of Hitler, although he himself would not have approved of it; in dark brown clay he looked anything but Aryan!

When the ironing-room was abandoned, Margaret and I took vacant possession, furnished it with two old chairs and a table from the storeroom, and hung decorative weapons on the brick fireplace. Hitler adorned the mantleshelf and he was sometimes joined by jars of aquatic creatures we had dredged from the lake. This was our main Cubby and it became the headquarters of the secret society which Margaret and I founded. For some now forgotten reason this was called The Favour-ites Club (-ites to rhyme with bites). Margaret and I were the only human members, which conveniently meant that our word was law. Among the other members were Popeye and her kittens, our bicycles, the Cubby itself, certain pot plants and so on. We invented a special dialect, which was a strange blend of pidgin English, baby talk and Italian. Exclusiveness was the main characteristic of this club – as of all clubs – and its only program seemed to be the waging of guerrilla warfare against those considered to be enemies of the Favourites, who were lumped together as Stinks. The main Stinks were Dorothy, Elizabeth and the current nurse (while nurses remained). Our tactics were confined largely to plotting, stalking and spying, so that the Stinks were largely unaware of the dangers which beset them.

Elizabeth was not a Stink unless Margaret was present, and she and I invented two imaginary characters, the Old Daddy and the Old Mummy, whose parts we played with gusto. They were a doddery and querulous pair, and the Old Daddy dribbled a lot and hissed through his lower dentures. A generation later my own children invented a similar archetypal couple, although these were less decrepit and had a family of sixteen children, and the general effect on our own family life was much more shattering.

THE WOODSHED

Back to back with the tennis pavilion was a big double shed. One half of this housed bins of chook food, nest boxes, ladders, rolls of wire netting, bunches of onions and so on. Alongside was the woodshed. Its walls were lined with stacks of grey box logs and stumps, its floor was inches deep in the soft chips and sawdust of years, and at its centre presided the battered red gum chopping block, with the axe wedged in it and a decoration of bloodstains from beheaded chooks.

The woodshed was central to the ritual of the wood fire. The ritual began when the wood merchant chugged into the backyard in his ancient truck and tossed several tons of twelve inch logs onto the gravel. It was left to Stan to trundle the logs into the woodshed in the old barrow and to stack them. He then split up loads of the rich pink firewood and wheeled it to the back door near the nursery where, in a little lobby, there was a large oak chest to be filled. When Stan wasn't there, I spent a lot of time chopping wood and slicing up kindling to work off steam and energy.

Of the eleven fireplaces in the house, about four were used regularly. The Esse stove in the study gave out a fierce heat, but the open fires were much more magnetic because we could prod the coals and make the poker red hot, or manufacture charcoal 'pencils' for drawing, or puff with the bellows, or make toast. It was natural to become a fire-worshipper, and on winter nights it was agonising to leave the warm hearth for the dark, icy passages and the cold linoleum of the back stairs.

TREES AGAIN

At Old Bishopscourt the trees had dominated everything, but in our new garden the planting had been more judicious. There were all sorts of specimen trees and shrubs which I found interesting or useful. The loss of the mulberrys and the horse chestnut had been a pain, but there was a pussy willow to provide springy bows for archery, and a holly (minus berries) for Christmas. A stand of cream bamboo was in constant demand for spear-handles, fishing rods, bird perches, flagpoles, high-jump bars, walking sticks, telescopes, flutes, blow-pipes and so forth. On the front lawns there were beautiful ornamentals, four superb liquidambars, two crimson Japanese maples, a large golden ash, a rhus and a silver birch. We added the memorial scarlet oak from the old garden. Autumns were technicoloured.

Popeye's palm near my bedroom was matched by two more spreading palms outside the front windows. These were raided annually by various vicars for Palm Sunday fronds and they seemed to thrive on their Lenten prunings. At the far end of the tennis court grew a rare deciduous swamp cypress and at certain times of year this feathery tree drew all eyes – to its new growth of vivid green in spring and to its blaze of pure russet in autumn. Mother discovered another specimen in the Botanical Gardens, labelled *Taxodium Distichum* (North America), but ours was the finer specimen.

Then there were the climbing trees. While adults are often nostalgic about the tree-climbing of childhood, they tend to forget the practical problems involved. The fact is that hardly any trees are both climbable and hospitable. At Old Bishopscourt the trees were too big. At the new place there was more hope. In the front garden there was a large New

Zealand beech with possibilities; it had smooth, well-spaced, horizontal branches, like a ladder, but when you reached the top there was nowhere comfortable to sit and not much to look at. Yet it wasn't bad for a stealthy leopard hunt with the air rifle.

The golden cypress behind the garage was congested, spiky, dusty and sticky with resin, but it was worth struggling up to the light for its top branches were cushions of golden needles resting and swishing on the garage roof, and it looked over the whole backyard, the street, the neighbouring gardens and the Croquet Club greens across the road.

But the silky oak nearby was the best climber of all. It grew beside Grove Street and we could swing up from the fence into its branches with two or three Tarzanic swoops. It provided seats and backrests and screens of leaves. Margaret and I spent long hours in the silky oak. We turned it into an arsenal with jam-tins of ammunition suspended from the branches on strings, acorns and green plums mainly, in theory to defend ourselves from the attacks of passing schoolboys, should they discover our hideout. In fact the schoolboys cycled past far too speedily to notice us, so warfare never broke out. We enjoyed other things about this tree – its golden spider flowers, its black seed pods, and its botanical name, which we rolled with relish over our tongues – *Grevillea Robusta*.

THE WILDERNESS NEXT DOOR

Although we no longer lived beneath the giant trees of Old Bishopscourt, there was now a backdrop of towering pines growing in the property behind us. Once again, any view we might have enjoyed across the lake was entirely blotted out. The house at our back belonged to 'The Old Ladies', two of them, and it was of about the same vintage as Old Bishopscourt, although much smaller and lacking a tower. Older residents of Ballarat claimed that it had in fact been the temporary abode of the first bishop, Samuel Thornton, when he arrived from England in 1875 and before the Old Bishopscourt was purchased. It, too, faced the lake across Wendouree Parade, with its own Cedar of Lebanon at the front. By our day, the back of the property had turned to a gloomy wilderness under the pines. Between them, Bishopscourt and the Old Ladies' estate took up the whole of the western side of Grove Street. The Old Ladies also owned a paddock along much of our western boundary.

For us children, the paddock and the wilderness provided the perfect foil for the carefully designed garden of Bishopscourt. Tennis balls and other missiles were always flying over our back fence, and we had to leg it over into that dark and mysterious region below the aged pines and the wild broom, where mouldering fowl sheds and wire-netting runs were rotting away under the damp pine needles. Blue periwinkle rambled over everything like a rash. It often took ages to find our balls in this dim jungle, and sometimes we gave up searching and crept closer towards the old house, crawling on all fours like Indians. Usually there was no sign of life, apart from the ghosts of the garden, but very occasionally we came face to face with an Old Lady – we would flee and nothing was ever said. The two of them wore felt hats in the garden, and to Margaret and me they were known as 'Brown Hat' and 'Green Hat'.

The paddock was quite different; it was an open and sunny place, sometimes inhabited by cows. In the summer, Father would ask the Old Ladies if the grass could be cut because of fire risk, and then a man would arrive with an old draught horse and a mowing machine. Elizabeth and I piled the swathes of grass into miniature haystacks with a pitch fork, feeling very bucolic. The paddock was a perfect place to muck about in. I generally wore gumboots in case of snakes or scorpions, although none were ever seen. With nets made from bamboo poles and mosquito netting, I went hunting for frogs, butterflies, grasshoppers and beautiful spiders, carrying matchboxes in my pockets for interesting captures. Buttercups grew there, and a most varied collection of wild grasses and a few delicate wildflowers – Early Nancy, Sundew, Native Bluebells, Milkmaids, Trigger Plants – which struggled up each year amongst the luxuriant growth. The little bush flowers in the paddock were the nearest thing to native plants we ever saw close at hand, apart from the 'specimens' in our garden like the *Grevillea Robusta*. Because of this sharp distinction between gardens and the wild, we never took the bush for granted. It was a place we went to for picnics and I always picked a bunch of pink gum-tips to bring home, if possible, so that the house was filled with the medicinal aroma of eucalyptus. Gum trees were, in a topsy turvy way, more exotic than roses.

Across the grassy lane beyond the paddock (Elliott Street) stood the Malthouse, where grain was malted for brewing, our city being the home of Ballarat Bitter. The Malthouse was a most intriguing place, supplied by horse-drawn waggons bringing fat sacks of grain, and giving out industrious noises and the rich smell of malt, while up and down the lane outside waddled a flock of ferocious, grey geese who kept intruders at bay and filled our world with a chorus of honking.

So, here we were, living in respectable suburbia, with trams at the front, and pavements, yet we shared all this with the animal kingdom – geese, cows, horses, chooks and ducks, birds and cats, and the wildfowl on the lake.

The Biggest Invasion Since the Gold Rush

THE YANKS ARE COMING!

The war ceased to be remote in December, 1941, when the Japanese attacked Pearl Harbour. The Japanese advance down through Southeast Asia was rapid and frightening. Hong Kong was bombed; Singapore fell; 'invincible' British warships were sunk. News of the sinking of the aircraft-carrier HMS 'Ark Royal' came through on our Speech Day. Margaret's father, arriving slightly late at the ceremony, whispered the dreadful tidings to my father, who was presiding on the stage. Father, in turn, informed the gathering and called for a minute's silence. This not only cast a pall over the prize-giving, but also gave promise of an anxious summer ahead.

Indonesia was overrun, as were the Philippines; New Guinea was invaded. The nineteenth of February 1942 brought the first of nearly sixty air-raids on Darwin, and in that raid five ships were sunk and nearly 240 people died.

At this very inauspicious time, Dorothy left school. Early in 1942 she went to Melbourne and spent two years at the Invergowrie Homecraft Hostel in Hawthorn. I inherited her bicycle and some of her books, but not the coveted bedroom which she still used during holidays and occasional weekends at home.

Suddenly the war was very close and we were doing all those things which Aunt Dorothy had described two years earlier in Britain. Signposts disappeared; sandbags were filled; some Melbourne schools were evacuated to the outer suburbs. Others shared campuses so that the military could use school buildings. Father joined an Air Raid Precautions' squad (ARP) and learnt how to fight incendiary fires. Mother went to First Aid classes, taking Margaret, Elizabeth and me with her (as giggly victims) to be bandaged and splinted and artificially respirated by enthusiastic recruits.

Then, in April, with about two days' notice, we heard that the Americans were coming! US troopships had arrived at Port Melbourne. We already had a RAAF training base on the outskirts of Ballarat, and now it was decided to turn our tranquil country city into a holding base for American troops. While a camp was being hastily prepared for them in Victoria Park at the west end of Sturt Street, the first American arrivals were billeted in homes throughout the town, wherever they could be housed at such short notice.

In the biggest invasion since the gold rush, over five thousand GIs homed in like a stupendous swarm of bees. Endless convoys rumbled up and down the avenues of Sturt Street, jeeps carrying white-helmeted Military Police dashed about at alarming speeds, the GIs climbed all over the staid old trams, clinging on wherever they could, even on the roof, and the local maidens were whirled off their feet.

We were told to expect two officers. The nursery came into its own, furnished with beds dragged out of the garage, and there was barely time to get it ready before the convoys started arriving. Our officers turned out to be army chaplains, which was surely no accident. Chaplain E. from Texas was a prim 'Episcopalian'. The word 'episcopal' was often used around our place (Latin *episcopus*, bishop), so we children worked out that American Episcopalians approved of bishops, which, in the circumstances, was just as well.

Chaplain P., however, was a dark and dashing Presbyterian from Indiana who, very soon after arrival, announced that he had to go out, and went – to minister to his troops, so we supposed. A little later we took Chaplain E. for a drive to see the sights and the first notable sight we saw was Chaplain P. on a seat in Sturt Street with his arm clamped tightly round a nurse from the base hospital. Chaplain E. averted his eyes and murmured that his colleague was a 'fasst worker'. Father could only agree, especially as Chaplain P. had a wife and family back home in Indiana.

The chaplains' kitbags disgorged quantities of dirty clothes, which had accumulated during their shipboard confinement. Mother took charge and the washing machine chugged away all the morning until the lines were filled with an unprecedented display of khaki shirts, trousers, socks, regulation underwear and tropical mosquito nets. She decided that, padres or not, war or no war, they could iron it all themselves, so she set them up with the iron and board in the Pughole and left them to it. They looked rather vague about the job, but at least they set off for the Pacific War in a state of cleanliness, if somewhat creased.

Our next American guest was a private from Pennsylvania who could have taught the chaplains a thing or two about laundering. Walter was very young, handsome and homesick. He had left the States with barely any warning and scarcely seemed to know what had overtaken him. Mother suggested an evening at the cinema, but Walter was quite disapproving of this – his Commanding Officer had told the men they were to have early nights. Walter politely declined to eat with us and asked if he could prepare his own food in the kitchen. Florrie granted him a portion of her territory and then watched in astonishment, and with some sniffing, as he doused raw vegetables in vinegar prior to eating them with every sign of relish.

He did all his own washing and ironing with professional expertise, and so was always superbly groomed. In the few days he was with us, he became anxious for our safety should the threatened Japanese air-raids eventuate, and he offered to dig us a slit trench. Father accepted his kind offer and provided him with a spade and a piece of spare garden near the ironing room. I watched Walter with admiration; in his white singlet and khaki trousers he dug neatly and quickly and in no time a deep trench was ready for us in the black soil. Fortunately, Walter had left us before the inevitable happened – he never knew that his beautiful trench filled rapidly with water. This, I imagine, was true of almost every slit trench in the town. Had the raids actually begun, there would probably have been more fatalities caused by drowning and exposure in the trenches than by enemy action.

As Walter departed, he distributed presents. For most of us it was a regulation toothbrush, but he gave Mother a whole carton of chewing-gum and was dumbfounded when she confessed that she had never chewed gum before – nor was she ever likely to, although she didn't tell him that. To her faint enquiry, 'Are you sure you can spare so much of it?', he chucked her under the chin and replied, 'Sure, Ma'am! It's all on the United States Government!' Many other citizens were enjoying gifts of nylons, orchids and chocolate from their American guests, but Walter was not one of those smoothies. I hope he came through unscathed.

For many people, including us, the arrival of the GIs was our first experience of culture shock. Everything about them was larger than life, or the life we knew. Their stylish uniforms made our own servicemen look rather homespun, and most of them were more socially at ease than Australian boys and so had no trouble in finding girlfriends to escort to the dances which were organised for their benefit. Many of them had excellent manners. One night Dorothy came home on a crowded tram and was alarmed when a GI followed her when she got off. He walked behind her through the blackout to our gate and, just as she was about to scream, he raised his cap, said, 'I wanted to make sure you reached home safely miss. Goodnight,' and vanished into the darkness.

We were introduced in person to the wisecrack, that sardonic, snappy remark which Groucho Marx had perfected on the screen. Ballarat was described as being 'half as big as the New York cemetery and twice as dead'. Our visitors did what they could to wake us up. The streets teemed with soldiers and the trams laboured up and down under their riotous burdens. Little old ladies were told they'd have to 'chuck their weight about' if they wanted to reach the exit doors. The copper name plates (BISHOPS COURT) vanished from our gate, but were returned with no questions asked when Father rang army headquarters. Even the old horse-drawn cabs enjoyed a last season of gaiety as the soldiers took the Ballarat girls out for a farewell spin, and no doubt many broken hearts were left behind in Wendouree and Sebastopol, Mount Pleasant and Brown Hill.

AMERICAN SOLDIERS
BILLETED IN BALLARAT.

In our last issue we spoke of the American soldiers billeted in the homes of the people in Ballarat. On their departure a letter was sent on behalf of the commanding officer. As it may be of interest to our readers we reproduce it from the Ballarat Courier. It was addressed to the Mayor and Citizens of Ballarat, and said:

"We of the forces who have been so fortunate to be billeted in Ballarat leave here with the greatest sorrow at parting from friends who, though new and of short acquaintance, have proven to be the finest in the world. We leave you for but a short time, and we leave you all with the same sincere adoration and love that we have left our own families. The beneficence and heartfelt consideration which you have extended to us are appreciated from the bottom of our hearts. It will be as victors that we return to your beautiful city and marvellous people. God bless you all for your kindness, and the day will be grand when we return, after peace is ours, to Ballarat to celebrate victory."

Ballarat Church Chronicle 13.4.42

Very early one morning, Margaret and her family were awakened by the sound of music. They were drawn to the front gate in their night attire, to see columns of Americans marching down Sturt Street to the Railway Station, where the troop train awaited to carry them off. As they marched through the eerie light of dawn, they sang 'Over there ... Over, we're coming over, and we won't be back 'til it's over, over there.'

FLAGS

Sturt Street was a grand and theatrical setting for processions and marches. With its dual carriageway and central gardens, there was ample space for crowds, brass bands and horses, and the buildings, following the example of the Town Hall, the Post Office and Craig's Hotel whose towers soared up proudly on the hill, all carried flagpoles for festive occasions. Father had a tall white flagpole planted in our garden so that he, too, could unfurl the Union Jack when he felt a surge of patriotism (quite often).

During the war, flags were constantly being run to the top of masts on towers and rooftops – the Union Jack, the Australian ensign, the American Stars and Stripes predominated, while the Anglican churches flew the cross of St George and the Presbyterian kirks the cross of St Andrew. Anzac and Armistice Days were marked with redoubled fervour. Father pinned on his medals and joined the columns of the First World War veterans marching down Sturt Street while we stood in the crowds to cheer or observe solemn silence. Little cloth flags on sticks were available for children to wave in the street.

The predominant flag was the Union Jack, the flag of Great Britain and the common flag of her empire. Its place in the corner of the Australian ensign was well understood, for Great Britain was our Mother Country. During the war, Mother England had her back to the wall and our patriotic fervour boiled over. Her war was our war and her flag was our flag, whether in its full glory or tucked in the corner of our own blue standard with its starry cross.

The make-up of the Union Jack was explained to us at school. Diagrams showed how the separate flags of England, Scotland and Ireland were cleverly superimposed in a composite design to symbolise their union as one nation. The word 'jack' was a naval term for flag, and from watching war films we all knew how important identifying flags were at sea if you didn't want to be blown out of the water by one of your own ships! More intriguing still, these three separate flags were in

144   Beside the Lake

fact the crosses of St George, St Andrew and St Patrick, the patron saints of the three nations. So, the Union Jack was a saintly flag. We had exercises in drawing it, carefully measuring the angles and proportions before colouring in the red, white and blue.

The other side had their flags too. Hitler and his henchmen were flag fanatics and they understood the power of massed red banners to arouse a crowd. There was nothing saintly about the swastika. To us, it was a symbol of evil. Its black, clawlike silhouette, seen against white and red, seemed predatory, cruel, and yet it was a fascinating shape to draw. Swastika doodles were common on my blotting paper. The swastika flag didn't appear in our edition of Pears' Cyclopaedia, that dumpy, red fount-of-knowledge in Father's study. The German flag shown there was plain and dignified red, gold and black. I pored over these brilliantly coloured pages in Pears' – here was another example of the ordering of things, serried ranks of flags in the alphabetical order of nations, each with its own symbolism in design and colour, including our own Southern Cross, reminiscent of Ballarat's very own Eureka flag.

Churches often had flags displayed inside, some of them tattered relics from earlier wars, others new. The older ones were often faded and discoloured, some even threadbare. I could almost imagine bloodstains! They could have been trophies from the Battle of Waterloo, or perhaps Agincourt, so old and decayed were they. Most churches displayed the saintly Union Jack somewhere. The warlike spirit was also manifest in certain hymns, none more so than:

> The Son of God goes forth to war,
> A kingly crown to gain;
> His blood red banner streams afar.
> Who follows in his train?

The last line encouraged jokes about railway excursions and the like, but these could never dim the blaze of that blood red banner.

DARK DAYS

These were exciting times, but inevitably they had their dark side. Having no immediate kinsfolk in danger, our family was spared the racking anxiety which so many others suffered, but our parents knew of many who were stricken. Elizabeth and I were sheltered from these tragedies, but I was aware of hushed conversations and sadness. Mother vanished to stay with a cousin whose son had been killed in action. Father drove to another diocese to take Sunday services for a similarly bereaved clergyman. A young friend from Adelaide, who had visited us while training at the RAAF base nearby, did not return from his overseas posting.

At school rumours were rife. Tokyo Radio had announced the arrival of American troops in Ballarat, it was said. Ballarat would be bombed; we had become a target. The Japanese were said to be indiscriminate bombers. 'What does indiscriminate mean?' I asked Mother casually, having a pretty fair idea of what it meant. She tried to sound reassuring, but whether the Jap bombardiers aimed well or not we lived only half a mile from the American camp, and the nearby lake was a perfect landmark from the air.

We tried to comfort ourselves with other scraps of misinformation. Perhaps their aircraft, being 'made in Japan' would fall to pieces. The Japanese themselves were said to have very poor eyesight – if they couldn't see, perhaps they would be incompetent fliers and get lost on the way to Ballarat. Our own airmen, of course, ate carrots, which enabled them to see in the dark.

Women, at their afternoon teas, discussed the possibility of setting off into the inland with their children. Mother reported that one respected matron had identified the need for a pair of sturdy nail scissors to keep one's toenails in trim on the long trek. In the meantime, every effort was being made to confuse the invaders, if they came, by removing or painting out all signposts or place names across the countryside.

At school, slit trenches were dug in one corner of the hockey field. Hanging beside our desks we each had a kitbag containing emergency rations and spare clothing. Around our necks we wore corks or rubbers on strings, to bite on when the bombs began to fall. Our kitbags were inspected at intervals, and nearly always, of course, the emergency rations had been eaten. Air-raid drill was sprung on us, and when the whistle blew everyone lined up in a double file down the long corridor. The smallest girl in the school (who happened to be Elizabeth) was paired off with the head prefect, and in this way the little ones were in the care of the eldest. Being in the middle of things, our class was left to look after itself as we marched – 'in an orderly fashion, girls!' – out to our appointed place in the trenches. Margaret and I found ourselves in a soggy corner which had very early sprung a leak.

Jenks had been sent to Melbourne to attend an ARP course, and when she returned she was put in charge of these daytime arrangements and also of precautions in the boarding house. The school was only a short distance from a power station and was therefore vulnerable to attack. Larks carried out the mammoth task of making blackout curtains for the boarding house, while Jenks instructed the girls and house staff in air-raid drill. The night shelter was the old cellar under Manifold House. The boarders went to bed with their kitbags beside them and their slippers turned upside down on the floor in case of flying glass. They were forbidden to run if the siren went.

At home, too, blackout curtains and screens went up. Ballarat had its first blackout practice very soon after the attack on Pearl Harbour in December, 1941. By 1942 we had settled into the Pughole and a large piece of masonite had been cut to fit into the window at night, so long as the threat of air-raids remained. Walter's trench was filled in and a sturdy wooden 'Mousetrap' shelter was built inside the house, where there was less likelihood of drowning. This shelter was fitted in at one end of the Pughole, of all places, because this room was under the back staircase. The Mousetrap was strong enough to withstand falling masonry and it was padded inside with old mattresses, so it doubled quite well as a cubby house while we awaited the wail of the sirens. We children also found its flat top useful as a stage or as a sort of dress-circle when conditions on the floor became too crowded. Its presence in the Pughole reduced the already modest floor space by about a third. In another corner Mother installed a second-hand knitting machine (never a great success, as it kept dropping stitches) and sometimes the treadle sewing machine was wheeled in as well. At all times there were four or five chairs and a round table, and very often a rack of airing washing. Life in the Pughole during the Second World War was extremely cosy, not to say tight.

Our tendency to gather in the smallest rooms of this extensive house became a family joke. The other most common rallying point was the tiny laundry, where washing and boiler duties often seemed to coincide. In the darkest days of austerity, however, the boiler went out altogether. Because of a shortage of coke, and also a shortage of time and energy for boiler stoking, Father decided to instal a chip bath-heater in the broom lobby near the back door. A hole was drilled in the wall and the spout of the heater was poked through this to emerge above the sunken bath in the former Maids' bathroom. Bath-time, under those conditions, was like an item from a Boy Scouts' manual. It was necessary to lay in a large supply of chips before nightfall and then to light the engine well in advance, for the Mallee Heater took its time in producing a reasonable amount of hot water. For that reason we often all dipped in the same tub, one after another. The testing time came at the end, after towel and pyjamas had been applied, for then one had to sprint through the icy kitchen wing and up the stairs to the chilly bedrooms and dive under the blankets before the warmth wore off.

Through all these domestic events, the wireless droned on. In 1942 we lived through more 'turning points' – the Battle of the Coral Sea in May and the Battle of Midway in June. We learnt a new litany of names – Corregidor, the Burma Road, the Kokoda Trail, Milne Bay, Buna and Gona. To the pictures of desert sand and North Atlantic blizzards were added those of jungle and palm trees and coral atolls. General MacArthur arrived flamboyantly in Melbourne and the convoys continued to rumble through Ballarat.

1941-42 Japanese forces reach Australia's gateway. (MH 15.8.45, VP Day retrospective)

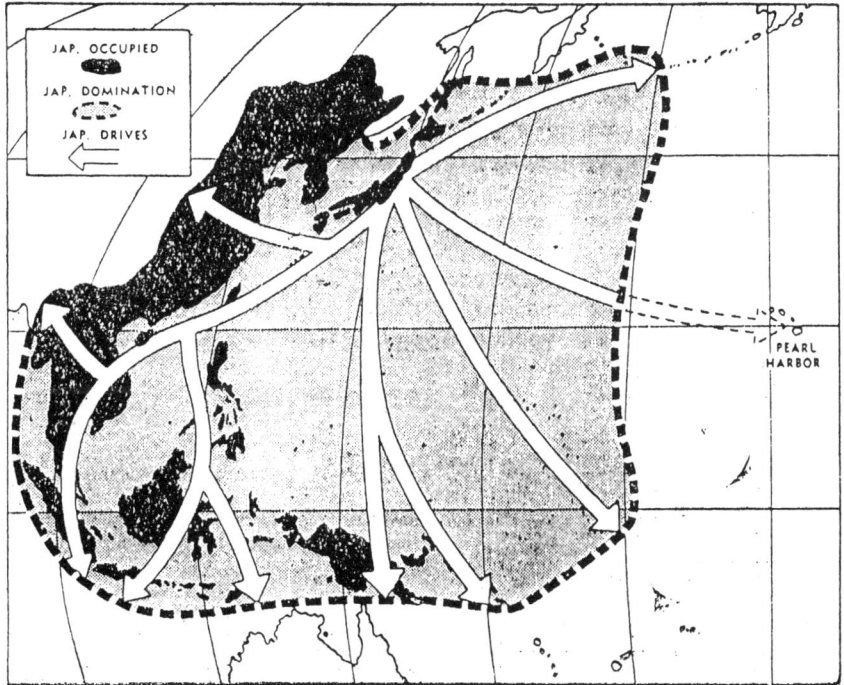

148   Beside the Lake

Over beyond Victoria Park the Guncotton Factory was built and marked our city's entry into war production. Margaret and I sometimes rode our bikes past the Guncotton Factory, intrigued by the mysterious activities behind its secure fences and closed gates. Nobody told me that guncotton was used in explosives, and not wanting to show my ignorance I imagined it to be a sort of cottonwool substance, perhaps used for cleaning gun barrels. Such a place gave us all a sense of taking part in the wider struggle.

So too did the popular weekend pastime of sitting in parked cars near the RAAF camp and watching the Avro Anson and Wackett training planes taking off and landing. (We named two of Popeye's kittens Wackett and Thumpit.) These planes were a far cry from the giant Lancaster bomber which visited Australia in 1943, presumably to keep us in touch with the miracles of modern aviation which were helping to win the war in Europe. When the Lancaster reached Ballarat, we were all herded onto the school hockey field to watch it lumber overhead, and to cheer.

Visits to the Railway Station were still exciting, especially at night, as the station was blacked out and trains carried only small lights low down over the wheels, so there was a somewhat infernal atmosphere of steam and sparks and an eerie glow. Trains were unpunctual and very crowded, the platforms usually swarming with soldiers and airmen humping their kitbags or clasping wives and girlfriends.

A War Savings Certificate, with explanation

WAR EFFORT

At a low level we children did our bit for the war effort. We saved up pennies for sixpenny War Savings Stamps, which were stuck on a card until we had enough (40=one pound) to convert into a War Savings Certificate. At school we were taught to knit strange khaki garments to send to 'the boys'. At our incompetent level in the middle school, we were confined to long, narrow strips called 'garters', knitted appropriately in garter stitch, although the older girls were let loose on socks and balaclavas. After school sometimes, Margaret and I visited Mrs Fairbairn (whose husband was a Wing Commander in the RAAF) to be taught how to make camouflage netting. This was a much more sensational operation than knitting; in no time the room seemed to be knee deep in netting. We helped to wrap up cartons of knitting wool and food parcels for the long and uncertain voyage to Britain. Fruit cakes of concentrated nourishment were hermetically sealed in Willow tins, wrapped in waterproof material, then sewn into hand-tailored jackets of canvas on which the names and addresses were laboriously printed in indelible ink. I like to think those fruit cakes helped to win the war.

LDT 1943

We are so thrilled with that marvellous cake. How dear & generous of you to send it; it arrived last week in perfect condition, & we haven't seen it's like in years! It has the most ravishing taste. I'll send a special note of thanks to Florrie who also seems to have taken a large part in proceedings. Cakes are never displayed here in shop windows now, & haven't been for ages, but if you stand in a queue, you can buy rather sharpe looking specimens at certain times of the day.

On more independent lines Margaret and I were inspired to hold fêtes in aid of wartime charities. We made toffee and sweets, organised lucky dips and jumble stalls, and set up shop in the front hall at Bishopscourt, having invited long-suffering committee members of the organisations concerned – the Red Cross, the Missions to Seamen, the Comforts' Fund – and anyone else we could browbeat into coming. There was no point in asking other children, as they hadn't enough cash, so our customers were the good ladies of the district who would return home bearing bags of stickjaw, cakes of Lifebuoy Soap and bunches of wilting flowers. What good sports they were!

The Depression had been an effective training ground when it came to practising the wartime virtues of thrift and making-do, and the war years were to foster the very opposite of our present 'throw away' mentality. From every quarter we were exhorted to economise and save – to switch off lights, grow food, save paper, support war loans, collect old aluminium saucepans and scrap iron. Iron railings and fences disappeared from public gardens, to be turned into guns.

Very little was thrown away and the packaging industry had not yet run mad. Milk bottles, which had just replaced the back-step billy, were strictly returnable. Bread, unsliced and unwrapped, was handed in at the back door or left in a tin. Meat came wrapped in white paper (our meat) or newspaper (catsmeat) and this wrapping was immediately used for firelighting. Fowl food arrived from the grocer in returnable sacks. Most perishables came in paper bags and these were put to good use, lining cake tins, covering jam jars, tying up seed heads in the onion patch. Greasy butter paper was also kept for cooking tins, while empty fruit cans were prized as scoops for the wheat bin, water tins for the chooks, or stilts for Elizabeth and me. All foil and silver paper was saved for the war effort, while a deposit system on screw top soft drink bottles ensured that they went straight back to the shop. Our garbage tin contained a meagre amount each week, thanks to the poultry, the compost heaps, the fires, the war effort, the deposit and return system, and the general absence of throwaway material, especially plastic.

There were shortages of everything, which led to irritation and frustration, although it could not honestly be said that we suffered hardship. In fact it was very beneficial to the character to have to save up, to wait, to earn things, to make do and be inventive and resourceful. I expect that even our teeth benefited from sugar rationing.

Chocolate was in very short supply and consequently became the subject of a wide community craving. It was always worth asking in any sweet shop whether the latest chocolate ration had arrived, just in case. Dressed in full clerical rig down to gaiters, Father visited a Melbourne sweet shop to ask just this, and when the shopgirl sheepishly handed him a block of Fruit & Nut Milk from under the counter, the other customers expostulated, 'But you told us that there wasn't any!' 'Yes,' she sniffed, 'but I couldn't tell him a lie, could I now!'

Father didn't appear in gaiters very often, as they were formal wear for high level occasions. Before the war he had bought himself a Harris tweed sports jacket of grey and white houndstooth, which he wore at home and in the car to keep himself warm. I thought it was the best garment he ever owned, as it made him look like a normal man even over his dog collar and purple stock. He owned just one suit of clerical grey, which became more frayed at the edges as the war dragged on.

At home, Mother made do in various ways. She took her old hats to Harry Davies Emporium to be reblocked and freshly trimmed for the coming season. She set us to work grinding wheat for porridge in the coffee grinder. This was pretty hard work and it resulted in pretty nasty porridge. There was one abortive soap-making experiment; fat and a number of other unpleasant ingredients were boiled up in a kerosene tin and eventually turned into shrunken, dung-coloured little blocks which sat on a shelf for months until someone had the courage to throw them away.

Rubber goods were, for civilians, virtually unobtainable because of the huge military demand for rubber. Tennis balls were more precious than gold and tyres and tubes were nursed along through many a puncture and blowout. When the old rubber hotties had perished, we warmed our beds with metal flasks or with warm bricks wrapped in flannel. The shortage of elastic gave rise to crucial problems, especially in the underwear department where we learnt to make do with buttons and hooks. There was also a shortage of suitable material for underwear and parachute silk was much prized as a substitute. Having seen a parachute at close quarters, I was astonished at the number of pairs of bloomers it represented.

For the young, austerity also had undeniable advantages. I belonged to the first wave of twelve-year-olds who were exempted from wearing regulation lisle stockings at school. This was comparable to being saved from a fate worse than death, and scenes of jubilation took place in assembly when we were told that we could wear brown sockettes! Mother decided to knit our socks, and the toes of mine were always finished off in another colour – blue or yellow – to save breaking into a further ball of wool. Coloured toes caused me embarrassment in the cloakroom, but anything was better than being encased in thick stockings and suspender belts. These trappings were the first signs of the approaching prison of adulthood; suspender belts led to girdles and girdles led to corsets, those whalebone monstrosities which our mothers wore! As with stockings, our virginal white speech day dresses were swept away by the war, never, mercifully, to reappear.

Ration books were issued for food, clothing and petrol, and children of a certain age and size received supplementary clothing coupons, most of which were swallowed up by school uniforms. Petrol was the first item to be rationed, in October, 1940. Motorists were disciplined by the petrol coupon and by a strict speed limit and they soon learnt to use their cars for essential purposes only and to drive slowly. Some attached hulking charcoal-burning gas-producers to their cars, but clergymen were allowed a fairly generous ration of petrol so our family was less restricted than many.

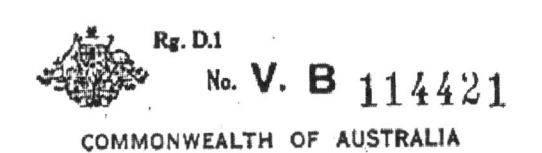

Rationing. The coupons (for sugar, tea, meat, butter, clothing) were snipped out by shopkeepers as used. Petrol coupons were much larger.

The indirect advantages of petrol rationing to children like us were enormous, for just at that time, when I was about eleven, I inherited Dorothy's big bike and Margaret acquired a new Malvern Star. Except for military convoys on the main routes, the streets of Ballarat were peaceful and almost empty. Public space was accessible to us and relatively safe from traffic and crime, a privilege we barely appreciated at the time. We rode our bikes to school, to the shops, to the lake, to the countryside, to anywhere. They were passports to endless freedom, exercise and adventure. We patched and pumped our worn tyres and tubes, and tied things together with wire and braked with our feet; at all costs those bikes had to be kept going, for one could scarcely imagine life without them.

While petrol rationing allowed children freedom of the roads, the war made it possible in other ways for us to enjoy this new independence. It freed us from nursemaids and the restrictive domestic regime of earlier times, and our elders' preoccupation with their work and the war effort meant that we were less strictly supervised than we might otherwise have been. Hidebound rules and conventions of dress began to relax, and with them those mid-Victorian attitudes which regarded little girls as demure, ladylike and passive, and even – in white dresses – angelic.

In a perverse way, it was beneficial to grow up in wartime. Life was rarely trivial or frivolous; there was always a serious purpose to it, a cause that people were prepared to die for. War taught us about sacrifice, co-operation, patience, thrift, loyalty, effort, discipline – outmoded virtues nowadays perhaps, but virtues all the same. The downside of humanity was also thrown into relief; we became aware, at a distance, of tyranny, megalomania, torture, cruelty, cowardice and the greed of black marketeers.

There was general admiration for the Russian people, the Red Army and for 'Uncle Joe' Stalin, all of whom did so much to withstand Hitler's assaults and to turn the tide of the war in Europe. Father, however, in articles, speeches and sermons, waged a relentless campaign before, during and after the war, against what he termed 'militant, atheistic communism'. The Cold War and the Iron Curtain came as no surprise to him.

A Port on the Yarrowee

ALL AROUND THE TOWN

The move to the new house had brought us closer to the city's heart. We now lived on Sturt Street, the main artery, instead of in the rural distance. At first I walked to and from school, but within a couple of years I was old enough to ride my bike, not only to school but also further afield. The layout of the streets and the character of the buildings came into much clearer focus.

Margaret's father claimed to have read in a school geography book that Ballarat was 'a port on the Yarrowee'. We young ones seized on this idea and laboured it to death, for the Yarrowee Creek was something of a joke. It was largely hidden from view, flowing through channels and culverts and beneath the buildings and pavements of Bridge Street. Bridge Street, of course! But who could guess that it was a bridge over anything? We couldn't imagine the creek's original rural character because it looked like a large gutter in the places where it was visible, yet it still divided the town into two halves, east and west, and the two halves were very different, as they always had been.

The West was planned as a grid, except round the lake where bends were unavoidable. The streetscapes in the East were more meandering and only Victoria Street, which made a brave entrance to the town as one drove in from Melbourne, could rival the dignity of the West. Victoria Street had brilliant flower beds and its fair share of trees and fine buildings, yet most of the prime historical sites in the East were tucked away in side streets – Eureka Stockade, the Old Curiosity Shop, St Paul's Church and Main Street wandering off to Buninyong. The nave of St Paul's had collapsed, undermined, in 1864, and Father told us about it so often that I think he must have felt edgy in case it happened again. Several churches were destroyed by fire in his time, so the added threat of subsidence would have brought him no joy.

We sometimes rode our bikes and often drove along Main Street, past the Chinese Joss House and the jumbled landscape around Sovereign Hill (in those days an abandoned mullock heap). It was slightly eerie, like riding through a forgotten cemetery, quiet and decaying, and it was here that one was most aware of the mines because the surface was so disfigured and untidy. Up in the West we were not aware of the tunnels which snaked about under the basalt below us. Now and then a subsidence would remind us of the subterranean honeycomb, such as the gaping hole which appeared in the school quadrangle, threatening the foundations of the assembly hall. This caused eager speculation as to whether the entire school population might slide into a deep lead during morning prayers, but no – the hole was filled in and lessons went on as usual, ho hum.

The streets we pedalled around bore names like a roll-call of early gold commissioners and police officers, commemorating Police Commandant Sturt, Captains Dana, Mair and Lydiard, Commissioners Doveton and Armstrong, Surveyor Urquhart, but at the time I had no idea of who they were. Dana Street was noted for its 'hill' which (as a pale imitation of the Newcastle steeps) swooped down from Lydiard Street towards the gasometers on the flat and was death to bikes with poor brakes. The Diocesan offices were tucked in under the Anglican pro-Cathedral on this hill and Father often parked outside on the steep slope. Sometimes we went into the office with him and crept on further into the old Chapter House, which was to have been the crypt of the great projected cathedral which was never finished. The Chapter House was cavernous, with fine stone arches. We children at once recognised its theatrical potential – sunken floor, raised platforms on three sides, gothic arches, massive pillars and stone steps – what a setting for Shakespeare! 'Romeo, ROMEO, wherefore ART thou, Romeo?'; or for Nelson Eddy and Jeanette MacDonald! We capered about on the stage, sat in the throne and hooted discreetly to test the thrilling echo, before being summoned back to the tilted car on the hill.

The hill ran across to Sturt Street, Mair Street and Camp Street, from where the Government Camp had watched over the diggings below. The hill gave to the West its air of supremacy, which was increased by the pile of impressive buildings on its shoulder, the scene of the flag-flying.

There were four department stores in Sturt Street where Mother did much of her shopping. Paterson, Powell & Sandford (now Myer), Crocker's and Harry Davies' were all draperies, while Tunbridge's sold furniture. These four occupied prime corner positions near the Town Hall and Mother spread her custom amongst them all. I associated Harry Davies' with hats, Crocker's with stockings and lingerie, and Paterson's with school uniforms, fabrics and haberdashery. At the rear of Patersons there was a mezzanine floor, hushed and carpeted (unlike the squeaky boards of the lower level). Miss Brown reigned in the school uniform department on the upper level, and there we went to be fitted for blouses, skirts, dresses and playsuits (for sport), which were mostly custom made. The school playsuits were of unbelievable design, considering they were worn by girls up to eighteen years old. They were combinations of shirt and long shorts, buttoned down the front of the shirt, across the waist and down the side of one leg, and therefore almost impossible to escape from in an emergency! Miss Brown's hair was arranged in two buns and she usually had her lips clamped upon a row of pins as she tucked and eased us into our garments, assuring Mother through the pins that she was 'allowing for growth'. How I squirmed.

The customers had high chairs and stools to sit on at some counters and nothing that Modom wanted was too much trouble. While Mother was trying on hats or choosing buttons, I watched the 'flying fox' which catapulted the money to the cashier. Like spiders at the centre of their webs, the cashiers sat in cages, linked by cables to all the counters. In Paterson's the cage was near the roof, out of the reach of bandits, I supposed.

Sometimes we had lunch at Craig's Royal Hotel, generally on a Sunday or when Florrie was on holiday. I was more interested in the menu than in the royal heritage as we mounted the splendid staircase towards the dining-room. This room had very tall windows overlooking Bath Lane, where Adam Lindsay Gordon had once run the livery stables. The numerous damasked tables were spaced out on shiny brown linoleum, and the elderly waitresses, in black and white uniforms, had a long walk to the kitchen with their heavy trays. Nevertheless they always asked if I would like a 'return', which I quickly understood to mean a second helping. As there was usually chocolate or ginger 'sinker' on the menu I invariably accepted their offer, and then felt guilty as they tottered off to do my bidding. All the same, they looked quite pleased when someone asked for more.

Beyond Craig's, at the end of the street, loomed the massive gateway of the city gaol, sitting companionably amongst the various churches, legal offices and the School of Mines. Those brooding bluestone walls evoked grim scenes of flogging and hanging, so that it was a surprise to see, from the street at the back, the gaol gardens terraced down the hillside and watched over by the little coolie-hatted stone towers in the surrounding walls. It looked as peaceful as a Chinese market garden.

The South Street Competitions took place each spring in the notorious Alfred Hall in Grenville Street. This eisteddfod was first held in 1879, while the hall was built (hastily) in 1867 in time for Prince Alfred's visit. Altogether it could hold about 5000 people, so that it was certainly the largest mark which the Prince left on the town plan. It was raised, appropriately, across the dividing line between Ballarat East and Ballarat West, which was of course the channel of the Yarrowee. In our time the Yarrowee still ran beneath it through a culvert, and on a wet night, with rain drumming on the iron roof and the swollen creek gushing beneath, the audience was hard put to it to hear what was happening on the stage. The draughts which whistled under the seats

Advertisement in the South Street Competitions Guidebook for 1941

in winter were legendary. Spectators arrived equipped as for a polar expedition, muffled up in boots and furs, bearing rugs and hot water bottles. No doubt it couldn't go on, but I for one am glad that I had the chance to be mentioned honourably in that extraordinary auditorium before it bit the dust!

The city buildings which we children visited most regularly and willingly were the cinemas. We called them 'picture theatres' and Ballarat had four. It must be said at once that two of them we scarcely patronised at all, for picture theatres were graded in our esteem as much for their decor and class as for their programmes. Ranked lowest was the Plaza in Camp Street. It had no 'upstairs' and was more like a hall, and so ruled itself out of consideration. The old Britannia, which was somehow entwined with the Mechanics' Institute and tucked in behind the shops on the Sturt Street hill, wasn't much better. It showed the 'Saturday arvo' serials, so you had to be an avid weekly patron to get the most out of that cinema, and in any case it was distinctly lacking in glamour. Her Majesty's in Lydiard Street South was acceptable because it had both dress and upper circles, and we went there sometimes if the film was very attractive, but the seats were hard. Our prime target always was the Regent at the other end of Lydiard Street.

The Regent was a modern palace of the 1930s, with a spacious 'upstairs', well-cushioned seats and no obstructing pillars. It had all the comforts of home – indeed it had a good many more, like marbled stairways and deep carpets, plaster 'sculpture' and friezes, and fake urns which could have concealed Ali Baba and his forty thieves. As children of austerity, we inevitably preferred the luxury of the Regent to the spare elegance of Her Majesty's, and as we hastened towards it I barely noticed the splendid series of Victorian banks beside us or the celebrated colonial verandahs of the George Hotel above, or the beautiful iron lacework on the balconies over the way, for our steps were bent towards a stirring afternoon with Nelson Eddy or 'Mrs Miniver' (a famous wartime weepie celebrating the evacuation from Dunkirk and starring Greer Garson). Cinema programs changed every week and for a few pence we saw a cartoon, a newsreel or two and two full-length feature films. At interval we bought an ice-cream or a Violet Crumble from the boy who stood in the aisle with a miniature sweet counter strapped over his shoulders.

'God Save the King' was invariably played at the conclusion of the program, and there was sometimes a rush to reach the exit before the opening drum-roll of the anthem froze everyone to attention. Once, when Father was with us, he rose to his feet as the King's image appeared on the screen, and boomed, 'Everybody STAND!' I stood and shrivelled up.

Opposite the Regent was the Art Gallery. Each year this building would come into focus when the results of the Crouch Prize were announced. This was an acquisitions prize financed by a local benefactor, R.A. Crouch, and it attracted numerous entries. Like the Sun Aria at South Street this art prize was something of a national event; our city moved into the cultural spotlight and we rather enjoyed the glow. Father would steer us down to the gallery to inspect the entries and the winner in the Crouch exhibition, and I enjoyed the ascent of the grand staircase and the overpowering presence of 'Ajax and Cassandra' on the wall of the central landing. By the time we had reached the top of the stairs, I felt subdued by the atmosphere of hushed reverence, which was a bit like going to church. Coming down again later, there was always a big temptation to slide down the banisters.

As a building, the Railway Station was less easily taken for granted than the architectural beauties of Lydiard Street, perhaps because visits there were emotionally charged with the excitement of journeys, arrivals and farewells, and the orchestration of steam and shunting. There was time to explore, to run across the overhead bridge and to appreciate the massiveness of stone archways and the weight of the iron barrier gates. If we were told to wait outside in the car, there was the architectural joie-de-vivre of the entrance facade and the clock tower to stare at, the tower with its four clockless faces, like blind eye-sockets.

The important clock tower in Ballarat was that of the Town Hall, always to be linked in my mind with the trams. The building was opulent, grey, solid, lordly. It was to become the scene, in my later years, of public examinations, when its marble staircases and echoing chambers swarmed with the jittery, clattering youth of the district, our uniforms all jumbled into alphabetical order on bentwood chairs as we underwent our common ordeal at the hands of the Public Examinations Board. But for me the Town Hall's raison d'être was its clock, the chiming clock with four faces and Roman numerals, visible for blocks up and down Sturt Street as we went about our business down below. We kept an eye on the clock, for the rhythm of a visit to the city was the twenty-minute rhythm of the trams. To miss a tram was a sobering experience, for twenty minutes was a very long time to wait, stamping cold feet at the tramstop or huddled out of the rain in the shelter. City visits therefore were punctuated by quick sallies out of shops or side streets to consult the old clock. On cold Saturdays, we hurried down from the Regent – what would the clock say as we rounded the corner? 'Quick! It's nineteen past – we'll just catch it if we run!'

The skyline of the city included an exhilarating mixture of towers, spires, turrets, minarets and cupolas. The upstanding towers of the public buildings bestowed an air of pride and optimism, especially when the flags were waving; but jaunty rooflines could be found on smaller buildings like bandstands and rotundas, houses and the three flag-waving turrets on the City Oval grandstand. It was sad when the tower at Old Bishopscourt was no longer among them.

We kept an eye on the Town Hall clock (left)

The Railway Station – architectural joie-de-vivre (right)

Ballarat was rich in Victorian and Edwardian houses, including a row of beauties facing Bishopscourt across Sturt Street West. This treasury of tiled verandahs, iron lace, bow windows and delicate picket fences or graceful barge boards I took rather for granted, or regarded as old-fashioned. Having lived in such an old house and known some of

Lacey balconies

the discomforts, I was more inclined to admire the latest cream brick models which offered sunrooms and wall-to-wall carpets and a more realistic approach to the Ballarat climate. One of the earliest of these was Mrs Tilly Thompson's house on the northern side of the lake – almost as eye-catching a landmark as the Arch of Victory with which she and the 'Lucas Girls' had been so closely connected after the First World War. Tilly Thompson had inspired the girls of the Lucas Factory (garment makers) to raise money for the memorial Arch, which was opened by the Prince of Wales in 1920, and also to plant the 4 000 trees in the Avenue of Honour. This was one of those inspiring stories of initiative, effort and local spirit which had given Ballarat much of its character. Mrs Thompson's house was a boomerang-shaped, functional house of the thirties, its long living-room almost entirely walled in glass, like the forward lounge on an ocean liner. Many conservative residents found this 'modern' style of architecture rather shocking, I suppose for its lack of privacy, and certainly something to be gasped at and to show to visitors – but how sensible Mrs Thompson was, for she captured not only every available sunbeam but also the lovely view across the lake. The same conservatism reared its head when the statue of Mother Earth appeared among the sedate Victorian sculptures of Sturt Street. But

162   Beside the Lake

Mother Earth settled in and before very long many a house on Wendouree Parade and elsewhere cautiously followed Mrs Thompson's example.

Pedalling or walking about the streets of Ballarat, I was intent on my own affairs and only subconsciously aware of the heritage of the past or of that feast of building styles spread around me. But I couldn't live against that backdrop and remain untouched by it, by the solidity, proportion and optimism of the Victorian buildings, by the weight of masonry, and the delicacy of ironwork in the hotel balconies, by the generous streets adorned with trees, statues and rotundas, by such eccentricities as the Alfred Hall and the Railway Station portico. The images printed on my visual memory then have never faded – images of bluestone baroque and colonial weatherboard, the Bastille face of the gaol, St Andrew's romanesque doorway and the classical columns of the Baptist Church in Dawson Street, not to mention the yawning gothic arches of the Roman Catholic Bishop's Palace, looming up from amid fields of grazing cows, and the charming Italianate Church of the Little Flower, smiling across the lake.

The Provincial Hotel – Byzantine detail

Schooling without Frills

'ONCE AGAIN ASSEMBLED HERE ...'

Children of the clergy carry a burden of expectation, for other people assume that they have been born with all the Christian virtues fully developed or have acquired them very soon after. For this reason it was something of a handicap being the daughter of a bishop, the expectations being even higher. In spite or perhaps because of this, I was decidedly naughty at school, as Father had been before me. He enjoyed recounting to us the tales of his misdeeds, such as raising an umbrella and standing under the shower in his best clothes, just as the family were about to go out visiting. I was greatly inspired by one of his school escapades; Willie (as he was then called) would ask permission to leave the classroom for a drink from the water bag (this in itself was intriguing to us, who were used to taps). He would quench his thirst, suspend the large canvas bag on the very tip of its hook, then place the school cockatoo on its stand directly below, so that when the next boy came for a drink and tipped the heavy bag forwards, glorious mayhem would ensue.

By the time we reached the middle school, Margaret and I were ringleaders of a small group who followed in this tradition of livening up the daily routine. I think I can safely say that our efforts were creative, not cruel. In later years, when we became prefects, our wise and venerable Latin teacher, Fanny Abrams, greeted the news with, 'Ah well, dears, there is much truth in the old adage "Set a thief to catch a thief!"'

Returning to a new school year in February after the freedom and bare feet of the summer holidays, we felt rather dazed and ill at ease in our tight shoes and new hair ribbons. There were new faces and new classrooms to get used to, a queue at the bookroom for new books and blotters and gold nibs, then ruling up the first virgin pages and learning all over again to manage a pen, amid the familiar smells of chalk and ink and the unyielding wooden desks which had been baking for eight long weeks in the hot, empty rooms. From outside drifted the new-mown scents of the hockey field, which our classrooms in the middle school overlooked.

'Lord, behold us with Thy blessing ...' we sang rather mournfully in first assembly, 'Once again assembled here' – but we were soon back into the swing of things. Classroom life went on, as ever, at two levels. New-chum teachers and girls had to be tried out in the usual ways – frogs in the teacher's drawer, lumps of crunchy coke under the hinged desk seats, rotten egg stinks in the wastepaper basket, shoes run up to the top of the school flagpole. The one thing which guaranteed newcomers their survival and acceptance was a sense of humour, for our intentions were rarely malicious. Notes were flicked and paper aeroplanes aimed across the room, while noughts-and-crosses contests raged under the desks. Of course it was fun to be back.

A full line-up of the school in front of Manifold House, 1941. Dorothy (7th from the right, back row) in her final year. Elizabeth (5th from the right, front row) just beginning. Margaret and I (extreme left, 2nd row) in Grade 6.

On the first day we elected a Form Captain (whose most important function was to hiss 'Shussssh! She's coming!' before lessons), as well as a Missionary Secretary and a Babies' Home Secretary. It was the Missionary Secretary's duty to collect one penny per week from each girl, for missions, and she did this by enquiring each Monday morning, 'Gotcha Mish?' The Babies' Home Secretary collected a similar amount in support of a Melbourne orphanage and also exhorted us to knit white garments or woollen squares for patchwork rugs. There were other occasional drives for charity, such as an Egg Day for the local hospital. Soon into first term we were issued with the Lenten boxes which signalled the season of Self Denial.

When the Easter holidays were over we settled down to face the winter. The cheerful open fires of Kinder and Remove had been left behind and in the upper school we were warmed by a central heating system fired by a furnace in the cellar. This was presided over by Mr Blight. Mr Blight's boiler was every bit as temperamental as the boiler at Bishopscourt, and he seemed to have no more control over it than we did over ours. Some frosty mornings we would dive upon the black classroom radiators to thaw out our frozen hands, only to find them stone cold. At other times they scalded our legs and burnished the seats of our tunics as we sat on them to warm our bottoms. The classrooms smelt richly of steaming serge and damp wool.

In the warmer seasons Mr Blight emerged from his cellar to sit on a large mowing machine behind a plodding horse and whirr up and down the hockey field, but in the winter the hockey field was often thickly rimed with frost, the blades of grass standing stiff and white. Gutters and puddles were motionless with ice as we puffed steamily to school on our bikes, or crunched along on foot. Feet were constantly wet; chilblains swelled and itched on fingers, toes and ankles, even ears. Before lessons we were sometimes given exercises to encourage the circulation, or sent forth in single file to run around the quad before settling down to the serious business of learning.

Except for official events such as Sports Day, the School Play and Speech Day, parents were rarely seen at school. Hardly any children arrived by car and there was no tuckshop duty to bring mothers through the gates (there being no tuckshop), so our home and school lives were clearly segregated, and at school we were free from parental surveillance. This deep divide was, I now believe, something of an advantage, to me at any rate. Having parents who were public figures was quite difficult to handle, and at school I was able to build an identity

166   Beside the Lake

and a life of my own. Some, but not all, of our school achievements and imperfections were revealed at home in the terse term reports which followed hard upon exams, for exams were held three times annually in the assembly hall; by the time we had arrived at Intermediate (Year 10) and our first public exams in the Town Hall, we were all seasoned campaigners. I don't recall anyone talking seriously about stress or nervous collapse, although I suppose most of us experienced butterflies in the tummy as we lined up outside the exam room.

EDUCATION THROUGH THICK AND THIN

Our school, like most others, had never been affluent or elaborate but the war ushered in a time of great frugality, even hardship, and many peace-time activities like school concerts, the Camera Club and excursions gradually faded out. As well as obvious intrusions like air-raid drill and slit trenches, there was a serious shortage of staff. Temporary teachers came and went; some of them were married to servicemen who had been posted to Ballarat for a short time, and when the men moved on their wives went with them. Some of the gaps were filled by the elderly, who came out of retirement to help; some were filled by the young and inexperienced, whom we treated with very little mercy. ('Please, Miss X, what does concubine mean?')

Towards the middle of the war, Father even contemplated sending me away to boarding school in Melbourne, as he thought my growing interest in science would be better served there. The possibility of such an exile loomed above me like a dark cloud, although I kept my nagging heartache well hidden. The threat was removed because of wartime disruption and uncertainty and my life became sunny once more.

By today's standards, our teachers worked under spartan conditions and were poorly paid. The staff room at Queen's was poky and there were few teaching aids; apart from simple demonstration materials such as a map, a bunch of leaves or a bone, our teachers confronted us with little more than a text book and a box of chalk. There were no films or videos, no 'resource' materials or cassettes or handouts, no photocopiers (so we transcribed everything ourselves with pens and pencils), very few excursions, and no library periods – for we had no proper library. About the only hardware in the school was a wind-up portable gramophone which provided scratchy music for folk dancing, and, in the boarders' sitting room, the big Tasma wireless (presented by the Old Girls in 1936) on which, when older, we went to listen to 'French for Schools'. There was no music department, no art room and nothing pertaining to craft, unless one counted a weekly sewing lesson in junior forms.

It must have been very difficult to keep organised sport going during the war years. Our school's stock of basketballs and baseball gear, kept in a big wooden box, was meagre at the best of times. As the war progressed, these things became very worn, and tennis balls were almost unobtainable – the few we had were used until they were bald. A corner of the hockey field was dug up for trenches, the tennis courts began to crack and sprout weeds, while the nets developed holes. Sports days went on as usual, for little equipment was needed for girls' athletics except legs, relay flags and a few balls. We did not hurl the discus or the javelin, or leap over hurdles and high jumps, and nobody wore spikes. On the other hand, we played baseball in a full-blooded manner and were not permitted to wear shin-pads for hockey. In our small school everyone was expected to play everything; sports periods were part of the time table and matches or practices took place after school. 'Gym' (really calisthenics) was a weekly period in the assembly hall, right to the Sixth Form (Years 11 – 12).

We were lucky that a few stalwarts remained at Queens through thick and thin and continued to educate us through those precarious years. There was Miss Woodbridge, for example, whose sister, an army nurse, was posted missing as the Japanese swept down on Singapore. Woodie carried on teaching us geography and arithmetic, until one day she was called from a lesson to the telephone to be told that her sister was a POW, but alive. The news raced through the school like a bushfire and everyone shared in Woodie's relief, but she soon had us back at work with our mapping pens and Indian ink. Geography was an important subject right to Year 10. The war, newspaper maps and newsreels filled in a mass of political and pictorial detail, but Woodie made sure we also knew about cut-off meanders, the winter solstice, flood plains, isthmuses and archipelagos. Her lessons on Holland, for example, paid no attention to Hitler's murderous bombing of Rotterdam, but enlightened us as to the unique features of the country – flatness, dykes, canals, windmills, tulips, clogs, and cheese. This was the essential Holland which would somehow survive the German occupation.

Nancy Wright, the sports mistress, was also at home teaching drawing or science or arithmetic, and her blackboard technique was enviable. Biology and botany lessons were full of exciting new information and terminology, with coloured chalk diagrams to illustrate osmosis, photosynthesis, the pulmonary system, intricate cross-sections of the kidney or the cerebellum. In fact, Nance equipped us with a working knowledge of most systems of the human body, excepting of course the reproductive. She also took drawing lessons, teaching us about perspective and how to draw ellipses and cones. These skills have proved useful in later life, but at the time I found more artistic satisfaction in drawing maps of the Zuider Zee or diagrams of the lung. In the higher forms, art could be taken as an extra after school. I think I would like to have 'done' art, but it didn't occur to me to ask about it for there were other things to do after school.

While history syllabuses seemed forever locked within the houses of Tudor, Stuart, Orange and Hanover, it has since proved valuable to know something of the aftermath of Henry VIII's marriages, of the rise of parliament, of Whigs and Tories, of the expansion of Empire. We followed all these through the dull textbooks, our pencils poised to underline and number the causes and effects of wars, treaties, rebellions, pacts and marriages. Sometimes a picturesque phrase or a romantic figure brought some animation to those desiccated pages, and we would seize gratefully on the Diet of Worms and the War of Jenkins' Ear, on Papal Bulls and the South Sea Bubble, on General Wolfe at Quebec (his men dipping their oars so silently), and of course on the Black Hole of Calcutta. There were also intriguing sayings like 'The Pyrenees have melted away!' (a somewhat free translation of Louis XIV's reported remark 'Il n'y a plus de Pyrénées', when his French grandson ascended to the Spanish throne). Sometimes the great narrative of human history took wings, but it rarely flew in the direction of Australia.

In about Year 9, however, part of our history syllabus was a brief survey of Australian Civics, so there was at least an attempt to show us how our political and civic systems worked. Unfortunately, the drab little text book was far from exciting and the way in which the subject was taught did nothing to help.

If Queen's had taken advantage of the Education Department's 'School Paper', which was a staple part of the state school curriculum, we might have discovered much that was interesting about our own Australian culture and background.

MUSIC

When Aunt Doris married and went to live in England, our family had inherited her walnut piano, a Ronisch. All three of us had piano lessons, and I plodded along on the violin, but none of us turned into performers. Our musical life and education were retarded, largely as a matter of history. On the one hand, the means of sound reproduction were crude and inconvenient until the 1950s, and on the other hand there came the war, which certainly curtailed our musical training.

When the war broke out, Miss Rehfisch ceased her weekly journeys to Ballarat and the magic vanished with her as there was no more ensemble playing. I think I was eventually almost the only string player left in the school. School music consisted of compulsory class singing, the school choir (voluntary) and piano lessons (extra), and the corridors and quad rang with scales, arpeggios and the works of the blessed Czerny, but that is largely where it all stopped, for orchestras and chamber groups are not built out of pianists.

Things would have been more encouraging had we owned the sort of hi-fi equipment which is commonplace today, but all we knew were wind-up gramophones with vicious steel needles and the 78 rpm records which hissed and blared as they raced around and had to be changed every three or four minutes. The sole gramophone at school was the portable model used in gym and folk dancing classes, while at home we had a larger cabinet model, on legs, which Mother had bought second-hand in Newcastle for one pound, mainly because it was handsome. Its storage shelves contained about five well-worn discs, all gifts, and we were always running out of sharp needles. It was taken for granted that we couldn't afford to buy any more records.

The most convenient items for recording were short ones which could be fitted on one or two sides of a 78 disc. Songs and ballads were therefore served up repeatedly on the radio. How often did we hear 'The Floral Dance' (Peter Dawson), 'The Bluebird of Happiness' (Jan Peerce), 'Open Road' (John Charles Thomas), 'Mother Macree' (John McCormack) and 'The Holy City' (Richard Crooks) for example? Or short instrumental favourites like the 'Minuet in G', 'Marche Militaire', 'Country Gardens', or anything by Fritz Kreisler. Handel's 'Celebrated Largo' was supreme in those music albums which lay on pianos bearing titles like 'Gems of Melody', or 'Well-loved Airs from Opera'. There was one on our piano called 'Great National Anthems of the World', which I enjoyed belting out in those days of patriotic fervour. Unfortunately one of the best tunes was Haydn's 'Austria', which the Germans had purloined for their anthem. However, it was also one of the great hymn tunes, so I played it in that guise, along with other hymns.

Country children of my generation were likely to be awakened to the world of serious music at the cinema. *Fantasia* was the prime example of this for me, but *The Great Waltz, Song of Russia, A Song to Remember* and *The Seventh Veil* opened other doors. Whatever they were like as films, they at least brought to us the music of Strauss, Tchaikovsky, Chopin and Grieg.

Before that we had heard very little of the world's great music properly performed, yet we were luckier than earlier generations who had no gramophone or wireless, and a great deal more fortunate than Franz Schubert, for example, who never heard some of his symphonic music performed at all.

BATTLE SONGS

The war may have retarded musical opportunities, but there was one area in which music flourished. As has often been the case in times of conflict, the combatants burst into song. The authorities were well aware of how vital it was to keep up morale, both military and civilian, and the world might not have endured those years so well without the songs which inspired communal effort or patriotic fervour, and those which made us look on the bright side and keep our peckers up. We were convinced that 'There'll always be an England' with 'bluebirds over the white cliffs of Dover'. There were revivals of First World War favourites and of older patriotic rallying cries like 'Rule Britannia'. We even borrowed from the enemy and sang 'Lili Marlene' in English. When America entered the lists, she brought with her a sense of irreverence to counter-balance the sob in Vera Lynn's throat, and those gutsy marching tunes like 'Anchors Aweigh' and 'The Marines' Hymn'

> From the halls of Montezuma
> To the shores of Tripoli,
> We will fight our country's battles
> On the land and on the sea ...

were now more commonly heard than 'From Greenland's icy mountains'.

Some of these songs were designed to sustain the decent feelings in a time of brutality and violence; they were sentimental, nostalgic for the domestic hearth, for the idealised natural beauty of bluebirds and white Christmasses. Others were more comical; Margaret and I were paralysed by the 'wit' of 'The Quartermaster's Store' where 'There were eggs, eggs, nearly growing legs', and tickled by the lighthearted, if pathetic reminders of food shortages – 'Say little hen, when when when/ will you lay me an egg for my tea?'

Radio and films spread these songs round the world. Concert parties for the troops, Sunday community singing in cinemas and 'Music while you work' programs for factories all helped to keep up morale and stir up patriotic zeal and effort. Vera Lynn, Gracie Fields, Bing Crosby, the Andrew Sisters sang their songs and everyone in the free world joined in, regardless of age ... Wish me luck ... When the lights go on again ... Bless 'em all ... Roll out the barrel ... Knees up Mother Brown ... Kiss me goodnight, Sergeant Major – they were out-going, purposeful, gregarious, tuneful, often witty songs.

In the cinemas, children were well catered for. Very few films were really unsuitable for general exhibition and there were many made especially for the young – *The Wizard of Oz*, the Disney classics, tear-jerkers starring Shirley Temple, Deanna Durbin or Freddie Bartholomew, the comedy of Mickey Rooney, Laurel & Hardy or Chaplin, and animal sagas like *My Friend Flicka* and *Lassie Come Home*. There were musicals galore and war epics which stirred only the finer feelings. No wonder our mothers were nervous of *Gone With The Wind*!

ENGLISH AND OTHER LANGUAGES

At the end of 1941, Miss Krome stunned the school community by announcing her appointment to The Hermitage in Geelong. She was replaced as headmistress by Miss Emily King, whose subjects were Latin and Mathematics. Miss King was one of those gifted teachers who frequently wandered down interesting sidetracks, so that the grind of a Latin declension suddenly blossomed into an exploration of the history of words. 'Now girls, *annus* is the Latin word for ... what? Come on ... think! Yes, it means year. So, let's make a list of English words which might come from that root? Hands up! ... right, annual, anniversary, annuity ...' Chanting declensions was similar to chanting tables. The most rollicking was the declension of *bellum*, war ... *bellum bellum bellum/ belli bello bello* and so forth, with the subsequent tracking down of English offspring like belligerent and bellicose.

Latin roots were fun, but more puzzling was the discovery that words in other languages had gender. For no apparent reason they were masculine, feminine or neuter, with different forms and endings to confuse the poor beginner. We began French in the middle school, as well as Latin, so the confusion was compounded. Nevertheless, studying three languages at once and becoming aware of their different systems was a useful grounding.

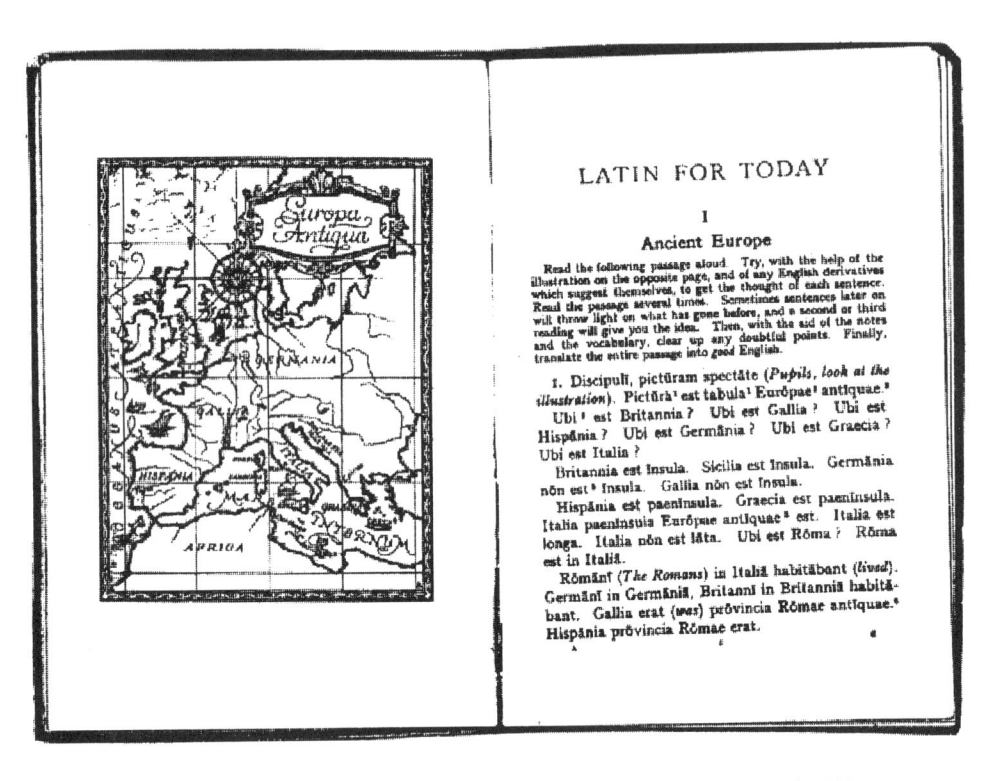

The celebrated first lesson in Latin, from *Latin for Today (First Course)* 1932

The subject known as English spread tentacles in all directions and took up a large number of lessons. Grammar had developed from the parsing in Remove to ever more complicated sentence analysis, for which we ruled our pages into columns labelled Subject, Verb, Object, Complement, Adverbial Adjunct (clauses of time, place, etc). 'Creative Writing' was not really an option – we wrote Compositions on set topics with careful attention to spelling, punctuation and syntax. There were lessons on vocabulary which harped on some of the common confusions, such as the difference between 'practice' and 'practise', or 'precipitous' and 'precipitant', or the real meaning of 'disinterested' (neutral, detached).

Long novels by such luminaries as Robert Louis Stevenson and Dickens were read aloud in class, generally by the best readers. This was sensible, if not politically correct, for these were literature lessons and not hack reading practice. One act plays and some Shakespeare were read aloud from our desks or occasionally acted out on the dais in front.

As You Like It was our first taste of the Bard, and by the time I left school I had studied seven of his plays, including four of the tragedies.

We would never have thought of morning assembly as an extension of our English studies, but it was there that we daily received a beneficial dose of 'Elizabethan' English from the King James' Bible and the Book of Common Prayer – improving not only for the character but also, I now realise, for the prose style.

English poetry fared well right through school, culminating in Chaucer, Milton, Pope and the Romantics. Earlier, we read poems aloud in unison, copied them down and learnt them by heart. It was no bad thing to absorb such lines into oneself with their throb of rhyme and metre, and to have the pleasure of recall in later life; to be able, like Horace Rumpole, to burst into poetic utterance at the apposite moment:

"Is there anybody there?' said the traveller,
Knocking on the moonlit door.
(W. de la Mare)

or

Out flew the web and floated wide;
The mirror crack'd from side to side;
'The curse is come upon me,' cried
The Lady of Shalott.
(Tennyson)

Poetry lessons sometimes blossomed into artistic endeavour as we were set to copy out poems and illustrate them. 'I remember, I remember the house where I was born ... ' (Thomas Hood) was ever a popular subject for this exercise, and the pictures were generally variations on a thatched, rose-entwined cottage in the Cotswold style – which only went to show how little we actually remembered about the houses where we were born! My poetry pictures were noted for hollyhocks, thatch, robins and squirrels, fir trees and daffodils, which were the stock-in-trade of northern hemisphere poets, reinforced by the Ballarat landscape. Wigwams, canoes and moonlight were features of Hiawatha pictures and fir trees were thick on the ground, inspired by the pine plantations surrounding our local water reservoirs at Moorabool and the Gong Gong.

LISTENERS

We still belonged to the age of Listeners; the Viewing age did not dawn until 1956, just in time for the Olympic Games in Melbourne. Before that, the wireless, as well as providing regular reports on the fate of civilisation, was also our chief source of entertainment, and, on the whole, the air waves were dominated by the speaking voice in news bulletins and commentaries, talks, plays, serials, panel games, quizzes and comedy shows. We concentrated on voices, sounds and the meaning of words, and the absence of visual material left room for the imagination. Language, as read and heard, was still by far the most important form of communication. The non-existence of television (and the Web) extended my childhood into the teens, because innocence was the more easily preserved without the intrusive screen. Fairly strict censorship of films and books reinforced this. With prolonged innocence went a prolonged sense of wonder and curiosity.

Radio plays were a highlight of the week. We gathered round the fire to listen to the ABC's Theatre of the Air, or the Lux Radio Theatre (during which we learned that nine out of every ten Hollywood film stars used Lux soap). Even more riveting were the serials which claimed us nightly, or at lunchtime in the case of 'The Lawsons', which later evolved into 'Blue Hills'. In the evenings there was a cluster of serials on the commercial radio; 'The Search for the Golden Boomerang', 'Dad & Dave', 'Mittens' ('A thrilling saga of the turf') and 'First Light Fraser' ('A drama of war-torn Europe') were favoured by us children, but the whole family gathered round for 'Martins' Corner'. Father revelled in the verbal warfare between Granny Martin and Mrs Ludlow.

For many children the top program must have been the ABC Children's Session. This ran for decades after I had grown up, but I knew it best in its earliest years when Elizabeth, Mac and Joe were in their prime. These three had a wonderful rapport and they were a talented comedy team when they chose; they were relaxed and liable to break into mirth, yet their programs were always solidly educational at base and maintained high standards of taste. Children were invited to send in contributions or to take part in competitions, so we posted off stories and poems and paintings, or parcels full of beetles and other natural phenomena to be identified by Jock the Naturalist. How exciting it was to win a Blue Certificate or to hear one's name and prose actually read out on the national network. On one matchless occasion, both Margaret and I had art contributions commended and described on the same program; it was not beyond the kindly Joe to have noticed that we lived in the same street and to have made a clever deduction.

The famous Argonauts' Club grew out of the Children's Session, Mac becoming 'Jason', captain of the good ship Argo, with Elizabeth as his No. 1 and Joe as 1A. From all over Australia listening children joined the fleet, fifty rowers to a ship, and were given crew names such as Agamemnon 23 or Xerxes 39. Mac's pronunciation of the classical Greek names was so meticulous that few Australian children, before or since, could have equalled us at rolling out the polysyllables of Aeschylus, Clytemnestra and Thucydides. Young rowers set out to win, through contributions, such honours as the Dragon's Tooth, the Golden Fleece and the Golden Fleece-and-Bar (on the well-recognised analogy of the DSO and the DFC). My sister Elizabeth rowed at No.12 in the good ship Polycrates, but I didn't join the Argonauts as I think I felt too old by the time they began, even though aged rowers of seventeen were fairly common. I also felt that the highly structured proceedings of the club smacked a little of school. Nevertheless I listened to most sessions and heard the songs of Orpheus (Harold Williams, out of disguise) and the combined wisdom of other heroes who spoke to us of poetry and myths.

I first learnt about cricket by listening to radio commentaries on one of Father's loud speakers when I was sick in bed, and by following play on a diagram in the newspaper. During the first England – Australia series after the war, in 1946, a whole new generation discovered the game for the first time, encouraged by nostalgic parents thinking back to the thirties. Father still bristled when the word 'bodyline' was mentioned. I became so engrossed by the exploits of Bradman, Hammond and their teams and by the spellbinding commentaries and back-chat of Arthur Gilligan, Victor Richardson and Alan McGilvray, that I kept a scrapbook of newspaper cuttings about this tour. New, peacetime heroes had begun to emerge – Lindwall and Miller, Compton and Bedser.

READING MATTER

Some of the stars of films and radio also featured in *Radio Fun* and *Film Fun*, two comics which managed to appear regularly in our newagencies despite the uncertain voyage from Britain. I thought them worth the outlay of threepence and a bike ride in order to follow the antics of George Formby, Laurel and Hardy, Abbott and Costello and the rest. Added to these were the comic strip adventures of *Ginger Meggs, Mandrake the Magician*, and the rhyming verse saga of *Curly Wee and*

Gussie Goose which appeared in the press. But another large slice of reading time was devoted to 'annuals'. These were huge, fat books which sensible aunts sometimes gave us for Christmas, with names like *Girls' Own Annual, Chatterbox, Tiger Tim's Annual*. They were a miscellany of stories, puzzles, serials, jokes, comic-strips, games, things to make-and-do, and pictures. They kept me going for months.

Neither of my parents was a recreational reader. Father read a great deal and his study walls were completely lined with books, but they all had to do with theology, international affairs, church history and so on. I never saw him reading a novel. But when he was in London in 1948, he discovered a new reprint of *The Fortunes of Richard Mahony* by Henry Handel Richardson. As the first part of this trilogy was set in the Ballarat gold-fields, he was curious to read it – and he was fortunate to have a long sea voyage on which to do so. He came home electrified, with two copies of this book, one of them for me.

Reading filled in all the gaps, especially in bed at night. To be able to read books gave one independence, the capacity to roam through time and space, to explore, to discover, to choose a mood.

When Dorothy left home in 1942 I inherited some of her books, including a row of Mary Grant Bruce, and I had acquired a few books of my own as presents and school prizes. One of the earliest prizes was *Black Beauty* in a lovely soft leather binding and with pictures, while there was also a *Book of Myths* in which I met some of those gruesome characters like Medusa, Grendel (and mother) and the three Fates passing their solitary eyeball from hand to hand. These were counterbalanced by the glowing ranks of heroes – Perseus, Jason, Beowulf and company, swords in hand, carving their way through the powers of darkness.

The fairy tales of Andersen and the Grimms were also decorated with sinister and frightening pictures, followed by Walt Disney in some of his film creations, especially the evil Black Queen and the grotesque purple witch in Snow White – far more alarming than Rhett Butler, did Mother but know it!

The most well-thumbed of my books was probably F.H. Burnett's *The Secret Garden*, another top gift from Auntie Flo (she of the croquet set and Chook Chook). Much of the book's appeal can be explained by its title and the similarity of this garden to our 'own' wilderness next door. In addition, many of the characters in the story were interesting, being sickly and neurotic, and I was absorbed to read how Nature had her way in restoring them to health.

Another gift was *The Desert Pool*, a Robinson Crusoe tale of the African veldt but told in a semi-documentary style with photographs. As I roamed the garden with my toy air rifle I identified totally with the lost boy in his cave and I found the strangely named animals enthralling – the gnu, the kudu and the terrifying black mamba.

Dr Pern, who took us sailing on the lake, was a Rider Haggard enthusiast. He summoned me to his house and handed out the precious volumes one at a time, starting with *King Solomon's Mines*. Another adventure which I read many times over, skipping the moralising bits, was *The Coral Island*. I identified with Ralph or Jack, while Elizabeth sometimes played Peterkin in garden re-enactments. R.M. Ballantyne's book would seem dated and unconvincing to today's children and has been replaced in their canon by Golding's *Lord of the Flies*, but between my childhood and theirs came The Bomb.

At school, there was a small room called The Library which was used by the few Year 12 girls for classes and study. This room housed a very few reference books and a collection of novels called the Boarders' Library, to which day girls had no claim. In a group of shops not far down Sturt Street, however, there was a small lending library which was a godsend to Margaret and me when we ran out of reading matter. Its shelves were stocked with popular novels, romances and travel books, and there was a junior section lined with Biggles, the William books, Ethel and Lilian Turner, Georgette Heyer and Baroness Orczy. On the adult shelves I made the discovery of whodunits, of Ellery Queen in particular. It cost a penny or twopence to borrow a book.

A 'good read' was like a drug. The more you read, the sooner the book was finished. I tried hard to put it away, to save further chapters until later, but the compulsion to devour just one more was often irresistible. I lay on the floor on hot Christmas afternoons, consuming the new Mary Grant Bruce, oblivious to all around me. By teatime it was finished and I felt bereaved – but at least there was a long line of MGB on my own shelf and I could return to Billabong as often as I wished. Re-reading a book many times was part of the magic – it became part of one's own life.

Being mischievous children, Margaret and I enjoyed books about other mischievous children, such as Richmal Crompton's William or Ethel Turner's Woolcotts. The Billabong set were not naughty – they really behaved splendidly and it is rather difficult to envisage them now as 'teenagers' – but there was enough light-hearted banter and pillow fighting and falling into the lagoon to save Norah and Jim and Wally from priggishness. I even envied them their ability to handle themselves with such assurance and modesty in adult company and always to do the right thing. How wonderful, I felt, to be like Norah of Billabong.

When I visited or stayed on a grand country property, I quickly realised that I was no Norah. It seemed to be assumed that I knew how to harness a horse and certainly how to ride it, that I would enjoy swimming in thick, muddy dam water, that milking a cow was no problem, and that I wouldn't turn a hair at seeing a calf slaughtered and strung up. (The latter process, which involved large-scale disembowelment, was in a different league from beheading and cleaning chooks!) My ego suffered many dints as I realised that I was not a real country girl at all.

'CREATIVE' WRITING

When we were eleven or twelve, Margaret and I thought of writing a book on the topic of our own escapades, which to us (alone) were screamingly funny. Fortunately the project went no further than a list of possible episodes, for we were far too busy being creative in the active sense to have time to write about it. For example, we invented a man-trap called a 'Shin-cutter & Stunner' in an attempt to capture a pumpkin thief who had raided Florrie's garden near the Grove Street fence and removed several prized Queensland Blues. Margaret and I inspected the scene of the crime, identified the most likely point of access and then set up our booby trap. At carefully measured intervals we placed in turn a trip wire, a sharp blade of metal (the shin-cutter) and a large rock at head level (the stunner). Nobody was caught, fortunately, for there could have been a malicious wounding charge.

Such creativity flowed into writing only when Margaret and I were separated by illness or absence on holiday. Then we wrote each other letters of enormous length and dramatic impact (some of which have survived) and in them we sometimes lapsed into Favour-ite idiom and flouted all the rules of grammar and spelling which bound us so rigidly at school: 'Me hab just got your letter thankumu yeyy much for the seaweed ...'. The letters free-wheeled from news of one's latest illness – 'My leg came up into a big blister and then busted in the night and a whole lot of awful pink muck came out (Ugh!) ... ' – to libellous remarks about one's family or acquaintances, to little jokes.

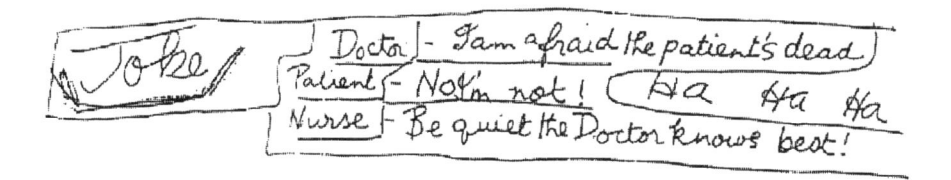

> Joke / Doctor - I am afraid the patient's dead. / Patient - No I'm not! Ha Ha Ha / Nurse - Be quiet the Doctor knows best!

or zany drawings:

Yore dorter *Yore Sun*

LM 1943

We played with language, revelling in hyperbole and trying out new words and polyglot phrases: 'Bong soya mon ancient dicotyledon' (bon soir old bean).

In a number of letters (especially those from or to the sick bed) we included one-act plays for the reader's entertainment. The characters were usually ourselves as heroines (MW and MJ), with well-known citizens, teachers, family members or the cats as villains or victims, and the plots were rather along the lines of the games of Consequences which we often played round the fire. This sort of thing

> Bing Crosby met/ (fold over)
> Queen Mary at/ (fold over)
> A Turkish bath/ (fold over)
> He said, 'How wonderful to see you here!'/ (fold over)
> She said, 'How dare you say such a thing!'/ (fold over)
> The consequence was they shouted one another a banana sundae.

(Unfold and read aloud to applause.)

In our plays, however, imaginary characters were sometimes included. In one play about sabotage on a plane (foiled by MW and MJ), the villains are Emil von Bonk and Adolf Hucklemayer, who speak in the 'guttural' manner which we picked up from comics and films:

AH: Are you going to blow upp der plane Emil?
EVB: Yes I am mit der aid off my leetle invention! Yes! No! ...
AH: What iss der bomb like?
EVB: Vell, you put der bomb unter someone's seat. It iss der time-bomb. It does not do anyting but make a beeg noise. Ha. Der person it iss unter vill also make der beeg noise and der pilott vill lose hiss head and come and see vot iss happening and der plane vill crash! Ha! Vee can jump vith our parachutes before it all happens through dis back door ... '

This sort of mad fantasy which we let loose in our very private letters was the perfect counterbalance to the solid grounding which we received at school. There it seemed that learning (like life) was basically a matter of rules and order. From tables and spelling we moved on to mathematical formulae and geometry, to Latin grammar and English syntax ('thou shalt not end thy sentence with a preposition or leave thy participles dangling'), to the metrical patterns of prosody and the harmonies of hymn tunes, and to the rules of sport which were accepted without question. Sometimes I sensed the beauty of a solved quadratic equation or of a geometric theorem, when everything balanced, came out right, although I wouldn't have thought of these solutions as 'beautiful', just satisfying. While such a system is frowned upon by more recent educationists, who favour creativity and self-motivation in learning, I have never regretted the firm foundation and the reassuring sense of structure and order which our no-frills education provided. It also gave us something solid to kick against, and there were many creative ways to do that.

REBELLION AND DISCIPLINE

Sewing, in my view, was the worst lesson of the week in Form IVA (Year 7), involving as it did the dismal process of hem-stitching and herring-bone on grubby little squares of cloth. Some girls sped through furlongs of exquisite stitchery with scarcely a crease in the cloth, but Margaret and I were not among them; our hearts were not in it. She and I sat next to the window, at the back, a much prized position. As each girl entered the classroom after lunch, the sewing teacher marked her present on the roll. Margaret and I discovered that by slithering out the window, creeping back into the building and entering the class again, we could cause a minor furrow to ruffle the lady's brow as she tried to mark us present – who were, it seemed, already present. To enter unchallenged a third time, if we could manage it, was some sort of compensation for the herring-bone.

The six main classrooms opened off a long corridor, which, after school one day, four of us decided to 'wash' by dint of turning on the fire hose and skating up and down the wet linoleum on cakes of soap from the cloakroom. Things had become very spirited by the time we were discovered by a senior member of staff, a humourless lady who quite failed to notice that the corridor was, in the end, much cleaner. Crimes of that magnitude led straight to the Headmistress's study, while more routine offences met with routine punishments – Friday detentions and lines.

One of our routes home took us past the state school in Pleasant Street. Its location was pleasant indeed, on the shore of the lake, but I viewed the school with deep suspicion as the haunt of 'rough' children, middle class prig that I was. For one thing, there were boys there as well as girls, and, being unused to boys, I was under the impression that their only aim in life was to form gangs and throw stones. We were also led to believe that punishment in state schools was harshly delivered by the rod or the strap. There was no corporal punishment at Queen's – as far as I was concerned, our school was a benign and happy place.

The three headmistresses of my school career were noted for having a twinkle in the eye. As I was being chastised, I sensed that they understood the high spirits of youth, maybe even secretly enjoyed some of our more creative misdemeanours. One such prank would have been an acid test, had not Dorothy foiled our plot. Miss Krome was to stay overnight at Bishopscourt, so Margaret and I thought it would be daring to short-sheet her bed and to load it with a bristly hairbrush. We were so excited about this, that we spilled the beans to Dorothy, who turned scarlet with horror and stood over us while we straightened out the situation. Dorothy was then a prefect.

I was sometimes spanked at home, although never at school. The usual punishment at home was to be sent to one's room, there to wait until Mother came up to deliver one of her 'little talks'. She wasn't a very skilful spanker, as it wasn't in her nature to inflict pain. In any case, the little talks were far more harrowing, especially after a long, lonely wait. Mother and most of our more effective teachers employed the 'more in sorrow than in anger' approach, which had the desired effect of making me feel either guilty or a failure, usually both. One had let down the side, whether it be the family, the school, the nation, the Allied cause, Christendom, or whatever, and the disappointment was intense. At home, Father rarely delivered little talks; his authority was reserved for really bad behaviour, such as being rude to Mother, and then his technique was short and to the point, with a slightly raised voice. Apologies were insisted on and were very hard to deliver.

Discipline and manners were intertwined. Good manners meant thinking of others and bad behaviour usually meant the opposite, so little talks often invited us to imagine how the other party might feel – 'How would you like it if someone ran your shoes up the flagpole?' or 'Please eat that all up, whether you like it or not – think of those hungry refugees in Europe!' Good manners became second nature at school; we very early learned to open doors and stand back for others, to wait our turn, to lend a helping hand without being asked, to give up our seats in trams, not to interrupt.

These small courtesies certainly oil the wheels of everyday life, and on the whole most of the rules we tried to obey made sense. They could be divided into those which had the welfare of others in mind, and those framed for our own safety. There were hosts of little practical tips aimed at safety, such as 'When carrying a knife or scissors, point them towards the ground and don't run.' 'In the bush, look before jumping over fallen logs in case there is a snake asleep on the other side.' Occasionally one tested out the safety limits, such as Elizabeth's forays onto the roof when Mother wasn't looking, but these limits made perfect sense.

WHATEVER WOULD THE NEIGHBOURS THINK?

When it came to the rules of etiquette, however, things were not so clear. Why did Mother flush with shame when I decided to cut my toenails in the presence of an elderly cousin? Certainly it was in the drawing-room, and the cousin was from Adelaide (which seemed to matter), but if she hadn't been there, Mother probably wouldn't have minded. 'We don't do that sort of thing in the drawing-room,' seemed to be the rule, but what was the reason? Seeing me cut my toenails didn't actually hurt Cousin B. She must have had toenails of her own to be trimmed, surely?

It gradually dawned on me that there were two levels of behaviour – carrying on naturally when nobody was looking, and moving up to a higher plane in public. This was called 'keeping up appearances' and I suppose it was meant to imply that one always behaved in a dignified and modest manner, at home as well as abroad. Class came into it, of course, because to be natural really meant to be vulgar or common, and that would never do. So, while it was wrong to trim one's toes in public, it was right to 'over-daint' with the teacups. It was all rather tiresome.

Convent trained girls were the exemplars of good deportment; the nuns saw to it that their every action was conducted with grace, dignity, modesty and humility. One could not imagine convent girls slouching, gobbling, using vulgar terms or removing their gloves in the street. Sometimes at school I was told to stand up straight or to pull my shoulders back, for I suppose I was sensitive about being taller than average, but we weren't made to walk round the room with books balanced on our heads, for deportment's sake, or trained to sit ramrod straight with feet together and hands demurely in laps. The main emphasis at my school was on manners, although good deportment was a mysterious state of being to which senior girls were meant to aspire and for which there was a prize.

Formality was common in our social circle, but Father's position made formal behaviour even more important in our case. Our parents were very aware of the dignity of their office; they were unlikely to kiss or embrace each other or us in public, for example, and even at home we were never (and still aren't) a demonstrative family in a physical sense. Similarly at school a formal barrier discouraged any familiarity between teachers and girls. It was unheard of to be on first name terms with a teacher, and in the wider world my parents were on first name terms with hardly anyone outside the family. Margaret's mother and mine remained Mrs Wilson and Mrs Johnson to each other, always.

Father was a man of simple tastes and quite used to stoking the boiler or eating in the kitchen. Nevertheless, having the bishop to stay for the first time must have been an ordeal for some people. One couple in the country carefully taught their small boy the correct way to greet the august visitor, but their lessons in manners were absorbed more fully than they guessed. 'How do you do my Lord?' said the child. 'Don't put your knife in your mouth.'

Propriety ruled that one didn't mention pregnancy or sex in front of the children. Discussions of that sort presumably took place, if at all, after the frequently given order, 'Now children, run outside and play. Mummy wants to talk to Auntie C ... or Mrs W.' Usually we were only too glad to escape, but certain areas of life remained closed to us and there was no television to provide the full, steamy story. Nor did I ever find out much behind the shelter shed, for other girls seemed to know as little as I. Questions could be asked of one's elders: 'Why can't girls ask boys to dance?' 'Because it's not done.' 'Yes, but why?' 'It would be very forward of them.' 'Why would it? Why isn't it forward for boys?' Sooner or later there would be a stonewall, no sensible answer, just 'That's the way things are, how things are done.'

The old principle that children should be seen and not heard still carried weight, so in the end one gave up asking and accepted the status quo. I didn't ever ask, 'Why don't we know any Roman Catholics?' Actually, we did. Pat, who sat in front of me at school, was one of them, and she seemed to be just the same as us. We were friends. Nevertheless the community seemed to be made up of little groups who didn't mix. The Anglicans didn't mix with the Catholics; the professions didn't mix with the trades; the kids at private schools scorned the state schools and the state schools kids jeered back; the Western District landowners kept to themselves.

We were often reprimanded, 'It's rude to stare,' and I knew myself that I disliked being stared at. But the poem by W.H. Davies called 'Leisure', an evergreen in school anthologies and pastel-leaved autograph albums, threw another light on the matter.

> What is this life if, full of care,
> We have no time to stand and stare?
> No time to stand beneath the boughs
> And stare as long as sheep or cows? ...

As I stared through the classroom window at the cow on the hockey field, who chewed her cud and stared back, I realised that rudeness applied only to staring at people, particularly those who were in some way different. Standing and staring in other respects was a sensible way of making discoveries and certainly preferable to learning French verbs.

L'ECOLE DE VIE

I had always been a starer, of course, as most children are. In Newcastle I stared at the waves and the blowhole, at Doris cleaning the grates and the laundress turning the mangle. Here in Ballarat, watching Florrie in the kitchen or garden was an education in itself, and we'd already seen the chapel being built. Then there were the tradesmen.

Despite Father's efforts, our leaky, worn down shoes needed regular visits to Mr Roberts, the cobbler near the corner of Pleasant Street. I would try to creep into his shop unobserved to stare at the whirring brushes, the stitching and the slicing and deft hammering, before he stopped to serve me.

Next door was 'Davis the Butcher'. When I inherited Dorothy's bike, my new duty was to buy the meat several times a week before school, to save Florrie on her way to work. At 7.45 am Mr Davis and his sons looked as if they had been at work for hours, as they doubtless had; the fresh sausages were being strung up in gleaming pink bunches, and everyone was busy sawing and chopping and making up orders from the long list in the book. The telephone on the wall rang frequently and more orders were written down by smeary red hands. The butchers handled their lethal weapons with skill and artistry, despite one or two missing fingers which suggested youthful exuberance! The butchering was done in full view of the customers (the blood, beheading and disembowelling being safely out of the way) and it was one of my favourite spectator sports – to watch the cleaving of a carcass down the backbone; the unearthing of gleaming kidneys in the protective suet fat; the whacking of an oxtail on to a hook to have its hide and tassel peeled off like a stocking; the boning and skewering of a rolled sirloin and sewing it up with a huge packing needle; the bouncy arrival on the block of a slithery, rubbery sheet of tripe to be chopped into squares. Butcher's shop anatomy.

Gentlemen in barbers' shops were well in view through the window, lathered in soap and at the mercy of the twirling cut-throat razor, whereas ladies' hairdressers veiled everything in mystery. I was taken to Mr Edwards's Salon for a haircut and discreetly curtained off in a private cubicle. Today, in a reversal of custom, ladies in rollers and towels and dryers are all in full view through plate glass windows, whereas the butchers have retreated behind screens and panels.

Our groceries were usually delivered right to the kitchen table, twice a week, but sometimes we visited Herbert's Grocery on the corner of Drummond Street. The shop was deep and dark, with a massive wooden counter, gleaming brass weights on the scales and a marble slab for the cheese cutting. The shelves were stacked with big, square biscuit tins, several of which were brought down and delved into if you asked for a pound of 'mixed'. (Chocolate Royals were only bought for parties or presents.) Bottles glinted on the far wall, their labels proclaiming Ruby Port, Invalid Port or Sweet Sherry, for Mr Herbert was a wine and spirit merchant, too. On the sawdusted floor were sacks and bins of sugar, flour and grains, and drums of honey, and somewhere at the back kerosene tins and 'metho' bottles were refilled. Mother sat on a high bentwood chair by the counter while her order was assembled, and this often took a while as most items had to be measured out, weighed, wrapped and even tied with string. There was no plastic or sticky tape, but grocers knew cunning ways of folding over the paper bags of sugar and sago to avoid spillage. Mr Herbert wore a white calico apron, and two or three cats snoozed watchfully among the sacks.

Of the tradesmen who called, the baker, the milkman and the 'garbo' had horses and carts. The baker's decorative cart had large wooden-spoked wheels which spun at a spanking pace, the milkman's cart ran on rubber tyres, while the heavy rubbish cart lumbered slowly behind a plodding draught horse which often had its face in a nosebag. Brewery wagons were still a common sight, and horse-troughs filled with chaffy water could be found in most streets.

The most irresistible of all our tradesmen was undoubtedly Ah Hung, the Chinese greengrocer. He turned up unannounced one Saturday afternoon, and continued to visit us for years. He was very short and round, with horny fingernails ingrained with dirt. He wore an aged black coat and a stained leather helmet, from which beamed forth his stubbly face with its creased-up eyes and semi-toothless grin. He would waddle towards the back door calling, 'Johnny, Johnny, Johnny!' to summon us, but as his wares were entirely of the vegetable order, which thanks to Florrie we didn't need, it was difficult to know what to buy from him. I don't think he would have minded if we'd bought nothing, so much did he enjoy our incoherent conversations. He and Father hit it off at once and seemed to be able to communicate by signs and shrieks of hilarity.

Ah Hung lived out beyond Black Hill at Nerrina and he travelled in a wooden cart drawn by an ancient horse which appeared to walk in its sleep. We often wondered how long it took them to complete the round trip. There came a time when Ah Hung failed to appear and news reached us that he was in hospital after an accident. Mother was hospital-visiting at the time and decided to call at his bedside. She was directed to a far corner of a ward and was rather shocked at the change in him. Without his helmet, and having been shaved and spruced up, he was barely recognisable. What was worse, in spite of being pleased to see her he seemed to have lost all his old joie-de-vivre; the conversation was very sticky, and he kept grimacing and rubbing his stomach. On her way out, Mother enquired about Ah Hung's progress. The ward sister looked astonished. 'Ah Hung? That isn't Ah Hung – he went home yesterday. That's Ah Gon!' Sure enough, in a short time Ah Hung was back on the beat, with a bandaged head but otherwise unchanged. He was eager to tell us about his terrible accident: 'Horse went gallop, gallop, GALLOP!' he demonstrated, waving his arms wildly. 'Me fall back over and hit my HAT!' We stared in wonder at the sleeping horse; whatever could have aroused it to a gallop?

He was very old and stiff with rheumatism, so Dorothy knitted him a pair of stout grey gloves to wear in the cart. This gift rendered him speechless, for once, but he headed out to his vegetables and returned with the mightiest cauliflower to press into her arms. He never wore the gloves in the cart, but he was seen on Sundays in Nerrina, even in a heatwave, walking along the road with his gloved hands held out beside him for all to admire. Those gloves might have been the only present he had received in half a lifetime.

Most of the tradesmen who called were interesting. Take the chimney sweep – in a two-storied house with about nine involved chimney stacks, his operations were prolonged and absorbing, but never as filthy as I hoped. As an early reader of *The Water Babies* I half expected to be sent up the chimney and to emerge blackened and unrecognisable, so that Mother would give me away to the sweep, but in fact he took very little notice of me as he puffed and strained up the dark tunnels with his immensely long, extensible brushes and scrapers. Big lumps of soot plopped spookily down on the newspaper spread round the hearth, but when the sweep had bundled it all up and tipped the contents onto the garden, there was scarcely any sign that he had been at all, except that the fires roared more loudly and there were black handprints on the Kalsomine.

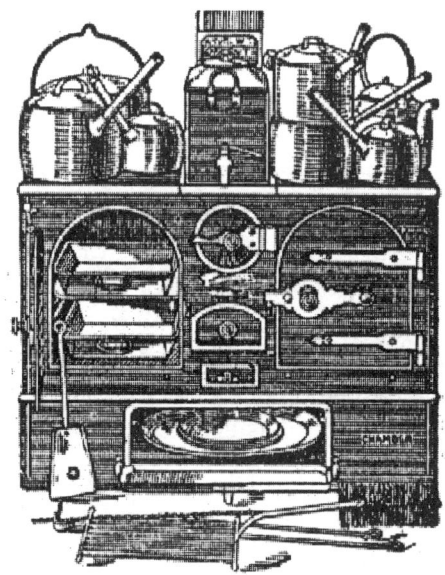

A cook's arsenal. From a 1941 advertisement for stoves.

In Sickness and in Health, with Visitors

VISITORS

While a stream of tradesmen came to the back door, an equally steady stream of visitors arrived at the front. They came for afternoon tea or a meal, for meetings, to be married in the chapel, or to stay for several days, and their presence had a crucial effect on the household routine. The humble Pughole was abandoned for the drawing- and dining-rooms, the boiler was primed in place of the chip bath heater, fires roared in the various chimneys, clothes horses were whisked out of the study, and we children had to mind our manners. Appearances were to be kept up.

Those visitors could be divided into the categories of Relations, Retreaters and Others. 'Others' comprised the largest and most varied group, ranging from archbishops and monks to our American soldiers, from children to the State Governor. The only time a bottle of whisky ever appeared in the dining-room cupboard was in preparation for the Governor's visit. At other times there was a decanter of sherry which was occasionally brought forth for guests, and a bottle of Invalid Port, reserved for invalids (of riper years) and wine trifles. Father never touched 'drink', although Mother enjoyed a rare glass of sherry. The children who came to stay were usually from clergy families in which the mother was ill, tired out or having another baby.

Many guests stayed overnight. Keeping them warm in winter was one of the main problems, although never so challenging as at Old Bishopscourt, and at times fires were lit in the guests' bedrooms upstairs. Even so, one American cleric, fresh from his native central-heating, could barely survive the chill of the passages and was not slow in saying so, but on the whole such thin-blooded and tetchy visitors were rare. The Archbishop of Melbourne's wife, Mrs Head, who stayed with us during a freezing Easter, was delighted to spend all her waking hours in the kitchen and to have Easter dinner on the big deal table by the range. In Mother's experience, the more 'exalted' people were, the more easily they fitted in. During the Archbishop of Canterbury's visit in 1950, the Archbishop's chaplain slept with the primatial cross of Canterbury under his bed. This treasure had never been out of England before and was insured for thousands of pounds, yet the visitors made no fuss about it and took full responsibilty for its safety, under the bed.

There was for a while a memento of Archbishop Fisher's stay at Bishopscourt, for, on his way to the chapel he had slipped on the wet cement and left a long skidmark. Elizabeth was quick to immortalise this skid with bright red oil paint. 'Would that she had chosen heavenly blue,' lamented the Archbishop. Three years later it was he who placed the crown on Queen Elizabeth II's head.

The Archbishop of Canterbury, Dr Fisher, with Mother, Father and Mrs Fisher in the backyard, 1950, setting off to an official function (hence the gaiters). Although it was late October, Mother's rugs and Mrs Fisher's fur coat suggest a chilly destination.

Monks made very interesting subjects for discreet staring. I examined their habits (garments) and decided that these solved a good many of the problems of dress, especially in a cold climate, and having peered furtively at their feet I was relieved to find that they didn't have to wear sandals in winter. Father Charles, a Franciscan from London, stayed with us during Easter week. He described the difficulties he had experienced over Lenten fasting with his previous hostess, who had plied him with superlative seafood and cream cakes as substitutes for meat. On Easter Monday, with Lenten self-denial safely past, we took Father Charles into the bush for a dinkum chop picnic.

The dining-room at Bishopscourt was large but rather taken up with heavy furniture – a table which could be extended to seat sixteen, and also a tall oak dresser and a matching pair of oak sideboards. Above the latter hung two very large etchings of classical Rome called 'Ave Caesar' and 'Circus Maximus', stirring Ben Hur-ish scenes of chariots thundering down the track in clouds of dust, flying wheels and lashing whips. To balance this pagan display 'The Passing of Queen Eleanor', pious and funereal, hung over the mantelpiece.

When there were very important guests or formal dinner parties (not often), we children were fed in the kitchen. We would then lurk in the passage hoping to ambush titbits of conversation or of food coming forth from the dining room, and before the door closed to glimpse the gleam and reflection of silver and glass in the mahogany table-top or, with luck, someone dabbling in the finger bowls, which were brought out only on the most special, over-dainting occasions. Quite often, however, we ate 'inside' with the visitors, one of us having first summoned the household by ringing a peal on the chimes in the passage.

Mother was convinced that everyone in the world needed feeding up, and vast platefuls of food would circulate round the table, causing gasps of awe and expressions of inability. Whenever possible visitors were treated to home-grown produce – a couple of roast chickens or ducklings, vegetables or salads in season, egg puddings and bottled fruit. Father sat at one end of the table and carved; he also kept the conversation moving, being something of a raconteur. Many of the visitors could match him, story for story, and we young ones didn't find it too difficult to sit still, being seen but not heard, as the anecdotes lobbed to and fro. For example, one irrepressible cleric who had been a prison chaplain had chosen 'Onward Christian soldiers' as a hymn for one service, and was then enchanted to hear the prisoners roaring, with enormous conviction: ' ... Brothers we are treading/ where the saints have trod!'

Being seen but not heard was our usual modus operandi when in company, but there were times when we children spoke up. An eminent bishop from overseas was mystified when he heard me shouting,

'Who's swiped Pop's lid?' as we were preparing to go out. The visitor wrote these words down as evidence of a strange dialect, and asked Father for a translation. This came as 'The episcopal hat is lost.'

Retreats were altogether different. We quickly learnt that being quiet was an essential ingredient of retreats, and those taking part vanished into the chapel a good deal. As a wartime child, I sometimes wondered if the clergymen in black cassocks who floated silently about the house were in 'headlong retreat' or was it merely a 'strategic retreat' they were beating? We were not allowed to eat with them, not even Mother, although she took the food into the dining-room and waited on them. As the door opened, we could glimpse the black cassocks sitting in silence while Father read to them out of a solemn looking book. I felt sorry for them, for it seemed rather like having a detention at school, but at least they were allowed to eat, and with Mother in charge they were not likely to starve, poor things.

There were usually three or four retreaters in residence at once and they slept in the spare rooms upstairs, or perhaps in the nursery. We children were rarely turned out of our bedrooms, but we relinquished our hold on the Green bathroom in their favour, using the White bathroom for the term of their silent visit. This led to some cross-purposes in the passage at bathtime; one peered out to see if any black cassocks were about before making a high speed dash from one end of the passage to the other, clad in pyjamas or towel (I don't think we owned dressing gowns). Generally I passed through the danger zone unseen, but once while taking the corner at full gallop I cannoned straight into a black cassock (which covered a pair of hard knees) and then fled in confusion to my room. The inhabitant of that particular cassock was a married man with small daughters of his own, so to him the collision was probably a happy reminder of home and family.

We had a very small collection of close relatives; our sole first cousin lived in England and we children had seen her only in photographs. This shortage was to some extent made good by hordes of second and third cousins on Mother's side, a few of whom turned up during the war when they were passing through or in camp nearby. But the relatives who came to stay most often were the paternal aunts and uncles, and grandmother Marmie, although after the war began she didn't leave Adelaide again. Father's sister, Aunt Doris, was married to Clive Carey, an English singer and producer of operas who taught at the Melba Conservatorium in Melbourne for the duration of the war. As they approached Ballarat for the first time we were warned to behave ourselves decently, because Uncle Clive and Auntie Dod were not used to children, having none of their own. As the world was full of children I found it hard to understand how anyone could be not used to them, and I wondered how this deficiency would manifest itself. I first saw Auntie Dod standing in my bedroom doorway, bearing a large stuffed lion which she had brought all the way from London for me. That seemed a fairly promising start and it turned out that she and I were at one in preferring animals (live or stuffed) to dolls, and I think she preferred them to some people, too. It was Aunt Doris in fact who had given me the beloved and hideous Binker many years before. The new lion, named Tawny, lived on my bed for years and is now in my guest room.

Aunt Doris was especially interested in cats. 'My dear!' she would exclaim in deep, vibrant tones, 'cats are psychic, you know.' She had a treasury of stories to prove this and it thrilled her beyond measure to find that my Popeye, distracted though she was by motherhood, showed every sign of being psychic, too. The Careys looked after Bishopscourt for us when we were away for the summer holidays once. During our three weeks' absence Popeye vanished entirely, but she reappeared on the day of our return and sat waiting at the gate. 'There you are, my dear,' purred Auntie Dod as we arrived. 'That cat is psychic too!' What an exciting word it was, psychic, and how wonderful that Popeye was one of the elect. During that holiday Auntie Dod taught Cocky to say 'Where's the Bishop?', but she never suggested that birds were psychic.

The nomadic Careys in Fiji, 1930

One thing which the Careys were not used to about children was their tendency to start the day early. Elizabeth was four at the time of their first visit; she woke with the birds and sang very loudly to fill in time. We were used to this, but to Uncle Clive it sounded like a busman's holiday of the worst order, so Auntie Dod painted a large notice, DO NOT SING!, and put it at the foot of Elizabeth's bed. Elizabeth pointed out that she could not read yet, so Auntie Dod patiently explained what the sign meant and left it there, to serve as a reminder and a first reading lesson. The dawn chorus was suppressed but then there was a heavy fall of snow, which turned Ballarat into a white wonderland. Elizabeth looked forth at an early hour, rushed downstairs and before long toiled back up bearing a bucketful of snow which she touted round from one bedroom to another, arousing the household with shrieks of excitement. The English visitors, to whom snow was commonplace, were not amused.

The Careys were flamboyant and surprising people, and Father used to mutter a good deal about 'the artistic temperament' after one of their visits, as though it were a mild infection. Doris painted in water-colours and oils, wrote sprawling, exclamatory letters to people, and had original thoughts. She favoured cloaks, interesting jewellery and bold colours like red and black. Clive wore a dashing black 'musician's' hat with a wide brim, and smoked cigarettes in a black holder. He was completely unassuming about all the famous people he knew, or had known at Cambridge. Years later I discovered that he had once tried (in vain) to teach Rupert Brooke to sing. Into our provincial lives the Careys brought a glimpse of the cosmopolitan, artistic world, but it was only a glimpse. I hadn't any notion of Clive's acquaintance with Rupert Brooke as I read, or recited: 'Stands the church clock at ten to three? And is there honey still for tea?'

GOOD PLAIN COOKING

Florrie was a 'good plain cook', but her good plain cooking was elevated to a noble status by the ingredients that flowed in from the back garden, all fresh and exceedingly organic. These were sometimes supplemented by offerings from the countryside, either gleaned by ourselves or presented to Father on his rural rides – butter from farmers, especially.

'Plain' cooking was the norm then, owing to our British heritage. Porridge, eggs and bacon, roast meat and baked vegetables, steamed puddings and custard, junket and stewed fruits, bread and jam were the accepted dishes. The post-war immigration program was still a decade away, so staple items of diet from other cultures – such as garlic, olive oil, yoghurt, the smellier cheeses, basil, capsicum, even table wines – were highly suspect or scarcely known. Rather bland curries were acceptable, perhaps because our English monarchs were also emperors of India, but rice and pasta (vermicelli, pronounced 'vermasilly') appeared more often in milk puddings than in savory dishes. Until wartime rationing took hold, meals were dominated by meat, foods fried in dripping, thick gravies, generous slathers of butter, sprinkles of salt and spoonsful of sugar (in tea, on porridge or desserts).

Play-lunches at recess were not much in evidence at school, and there was no tuckshop, so we were ravenous and rumbling as we rode home to lunch. Daygirls who lived within reach of school usually went home for about an hour, and many working adults did the same. Housewives and cooks spent the morning preparing a hot midday dinner.

Florrie had the meal ready to the minute as we puffed in and it was generally served in the Pughole by the fire, to the accompaniment of the ABC News and then the latest episode of 'The Lawsons' (later to evolve into 'Blue Hills'). Lunch always consisted of a hot meat and vegetable course, then pudding, and it sometimes began with soup, thick with vegetables and barley. Florrie's repertoire was strong on variety meats and stews such as shepherd's pie, brains in batter, sea pie (stew with dumplings), and legendary steak-and-kidney pies and puddings. We rarely had grills (they took a lot of coupons, whereas offal took none), and roasts were reserved for Sundays or visitors.

At night we were thrown upon our own initiative. Mother was often late home from meetings and would be met by one of us at the gate asking, 'What's for tea?' Soup, eggs and cheese ('mousetrap' or Kraft) were great standbys, while bread and jam filled up the cracks. In spite of this nourishing regime, well padded out by Florrie's offerings of cakes and biscuits, I was often overtaken by further pangs of hunger at bedtime and forced to creep down to the kitchen in search of bread and Marmite. This condition was referred to as 'Night Starvation', which we children considered a highly witty allusion to the famous advertisement, 'Take Horlicks for Night Starvation!' Night Starvation became acute when Margaret and I 'stayed the night' with one another. Supplies were smuggled into the bedroom wardrobe during the day with much giggling and excited anticipation, for a midnight feast was just as much fun to plan and assemble as it was to eat.

As very few households owned refrigerators or freezers until after the war, preserving food was mostly a matter of salting it down, making jams and pickles, or bottling fruit. Lack of refrigeration also meant frequent shopping for fresh food. Nearly everything was home-cooked. Things we now take for granted, like frozen TV dinners, would then have been in the realm of fantasy as there were no freezers and no TV. Even a packet of crumpets was a rare treat because of the expense. The only take-away foods were fish and chips and meat pies. I don't think we ever had fish and chips, as Ballarat was rather far from fish markets, but pies were sometimes allowed as a special indulgence. At Askgar's shop in the city the pies were made before your very eyes on a large table. The performance resembled bed-making as a huge sheet of pastry was unrolled across the rows of pie tins. The pieman deftly firmed this into each tin with his fist, filled each hollow with meat, then whisked another pastry sheet over the top before trimming round each tin with a knife. At school the prefects very occasionally organised a 'pie day' in aid of some worthy cause. A tepid, soggy pie and sauce at recess was a blissful experience.

Soft drinks (especially raspberry vinegar) were restricted to parties and feast days, although a bottle of Kia Ora 50-50 cordial was sometimes added to the larder and used very sparingly. Home-made lemon barley water was more likely to be available in the summer, and we were encouraged to drink milk. Otherwise there was water in the tap. I disliked plain milk, but the joys of flavoured milk were revealed to us at the Modern Dairy in Ripon Street which, during our teens, became a regular haunt after school. Behind the milk-bar Mrs Mitchell dispensed half-pints – twopence plain, twopence-halfpenny coloured. Mrs Mitch's system was simple; she tipped half an inch from the half-pint bottle into her big can and then topped up the bottle with a ladle of syrup. We drank from the bottle through a paper straw. Milkshakes (sixpence and rarely affordable in our early teens) were whizzed up and served in their metal beakers or a glass, and Mrs Mitch spent her spare moments washing up at a frothy sink in the corner. Only the paper straws were thrown away at the Modern Dairy.

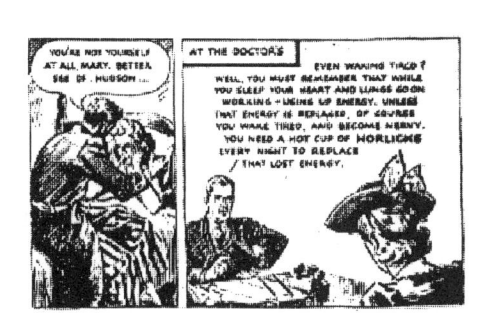

From a 1945 advertisement

CONFINED TO BED

Despite our sustaining diet, gales of fresh air and plentiful exercise, we were often ill. On the bookshelf sat a fat red book called *The Modern Home Doctor*, which we sometimes consulted. Among other things, it suggested the use of leeches as a remedy for various conditions. This was, I suppose, a comfort, for the lake was well stocked with leeches, but it made us wonder about the word 'Modern' in the book's title. Nonetheless, in those days before antibiotics there were many interesting ramifications to being ill or wounded, although we never actually had recourse to leeches.

Without antibiotics to stop infections in their tracks, illnesses were apt to drag on as everyone waited for Nature to take its course. Much of the time one lay in bed, feeling awful and contemplating symptoms – the rashes, spots and swellings, or the splints and dressings, or the bloodshot eyes and lurid tonsils (via mirror and torch). I learnt very early how to take my own temperature, as Mother unfairly insisted on concealing the bad news from the patient. If I were going to be the star of a sickroom drama, I wanted to know the scale of the drama in order to make the most of it.

At New Bishopscourt I soon understood the connection between the words 'patient' and 'patience', for our upstairs rooms were very isolated from the activities below. Being confined to bed was a dreamlike existence, listening to dim voices and footsteps, the distant ringing of

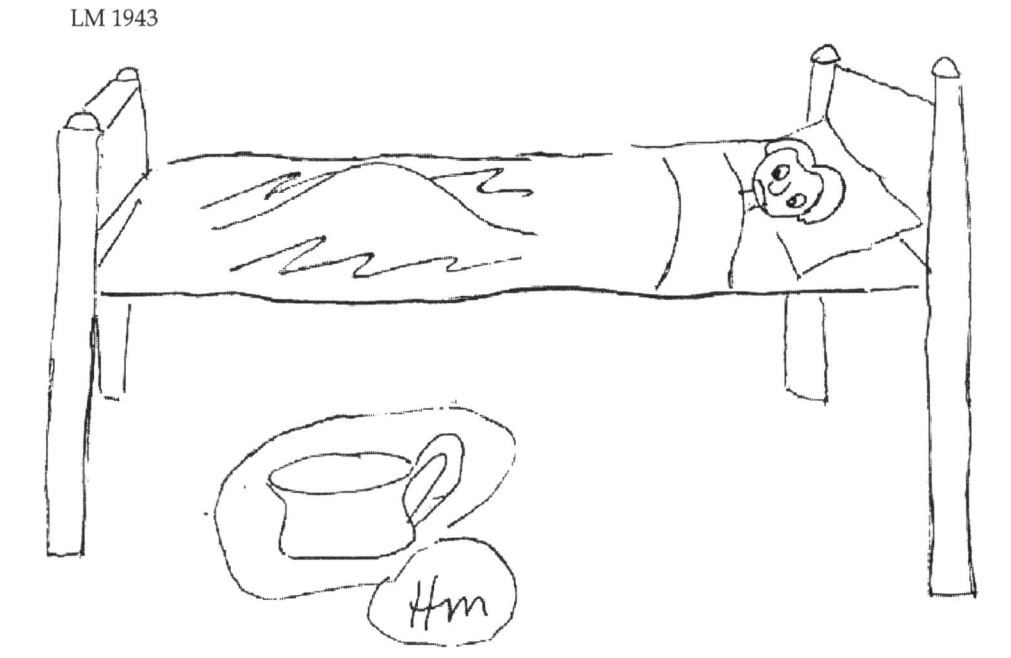

LM 1943

bells and shutting of doors, but unless one were on the brink of death visits from downstairs were infrequent. When trays were laboriously carried upstairs at mealtimes, I felt slightly guilty but also very pleased to see someone from the substantial world of knives-and-forks and mashed potato. The times I most looked forward to were those when Mother could spare half an hour to play patience or Bézique on a small bed-table laid across my knees. I learned the rules of patience and played games myself during the long hours, musing, 'The patient patiently played patience'. The patient also patiently read books, wrote letters and plays to Margaret, did jigsaw puzzles and made Meccano models. It was harder to remain patient with the Meccano set as its fiddly nuts and bolts were apt to vanish into the bed.

Illnesses were either minor (like dirty colds) or very nasty indeed. Our elders still talked emotionally about the Spanish influenza epidemic of 1919, which had killed millions less than twenty-five years before. One archdeacon, who had caught it then, recalled how he complained feverishly of the incessant noise of horses in his head and how his wife refrained from mentioning the procession of horse-drawn funerals pulling up at the church next door. We talked of germs rather than viruses, and the bogey words of my childhood were not so much cancer and coronary, but meningitis (Aunt Doris almost died of it in 1942), tetanus (Father's young brother, dead), typhoid, consumption (TB), diphtheria, smallpox, pneumonia, convulsions. We were reminded of the war by seeing the wounded from the Army Convalescent Hospital as they went about the town, very often on crutches or in their dressing gowns, while the sight of children in cots and wheelchairs reminded us of the threat of infantile paralysis (polio). In 1937, the school year had finished early because of the polio epidemic, and did not recommence until March 1938. Speech Day was limited to the senior school and no parents or friends were invited to attend.

We were threatened with hydatids if we ate grass or touched animals, and with worms if we ate raw meat, while the possible threat of hydrophobic dogs and rusty nails lurked round every corner. Visits to the doctor for anti-tetanus jabs were fairly common in the wake of rusty nail or garden fork mishap, but the first mass inoculation program which we experienced was during the war, when the whole school lined up for BCG vaccinations against tuberculosis. Everyone expected to catch the usual juvenile plagues – measles, rubella, mumps, chicken pox, whooping cough, scarlatina, although I escaped mumps and caught them from my own children a generation later. One of my first contagions was ringworm, which was a social disgrace for some reason. Rubella was considered a minor complaint until the 1940s, when its connection to congenital defects was established.

The possibility of quarantine for any of these ailments was a happy prospect in that it meant missing school, but it also meant that playmates were kept apart. Once, quite innocently, I led Margaret in to visit Father, who was in bed with a swollen face, and within the hour Dr James came to diagnose an episcopal case of mumps. Poor Mother had to then inform Margaret's mother that she was about to have a daughter at home for three weeks in quarantine, and even then none of us caught it. As epidemics swept through the school boarding house, one usually had at least one stretch of quarantine annually, and if this developed into the disease itself, the holiday from school became quite prolonged.

I was the first in our family to encounter the new Sulpha drugs in 1943, when I developed a temperature of 105°F. For once the information was withheld, for I was too sick to read the thermometer, but I remember a quite pleasant sensation of floating about the ceiling while actually lying in bed. The infection eventually declared itself as an abscess on the knee, just as Dr James was beginning to utter the dread word Meningitis. The large Sulpha tablets were about as easy to swallow as a plate. They were used to treat bacterial infections before the advent of antibiotics, and eventually did the job of curing me, although I missed five weeks of school and was very debilitated.

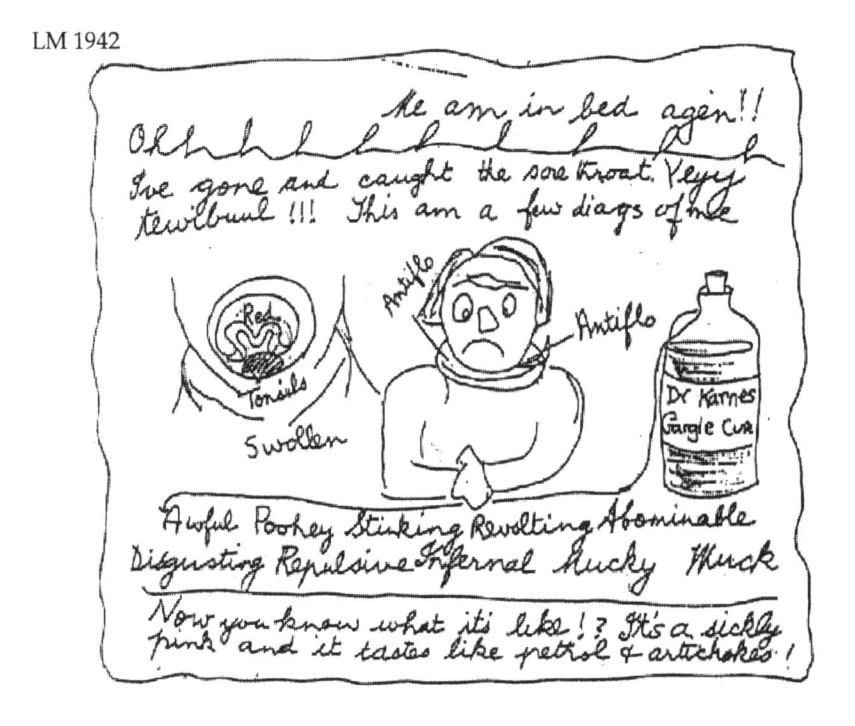

LM 1942

Ailments were often treated in outward and visible ways. Take, for example, the poultice – the bread poultice, the mustard plaster, and especially the Antiphlogistine poultice. The latter we called Antiflo. I had it plastered at different times on the knee, on my chest, on my neck, the principle being to apply heat and 'draw out the poisons'. Applying Antiflo was an enthralling operation. The Antiflo tin was placed in a saucepan of boiling water to be heated up; then Mother with a table knife spread a piece of old linen with slathers of the stuff, which resembled thick grey mud or lava, just off the boil. After testing for heat, the steaming poultice was slapped on to the victim in the appropriate spot. When the Antiflo had cooled down, it tended to behave like putty and next morning the bed would be full of little grey globules. In less extreme cases of chestiness, Vicks was liberally applied all over the front and back and one lay abed in a miasma of camphor and menthol. A more savage method of 'drawing out the poisons' in boils was to cover the spot with the neck of a warm, empty bottle; as the air cooled and contracted, the boil was drawn, rather painfully. This home remedy was never tried on us, partly because we didn't have boils. For earache, which usually occurred in the lonely hours before dawn, warmed glycerine was poured into the earhole and plugged up with cottonwool. It didn't do much good, but it was better than lying alone in the dark, and the treatment was diverting – especially for Mother, who had to get up and perform it.

The trusty standbys for minor cuts, grazes and skin irritations were iodine, boracic acid and vaseline. Sticking plaster was rarely seen in our house; money wasn't spent on luxuries like that when torn-up strips of an old sheet would do for bandages. We all managed to grow to maturity without Bandaids, which hadn't been invented.

Internal potions were, almost without exception, exceedingly nasty. You gulped them down and then rammed in a toffee to neutralise the taste. Bitter cough linctuses had none of the banana- or blackberry-flavoured attractions of today's mixtures. Milk of magnesia and cod liver oil (for 'building up') were both repulsive, while evil is the only word for castor oil and cascara. These purgatives were still in vogue, but luckily in our household they were reserved for moments in extremis. Castor oil was often disguised in orange juice, which had the effect of putting one off oranges for years. Even the beautiful royal blue castor oil bottles retained unpleasant associations. We didn't go in for salts much, although Florrie gave large doses to the chooks if she thought they were under par. But for some the use of salts for 'inner cleanliness' was a ritual which could become confused with godliness

– 'Oh Lord, make clean our hearts with Eno's'. Florrie's recipe for a clear, pimple-free skin was a large spoonful of sulphur mixed with treacle, every Saturday morning. It didn't work.

Most patent medicines were jocularly familiar to us through advertisements rather than first-hand experience. Bile Beans we mocked with a parody of our own called Belly Jelly; Doan's Backache Pills ('Every Picture Tells a Story') called forth heart-rending demonstrations; as exams approached, we announced a craving for Clement's Nerve & Brain Tonic. Rarely did aspirin pass our lips; temperatures were left to bring themselves down and often took their time, as we were smothered in piles of blankets for fear of chills. I had measles on that occasion when Elizabeth carted a bucketful of snow to the various bedsides. This was first-rate treatment for a fever, if not for the bedding.

Sal volatile was good for a laugh, partly because of its name and also because it was associated with swooning. We regarded swooners as rather feeble, nevertheless Fainting in Church was an awful possibility, although I never managed to bring it off. Margaret achieved it once and came close several times more and, as I watched the turmoil in her pew from several rows behind, I rather envied her the privilege of being encouraged to lie at full length on the seat while the service was in progress. Once or twice someone was half-carried out, while adults went on praying or singing with redoubled fervour as though nothing was happening. How could they be so unfeeling while bodies were being removed down the aisle? But of course they were being Tactful – this was one of the prime occasions when it was rude to stare. We were well versed in what to do if we 'felt faint'. Firstly, you took precautions by eating something before early church, and then if you felt it 'coming on' you stuck your head between your knees.

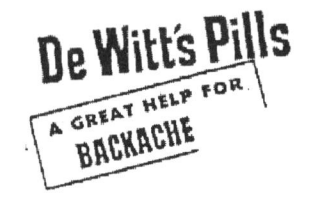

Going to hospital for most children was associated with having one's tonsils out. When this subject arose, adults talked loudly and cheerfully of icecream and jelly, which, we were led to believe, came in basinsful to the bedside and made hospital seem like one long party. Friends who had been de-tonsilled were fairly unenthusiastic however, and my own experience of hospital, to have a broken arm set, confirmed my suspicions. The anaesthetist appeared, alarming sight, in a huge rubber apron, and when I woke up I found my splinted arm roped up to a sort of gallows above the bed. Subsequent developments were more entertaining. My arm stuck out in an 'aeroplane splint' for several months, requiring a double bed for sleep, a double desk to myself at school, two seats at the pictures, a visit to the blacksmith to have a new splint made to measure, and then visits from the physiotherapist to have the gaunt limb restored to action.

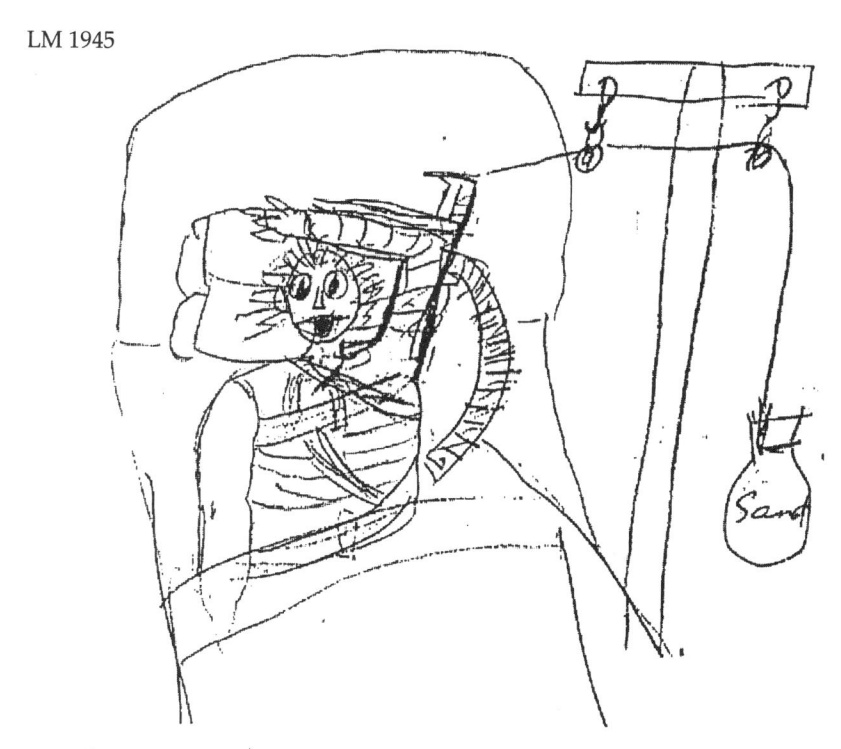

LM 1945

To have medical attention from a blacksmith was certainly diverting, but one could never say that of visits to the dentist, even though he was Margaret's father and made cheerful faces at me as I lay back in the chair. Beyond making the appointments with great regularity, Mother had little to do with our dental care. Elizabeth and I caught the tram and endured the long, slow rides to our doom, then climbed the steep, dark stairs in the old building at the foot of the Sturt Street hill, and waited. The waiting was very bad; footsteps approached and disappeared, there were distant clinks and brr-rr-rrs and hums of conversation, whiffs of gas and antiseptic smells, then suddenly there was Margaret's father in the doorway, beaming over his glasses and beckoning. Sessions could last a long time as the slow old drills chugged away and amalgam was pounded up by pestle in a mortar. There was no choice about injections – they were reserved for extractions only. I didn't much mind, as I was sure that the needle was worse than the drill. There was no piped music to soothe the nerves, no vacuum to whisk the mouth clear of rubble and the dentist pumped the chair up and down with his foot – but it was worth enduring all this for the euphoria of racing down the stairs to freedom and fresh air.

Margaret and I sometimes visited the surgery not as patients but as 'family', feeling smug as we passed the victims in the waiting room, thumbing through their magazines. We could go out through a back door onto the old roof among the chimney pots, or visit the mechanic in the room where he made the dentures, all pink and white and grinning. The room smelt of wax and gas, and the disembodied teeth were unnerving; it was a relief to race up and down the long stairs, or to go to the nearby milkbar for an ice cream.

If I wasn't ill or wounded myself, it was always possible to read about other people's sufferings. Harrowing descriptions of illness and accidents in literature were quite plentiful and rather scary. I was introduced to cholera in *The Secret Garden* (or at least to the fear of it, for no symptoms were described – just sudden death), and also to a hefty dose of neurosis. Scarlet fever and consumption were apt to rage in other books of that vintage. I read with morbid fascination the account of Dick's accident and subsequent paralysis in *Dick Lester of Kurrajong* by Mary Grant Bruce; there was much agony and sweat, and Dick behaving bravely through it all until cured by a do-or-die operation. Similar episodes in the Billabong saga (usually the result of accident) were always a satisfying compound of severe pain and cheery fortitude, and were good for endless re-reading as they all, save one, had a happy outcome. The exception was in *Mates at Billabong* when Norah's pony, Bobs, was ridden to death by contemptible cousin Cecil. While the death of a horse may seem out of place in a catalogue of human ills, this episode helped to stiffen me for the ultimate tragedy – the death of Judy in Ethel Turner's *Seven Little Australians*. Among all these agonising chapters, this was the one to be pored over again and again, in private, under the bedclothes. Here was a heroine I could so readily identify with – not a saint or a prig, whose demise could be borne, but a tomboy just like myself and killed by a falling tree!

Opposite: Lake Wendouree, south-eastern shore

Out and about

BESIDE THE LAKE

The shore of Lake Wendouree was only a step away down Grove Street, but as soon as Margaret and I acquired our big bikes the whole lake region became our territory. No-one ever seemed to worry about us drowning or about teaching us to swim. Sometimes they might have said, 'Try not to fall in, dears,' and in this we were happy to oblige, for the lake's bottom was squelchy, its waters when disturbed eddied and squirmed with mud and weed and wrigglers, and worst of all there were the leeches. But for such a large and accessible body of water, Lake Wendouree seemed to be far less threatening to our parents' nerves than mine shafts and mullock heaps. After all, it was at bottom only a swamp, shallow and even-depthed and innocent of rips and currents, although it could produce minor waves.

Creswick, about twenty kilometres away, was another of the old gold towns of the district, and sometimes we went there to picnic by the 'swimming pool', which had originally been a mine. The mounds and hillocks around this waterhole had become clothed in pine plantations and straggly bush, and the banks were fringed with reeds or edged with causeway paths and wooden decking. One safe area had been enclosed for small children, but the rest of the pool was open to anyone who dared to plunge in. I can now admit that the Creswick pool unnerved me, for its waters were deep and unbuoyant. At one side there was a small 'bay' encircled by steep, white banks, and here we were forbidden to go for there were legends about its murky depths in the mine. The water there was black and cold. Some said it was eighty feet deep; others said it was bottomless. I would watch anxiously as dare-devil swimmers stroked across the dark surface. Would they vanish into the grim depths? Was there a monster lurking below?

The Creswick pool stirred the darker recesses of the imagination, but not so Lake Wendouree. The lake's bottom was slimy, but it was mostly within reach, and no monsters could have lurked in those shallows. Even the leeches were midgets, as leeches go. All in all it was a friendly stretch of water. The sportsmen of the 1860s who eyed Yuille's Swamp as a potential playground for anglers and rowers, endowed Ballarat West with its finest public asset, for to live within sight of water is one of life's bonuses. The best thing about the lake and its surrounding parklands was the sense that they belonged to everyone; there were no fences or admission charges or Keep Out signs. One was never aware of any authority policing the area or making rules. It was our lake.

Yuille's Swamp was exactly the right size to become a town lake. It is small enough to take in at a wide glance, without losing the abiding sense of space and sky, and it is large enough to accommodate Olympic eights or yachts in regatta, lazy dinghies and fishermen and nesting waterfowl. We knew it as a setting for brilliant sunsets – as the sky reddened over the dark trees of the Botanical Gardens, the fiery colours were held in the water and inlaid with the black shapes of swans, boats and anglers.

Few things are so satisfactory as a circular six-kilometre walk along a meandering path beside water, and this is what the lake offered at all seasons. One could run or cycle or drive around the same magic circle. The circumnavigation of the lake was a local ritual; freed from the pressing business of school, work or daily chores, people were apt to say 'Let's go round the lake', and even in wartime there was usually enough petrol hoarded for a sedate Sunday drive around Wendouree Parade. Lakeside walks were full of pauses, to skip flat stones across the water, to talk to swans or feed them, to bounce in the springy piles of water-weed heaped on the bank, to watch the scullers and fishermen, to search for pond life in the backwaters, armed with nets and jars, to sample the swings and slides and to climb on the cannons. If we were on bikes, there were further attractions – scooting through the soupy puddles with our legs in the air, teetering in single file through Fairyland or around the smooth asphalt rim of View Point, that small promontory near the larger boatsheds on the eastern shore.

View Point was furnished with willows, lawns, seats and the odd cannon, and its edge was smoothly paved and bordered with white posts like teeth. Adults took View Point literally and went there to absorb the view. We children went there to investigate the water level of the lake. In a wet season the water sometimes swished right across the asphalt rim and lapped at the lawns, and from a distance View Point appeared to be sinking, leaving only its hairy trees and white teeth behind. On high water occasions we could churn around the asphalt on our bikes in a flurry of foam. When the lake level was low, however, there was a big drop from the asphalt rim to the water, and then it was mandatory to ride the bikes to within an inch of the edge, or to sit on the brink and stretch our feet as far as possible towards the surface without actually falling in.

Off View Point

The Old Bishopscourt shoreline, which we knew first, was on the north-west side, sheltered from the cold southerlies by the great bank of reeds across the lake's middle. This side was rural and wildish and it harboured most of the swans and waterfowl, who nested on the islands and strolled about the parkland in search of pickings. When we moved to the other side, we found that the eastern and southern areas belonged to the boats. Several impressive, two-storied boatsheds housed the rowing clubs, and sailing craft were kept in clusters of smaller sheds. Two fleets of rowing boats, brown and blue, hired out by Mr Taylor and Mr Gill, were tied up to piers in summer, and the three paddle steamers lived in dark, cavernous sheds behind them, emerging in the warm weather to churn to and fro across to the Gardens.

The boating side of the lake had to be kept clear of the reeds and water weeds, which grew with great swampy enthusiasm, and a familiar sight was the reed-cutter, a puttering, raft-like boat fitted with a device like an underwater hedge-clipper. It could be seen chugging along on its endless mission, its elbows pistoning up and down like an aquatic grasshopper. Mowing the lake was a long and leisurely process. The cut reeds rose to the surface and gradually floated towards the shore, building up into a thick brown mat round the edge. It lay there for some time, while feeding coots and moorhens plodded about on top. Eventually men armed with rakes and hooks would haul the weeds into piles on the bank, to lie for weeks draining and smelling dank before being carted away in trucks – to some giant municipal compost heap, I hope. The central reed bed was left alone, save for a couple of straight channels carved through it for the rowing boats. These channels were quiet, warm and sheltered after the brisk breezes of the open water, and we usually aimed for them when we went rowing.

Rowing was one of those practical skills picked up in passing, but I think Father taught us the rudiments of steering and handling oars as I recall his stern remarks about the ignominy of 'catching crabs'. We tried to avoid this disgrace as we heaved across the open water to the reed beds in one of the boats hired for a shilling or so from Mr Gill or Mr Taylor. Margaret and I also had a few sailing lessons from a retired doctor who invited us, with parental permission, to join him sometimes as 'crew'. After school we would scoot on our bikes to a boatshed near the Yuilles' monument, where Dr Pern would be busy rigging up his small boat. The main lesson we learnt was that of ducking the boom when tacking, but sometimes we were allowed to take the tiller. (Dr Pern was also a boomerang enthusiast. He had given throwing demonstrations at school and he gave us some private lessons and made me a boomerang of my own. It was in the form of a cross and it wheeled around the sky at great speed.)

Elizabeth was lucky to have a friend, Pat, with a sailing boat of her own, and the two of them spent most of their spare time on, beside or in the lake, while at home Elizabeth's bookshelves filled up with the works of Arthur Ransome, starting with *Swallows and Amazons*.

Rides on the paddle steamers were less exciting as we grew older and became capable of independent voyaging, but the old churners still had their uses. One Saturday afternoon Elizabeth left home. She ran away, owing to some act of domestic injustice. It was some time before anyone noticed that she was missing, for on the large Bishopscourt campus it was normal for children to be unseen for hours without anyone worrying. When her absence was confirmed, Father, Dorothy's fiancé Fred, and I set off in the car to comb the streets, while Mother and Dorothy waited at home for news, Mother probably preparing herself for a dragging of the lake. It was remembered that at the height of the tantrum Elizabeth had threatened to go and live with Ah Hung, so we drove to Nerrina to see if she had. She had no way of getting there, of course, but nobody was thinking very clearly, and no, Ah Hung had no news. We circled the lake several times, scanning the shallows for corpses, before giving up and returning home. Elizabeth walked in soon after, having spent the afternoon seated in the prow of 'The Golden City', steaming to and fro from View Point to the Gardens until her funds (stolen from Mother's purse) ran out.

A meandering path. The lakeside at the end of Grove Street.

Elizabeth afloat in the reed bed, with a large bag of supplies, c. 1946.

The school boatsheds came to life every autumn as the boys prepared for boatrace day – the Head of the Lake. Racing shells and singleted youths skimmed about in various corners of the lake as the weeks of training went by, and rumours reached the girls' schools about the 'form' which their heroes were displaying. The day came at last, the Saturday afternoon when we all climbed into our school uniforms, bedecked with partisan ribbons, and gathered at the big rowing club sheds on the eastern shore. Each school and its supporters had free run of one shed for the occasion, with the appropriate school flag flying above, and here we assembled on the rather rickety decking or on the even more dubious balcony above, and strained our eyes across the gleaming water to the starting positions on the far side. (The direction of races has now been reversed.) A tiny puff of smoke from the starter's pistol and the foam from the referee's motor-boat signalled the start of the races. For a long time we jumped up and down trying to guess which crew was in the lead, and the boys burst into primitive war cries which the rowers couldn't possibly hear. Eventually the tiny blobs in the distance grew larger and the colours of their singlets came into focus. The shouting intensified as they skimmed towards the line. Our angle of view made it difficult to tell who was in the lead until the last few strokes before the finishing gun was fired, by which time the shrieking crowds were leaping up and down, the old jetties bouncing in unison.

The Wind in the Willows was a natural accompaniment to life near Lake Wendouree, as we read of Ratty 'mucking about in boats' or sang of ducks 'a-dabbling, up tails all'. Up-tails-all was a common sight on the lake as the swans plunged their long necks to the bottom in search of food, their webbed feet waving wildly in the air to retain balance. It was less common to see swans in flight, but sometimes they took off in a flurry of wings and water and steered away to the country, necks stretched and white wing-tips beating. Birds animated the waterscape – coots and water hens scooting and chinking near the weedy edges; shags silhouetted in the island trees, their wings held out to dry; lone white egrets shining in the bare willow tops; the grey heron poised in the shallows, ready to stab; solitary and bizarre musk ducks living their strange, submarine existence. One day in wartime the pelicans arrived from the droughty north. Silently they wheeled above the lake in splendid formations and then came down along the edge of the reed beds to gorge on the fish. Mother was hanging out the washing when the first squadrons came over and for a moment of panic she thought the enemy air-raids were about to begin. But these 'bombers' had no engines; they were silent, and all the more sinister for that. Gliders, paratroops, invasion!

The lake was a magnet at all seasons. Its image was constantly changing – the water level rose and fell; the surface moved from silky blue to choppy grey; willows and poplars performed their seasonal changes of costume against the black backdrop of the pines, and small processions of woolly, grey cygnets, led by mother and tailed by father, glided by on the water to announce the spring. Bare willow trailers whipped to and fro in the winter squalls, and cycling round Wendouree Parade we had to stand on the pedals and push into the gale with all our might until we could sink thankfully into the haven of Grove Street, arriving home with drizzling eyes and noses, blue hands and heaving lungs.

HUNTERS AND GATHERERS

One of the farewell gifts from Newcastle was a fully equipped hamper, with plates, cutlery, cups and food containers all neatly clamped into a sort of suitcase. Father loved picnics, so we used the hamper a lot in the early days, loading it up with bread and butter, hard boiled eggs, sliced meat and salad, and then spreading everything out on a rug in some favoured spot. Moorabool Reservoir was a frequent destination, and I loved bounding through the dim, carpeted aisles beneath the pine forests, collecting cones for the fires at home. When war broke out, the reservoirs were locked against the public in case of sabotage.

As the situation grew darker from 1940 on, we became hunters and gatherers in earnest. Outings generally had some practical purpose. Rabbiting, for example, was a patriotic way of spending a Saturday

210   Beside the Lake

afternoon for it helped to rid the country of pests as well as boosting the meat ration. Father enjoyed taking his shotgun out to the bush to bag a rabbit or two, but there was no ammunition during the war. Then he discovered that Stan, the gardener, owned a ferret, nets and all things necessary for a rabbit hunt. Father offered transport if Stan would supply the ferret and the gear, and some exciting expeditions followed. Mother rarely came, for such blood sports were not to her liking, but the back seat was always occupied by eager, wriggling girls – us, sometimes our friends and Stan's daughter too. The ferret, smelling rather rank, rode in its own box at Stan's feet. It was a mean creature, yellowish-white and sinuous, with needle teeth and bad manners. I could understand why Toad was so mortified to learn that the ferrets and weasels were squatting in Toad Hall.

There were rabbits everywhere – they had burrowed their way through the continent – but we most often went out in the Learmonth direction, on the slopes around Mount Misery. The warrens were bare,

View across Lake Learmonth towards the rabbiting slopes.

lumpy patches on the hillsides, and as we tramped towards them, carrying sacks and spades and one of us proudly shouldering the ferret box, we watched for evidence of recent scratchings or fresh 'tracks' (Florrie's euphemism for dung). Having chosen a likely area to beseige, we searched for every burrow and hidden bolt-hole, covering each with a slip-net well anchored by a wire peg. Stan did a final check of the nets and then pointed the ferret into one of the holes, while we all withdrew into a ring round the warren, like alert fielders in a cricket match, and waited. No two warrens ever 'blew up' in the same way. Sometimes nothing happened at all and the ferret would wander out of a burrow blinking, having found nobody at home. Sometimes he stayed underground for so long, that we had to dig him out. But when there was a positive result, rabbits would explode into the daylight from different exit holes, rocketing into the nets with such force that the drawstring pulled tight. Our job was to pounce on the thrashing victims and hold them down until Stan was ready to deal with them. He was expert at disentangling them and swiftly breaking their necks, but this was something that none of us wanted to learn.

Stan would clean the rabbits on the spot, leaving their innards on the hillside for the scavenging birds. Then he would slot their back legs together and on we would go, with the floppy brown bodies swinging from a rope. Stan skinned them at home and stretched the pelts on wire to dry, ready to sell. How weird to see the fur peeling off like a glove. What had these hard, shiny, pink bodies to do with the soft furry creatures of the hillside?

A large haul often condemned us to an intensive diet of rabbit meat, roasted, fricaseed, casseroled and pied, so after one particularly bumper afternoon Father decided to take some of the catch home alive, to be slaughtered later. They were emptied into a tiny shed where the mower was kept, because this had an asphalt floor, but the experiment was not a success (and probably not legal either). The smell issuing from the shed became daily more noisome and Florrie's nerves daily more frayed as she forecast a mass escape into her lettuce crop, so the rabbits were executed and distributed as fresh game around the neighbourhood.

Problems of excess could also arise during yabby hunts and the haul, seething and murky, would be tipped into the white bath in the Maids' bathroom. But even Mother enjoyed yabbying, up to a point. One suitable waterhole beside the road to Buninyong was easily accessible and picturesque, and usually we went no further than that. Margaret often came with us to stalk the yabby. One cold day she wore her best winter coat. We unloaded the gear, tied the hunks of meat to our strings and gathered round the pond to begin. Margaret flung her string over the bank, slithered in the mud and followed her bait to the bottom. It was a thorough ducking, so we wrapped her in a rug and took her home to her mother, without a single yabby in the bucket.

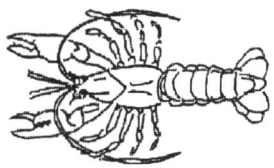

This sort of thing rather put Mother off the chase. She was a gatherer rather than a hunter and more inclined to make raids on the vegetable kingdom. At one stage, when she had acquired a spinning wheel, she was a keen gatherer of wool from barbed wire fences, but this could hardly qualify as a blood sport.

The fields around Mount Rowan or Newlyn were our target for mushrooms. The excitement of finding rings of 'mushies' poking through the grass took our minds off cold winds and wet feet. Sometimes, with shrieks of disbelief, we found monsters the size of dinner plates, but our parents insisted that the baby pink ones were the best to eat. Unfortunately they were usually served up as a blackish mulch in thickened sauce, and the pleasures of mushrooms sautéed briefly in butter, or grilled, or raw in salad, were unknown to us.

Harvesting blackberries was rather more tedious and damaging, but one put up with that because it meant a picnic. We discovered by accident a most romantic picnic spot beyond Mount Buninyong. Father turned off the Geelong road onto a gravel track and then onto a very tentative wheeltrack down a grassy slope towards an inviting clump of willows. The car lurched to the bottom, amid anxious clucks from the front seat and gleeful noises from the back. Had Shakespeare been on board, he would undoubtedly have begun, 'There is a willow grows aslant a brook ... ', although in fact there were several willows and the brook was scarcely deep enough to drown a mouse, let alone a sturdy Ophelia. The little stream burbled between banks of mossy 'lawn' and the old willows rested their elbows on the earth. We children climbed onto the springy willow branches and spent the afternoon bouncing, bucking and singing. Further along the stream, blackberries grew with their feet in the water, and this became our perennial blackberry patch, where the fruit was plump and juicy.

Mother romantically named this place 'Dingley Dell', in homage perhaps to its English-ness. We never saw another living soul there. Occasionally Margaret and I puffed as far as Dingley Dell on our bikes, and once we partook of a private banquet seated under the willows on the moss. The first course was cold roast pigeon (from my pigeon house in the belfry). We had a bird apiece, cooked for us by Florrie. Dessert consisted of fresh blackberries served with the sugar and cream we'd brought with us. I felt rather sick after this orgy and the hilly ride home was a big effort!

One quite different sort of expedition was the Girl Guide hike, for when I was about eleven a guide company was formed at school and we were kitted out in blue dresses and shapeless hats, ties which unfolded to become slings (in case of an epidemic of broken arms, presumably) and all the various badges and ribbons which had to be sewn on to identify us. Margaret and I belonged to the Magpie Patrol. As Girl Guides we learned to tie knots, knots called sheep shank, clove hitch, sheet bend and such. One or two of these have always proved useful, especially the trusty reef knot; the rest might have come in handy if we had later taken up ocean racing to Hobart. We also learnt to make beds (which I could already do), to light fires with one match and to track. The company set off into the bush near Nerrina, where we all attempted the one match trick, cooked chops and potatoes, and then tracked one another very noisily through the undergrowth. Why only one match? – the question nags me still. If one were lost in the wilderness, one would either have a reasonably full box of matches, especially if one smoked a pipe, or (more likely for an eleven-year-old female) no matches at all. It would have been more useful to teach us how to rub two sticks together.

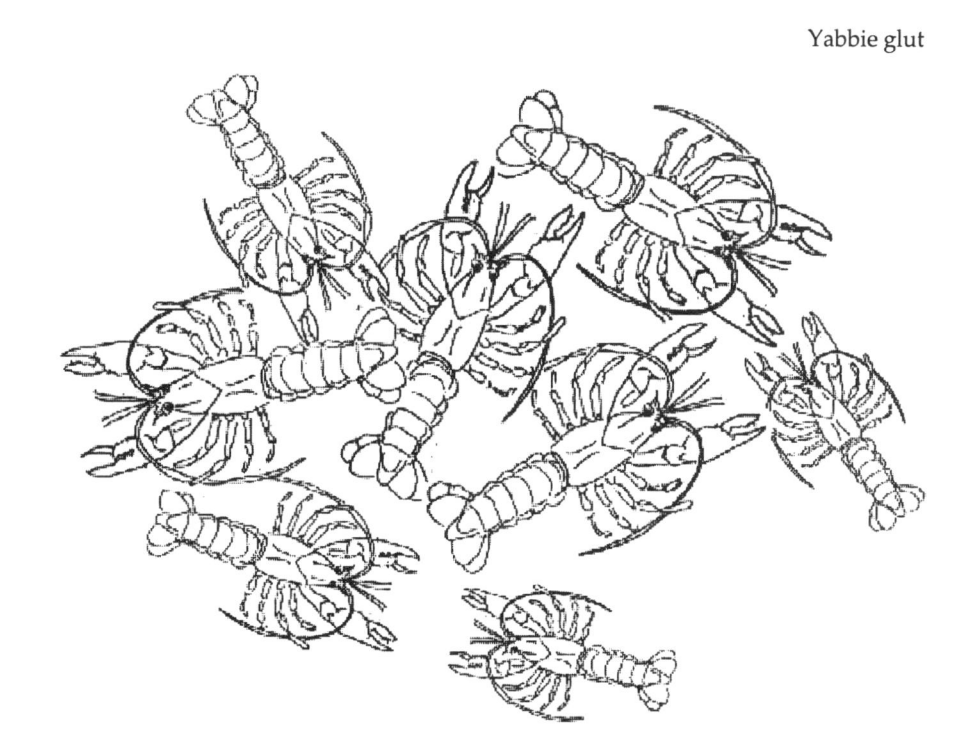

Yabbie glut

Holidays

THE BIG SMOKE

Trips to Melbourne were arduous. It took over two hours to cover the seventy miles of narrow, winding highway, negotiating the fogs of Ballan, the steeps of the Pentland Hills and the frustration of military convoys in wartime. Landmarks were the tiny pig farm near Gordon, Pike's Creek Reservoir, the halfway 'comfort stop' at Bacchus Marsh and the sweep up from there through Anthony's Cutting. When the radio masts near Melton and Rockbank came into view, we knew we were getting closer. The red brick flour mill at Albion was the first real building in Melbourne; we crossed the railway into Sunshine and were no longer in the country. Rich tannery and abattoir smells around Footscray and Newmarket elicited much ribald comment and nose-holding in the back seat, but soon afterwards we were in the city, negotiating the traffic lights and gaping at the hordes of Melburnians surging across the intersections.

Melbourne was very stimulating; everything was bigger, faster, noisier, more modern than in our rural city. When it came to public buildings we were used to Victorian splendour, although Melbourne had more of it. To me the awesome buildings were the modern ones, such as the Manchester Unity and the T & G and the brand new Police Headquarters in Russell Street. These all towered overhead and seemed not far short of New York skyscrapers. The elongated trams came in endless processions, clanging their bells impatiently. There were express lifts and escalators in the big shops and policemen on point duty. Sometimes we stayed overnight at the Windsor Hotel in Spring Street or the Victoria Coffee Palace in Little Collins Street. The cafeteria at the Victoria was a wonder of the world – my first experience of 'self serve'. Dazzling newcomers on the block were the twin restaurants, Russell Collins and Elizabeth Collins which set a new fashion for immense garden salads and for banks of flowers, especially gladioli. The main door into each was operated by electronic beam – that was modern, if you like!

Father took charge of Elizabeth and me, while Mother and Dorothy went shopping in Buckley & Nunn, the Myer Emporium, Georges and the Mutual Store. Father hung on to us and told us to ask a policeman if we got lost, although what we were to ask him I was never sure. Our chosen destinations were the Zoo, the Museum, Tim the Toyman's (to choose more model animals for my collection or new bits for the Meccano set) and, best of all, the newsreel theatrettes. These 'hour shows' embodied the sophistication of the metropolis. In smart, busy Melbourne you could dive into a dark newsreel cinema at any time of the day or evening and watch one 'short' after another, until someone hissed, 'This is where we came in.' You could stay and see them all over again if you wanted to – the Goofy and Donald Duck cartoons, the March of Time, Movietone and Cinesound newsreels to keep us up to date with the war, and Pete Smith specials. When it was over, there were three more theatrettes close by; we were even known to go to two in one day and they rarely showed the same offerings.

Full length films were not often on the agenda, for we could see them at home, but we made a special pilgrimage to Melbourne to see Walt Disney's *Fantasia* at the Savoy. At this cinema even the interval was enthralling because the management served tiny trays of tea and biscuits which were brought round to the patrons in their seats. The colour and animation of *Fantasia* bowled me right over, and it opened wide the door to serious, powerful classical music, even Stravinsky's 'The Rite of Spring' (starring dinosaurs, a forerunner of Jurassic Park), but especially Beethoven's 'Pastoral Symphony'.

Father loved pantomimes and took us to several in those years. I felt some confusion about the Principal Boy of the panto tradition, for 'he' was obviously a girl dressed up (why?) and (s)he was usually clad in silly satin garments, and the 'Dames' were men dressed up as ugly old women. The confusion soon wore off as I learnt to accept theatrical convention and cross-dressing.

The trip home to Ballarat seemed longer than ever, for there was the slow, grinding climb up from Bacchus Marsh, past Werribee Gorge and the solitary stone church on the windswept ridge of the Pentland moors; then more landmarks – the sleepy hollows of Myrniong and Gordon, the Wallace Butter Factory, the signpost to Korweinguboora (which vanished during the war, but was still a funny memory), and finally as we came over the brow of Woodman's Hill we would see our own city spread out below us in the Yarrowee Basin. Despite the bustle and glamour of the Big Smoke behind us, I was always glad to be home.

RURAL RIDES

When Elizabeth was old enough, Mother sometimes accompanied Father on his Rural Rides. By then, Dorothy had vanished to Melbourne, so Elizabeth and I were left in the care of Florrie, who slept at Bishopscourt and spoiled us unashamedly by cooking our favourite foods, notably steak and kidney pudding and apple turnovers.

In school holidays, however, we children sometimes climbed into the car and went too. We stayed in all sorts of places, farms, vicarages, station homesteads, country hotels. Mrs Powell's hotel at Sheep Hills was my favourite, although I stayed there only once. Father was a more regular guest and he returned home with wonderful tales of Mrs Powell's birds and pets. Then, after another visit, he returned with Cocky in a box, a present from Mrs Powell for me, so I was her devoted slave before I even met her. Father told mouth-watering stories of the hotel's magic menu, which always offered him a choice of turkey, goose, duckling or chicken, as well as beef, lamb and so forth, and on my one visit the same list was produced. There were few if any other guests, for Sheep Hills was a tiny hamlet, and there were no freezers. Did Mrs Powell really cook such a banquet every day, just in case? The mystery remained unsolved, as all good mysteries should.

Visits to station homesteads in the Western District could be intimidating. The owners were the nearest thing Australia had to 'landed gentry' and they modelled themselves to some extent on the English system, sending their children to the more exclusive private boarding-schools and living in a fairly closed society of their own. Father still referred to them sometimes as 'squatters'. Nevertheless, some of them were very generous to him and to the diocese and he had good friends among them. Several times we were invited to stay at Kongbool, a homestead near Balmoral belonging to Lady Smyth. She and her late husband, Major-General Sir Nevill Smyth VC, KCB, CB, were not colonial copies of the English gentry, they were the real thing, having settled in Victoria after a lifetime of serving the Empire. There was a mini-ballroom at Kongbool, with gilded chairs around the walls. On the floor of the wide entrance hall lay tiger skins with snarling heads, while other trophies of the big-game hunt decorated the walls.

Our visits were during the war years; Lady Smyth's sons and daughter were all away in the services and she was running the property herself with very little help. During the day she could be seen riding or striding around in her old jodphurs and shirts, but in the evening we all changed for dinner and foregathered in the smoking room for a drink while awaiting the summons on the gong. She would usually appear in a long evening dress. The large dining table was crowned with a 'carousel' for the cruets. Elizabeth was fascinated and gave it such a spin that the salt cellar flew off at a tangent, scattering its contents far and wide. Cringe.

No-one was exempt from helping round the property during the day, and one summer Lady Smyth had the bishop, his wife and family all out rolling hay in near century heat. Nobody dared to protest for this was all part of the War Effort. Elizabeth and I were able to cool off in the muddy dam, but Mother, being unused to farm labouring, had to lie down to recover. On one visit I was given the reins while we were driving about in a cart. Having never handled a horse and cart before, I managed to drive into a dead tree, breaking some vital piece of tackle and arousing the wrath of the farm manager who had handed me the reins in the first place. I loved visiting Kongbool, although so often I felt inadequate and 'colonial' in that outpost of the British Raj. How appropriate that its neighbouring township was Balmoral, Victoria.

We almost never went to the Otway Ranges with Father, perhaps because of the tortuous roads and car sickness. Our scene was much more often the flat and friendly Wimmera, where we strained our eyes for the sight of the next grain silo. These, like grey lighthouses, marked the way across the endless sea of the wheat belt.

Elizabeth and I were often perched on pillows in the front seat, where we were less likely to feel sick. I learned to read the road maps in the glove box and very quickly mastered the names and order of all the towns strung along the Western and Glenelg Highways like beads on a necklace, and the mileages between them. Other friendly landmarks were the mountains – some, like Mount Emu or Mount Arapiles, standing in solitude on the plains, and others joining hands along the Great Dividing Range from Beaufort to Horsham. Their profiles remain imprinted on my mind – such as the beautiful skyline of the Pyrenees, especially as seen from the main street of Ararat. We just called them 'the Ararat hills'. I wondered idly about Noah's Ark, which was said to have foundered on another Mount Ararat. Could Noah have possibly landed here too, to let off the kangaroos, wombats and blue wrens? How else could they have got here?

This handsome range pointed the way to the Grampians which, apart from Buninyong and Warrenheip, were my favourite mountains, rising blue and jagged out of the western plains in a series of peaks and massifs which enlivened the flat horizon for travellers in many directions. Mount Abrupt and Mount Sturgeon were twin sentinels on the Glenelg Highway. Father explained that a sturgeon was a fish, and we could make out the shape. In the middle of the range Mount William was special because he was the biggest, sometimes even snow-capped, and he had the same name as Father. At the north west extremity sat perky little Mount Zero.

Here and there across this landscape were monuments to Major Mitchell, the early Surveyor-General of New South Wales – stone obelisks each surmounted by a cement arrow and bearing the inscription MAJOR MITCHELL PASSED THIS WAY. These reminded me of our tracking exercises in the Guides, scratching arrows on the ground. The Major's arrows pointed in all directions and he seemed to have been everywhere, even to the top of Mount Zero, from where he had seen a fair bit of Australia Felix spread out below. Such monuments reinforced our school lessons about the explorers, but we couldn't imagine Australia Felix as he must have seen it, for the monuments were now set beside main highways and their arrows pointed across well-settled land.

Just before the war, our Ford V8 was replaced by a dark green Chevrolet (AK839) and this faithful car criss-crossed Victoria for the next ten years, somehow surviving the rigours of wartime motoring. Some of the journeys in the green Chev seemed interminable, especially when fuel-conserving speed limits and threadbare tyres kept us down to a snail's pace. If Elizabeth and I grew too wriggly and cantankerous, Father would stop the car and sternly order us to get out and walk. It was never made clear whether we would have to walk home or not, but the car always vanished round a distant corner. Being old enough to have some insight into parental behaviour, I was fairly confident that the car would be parked around the bend, and as we trotted along I did my best to stiffen Elizabeth's tremulous upper lip. The car, of course, was always there, so we soon found ways of getting our own back by loitering along the roadside to pick wildflowers, examine hollow trees and look for lizards, little realising that this is exactly what Father had in mind.

As a means of keeping me occupied on long journeys, I was given a mouth organ. It played in C major on one side and D major on the other, and it was sometimes possible to play accidentals by rotating the thing very rapidly and hoping to land on the right note. (With Larry Adler in mind as a role model, Mother once took Margaret and me to the mouth organ competitions in the Alfred Hall.)

Mother was given a book, *Wildfowers of Australia*, by the happily named Thistle Y. Harris. If the author was agreeably named, so too were some of the flowers she had painted and which we found by the roadside – Egg and Bacon, Running Postman, Prickly Moses, Blue Devil. It was often necessary to stop the car, while crossing the Great Divide, to gaze at the golden wattles close up and to drown in their sweet, peppery scent. I think Father's favourite plants were the great river red gums, some of which were as much landmarks to him as the mountains or the buildings which he passed.

WHAT BIRD IS THAT?

One of Father's inspired presents was Neville Cayley's *What Bird is That?*, which he gave me for my eleventh birthday. The book was the first thing to go into the car before journeys and it kept me occupied for hours. Birds added another dimension to the landscape. There were brolgas near Lake Bolac and avocets near Kaniva, if we were lucky. Pairs of mountain duck patrolled the dams on the plains around the Grampians, while flights of galahs and cockatoos wheeled against the backdrop of the blue peaks. Flying-boat formations of pelicans lumbered down to settle on the lakes, painted parrots streaked through the grey gums, and fences were festooned with the corpses of wedge-tailed eagles, killed by farmers when they preyed on newborn lambs. The surviving eagles cruised in the stratosphere overhead.

When nothing much was flying by outside, I pored over the book and absorbed the nomenclature of the bird kingdom, a rich collection of nouns and adjectives, descriptive, whimsical and poetic. There were families of babblers, chats and knots, of stilts, stints and crakes, weebills and pardalotes, rails and quails and terns, godwits and ruddy turnstones, tawny frogmouths and spangled drongoes. They were not merely red, white or blue; their colours moved beyond those of the spectrum to those of poetry – roseate, leaden, pearly, pied, dusky, pallid, sooty, rufous and buff. In shape they were needle-tailed, long-toed, spoon-billed, spur-winged; in character noisy, garrulous, sad, shy, laughing, even sordid. Word combinations were almost limitless – lavender-flanked, lilac-crowned, little-yellow-spotted, lesser-black-backed, greater-chestnut-rumped ... it was only a short step to parody, inventing terms of friendly abuse like 'You great purple-bellied flat foot'.

But as well as the birds, there was always something interesting to look at from the car. Mighty thatched haystacks, like ships at anchor in the paddocks, were rural works of art or architecture, created by men with pitchforks tossing hay from waggons drawn by Clydesdales. Teams of these noble horses pulled ploughs in the winter, drawing patterns across the land. Winding creek beds were outlined by basket willows, pink in late winter, yellow in autumn, while wind-breaks of black pines or sugar gums marched along the boundary fences. We met swagmen plodding along the roads. If there were floods I was sometimes put out in my gumboots to wade ahead of the car, checking for washaways. Once in the Little Desert we met a travelling circus moving along, the elephants swinging grandly down the middle of the road among the Mallee scrub, and there were always the normal animals of the countryside to look at – hundreds of white lambs, curly red bulls, or gaggles of matronly geese on the dams below the whirling windmills.

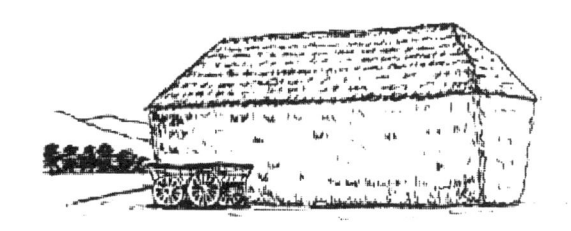

BOUND FOR SOUTH AUSTRALIA!

Marmie was our one surviving grandparent, so when we moved to Ballarat in 1936 it was inevitable that summer holidays would be spent in Adelaide, where she lived. She was then about seventy and she seemed extremely old to me. She wore black or dark colours, she walked with a stick and she rested a lot. I don't remember her as a very cuddly sort of granny, as she was reserved and dignified – but old ladies seemed to be like that in those days and most of them were rather alarming, I thought.

These holidays gave Father the chance to introduce us to the haunts of his youth and the beautiful beach at Brighton. Marmie lived in an extraordinary Spanish Mission house with marzipan walls and curly red roof tiles, and the front garden featured large, prickly cacti alongside a bouncy buffalo-grass lawn. There was never any question of us staying with Marmie; her house wasn't large enough, and in addition she was always referred to as 'delicate'. Instead, she found neighbours of hers who were willing to rent out their houses to us for the summer. One of these was directly opposite Marmie's. It was a sort of Californian bungalow, but I remember it chiefly for the pianola in the front parlour and a generous supply of piano rolls which the owner had left for us. I had a magical time 'playing' Liszt, Offenbach, Strauss and music hall medleys, watching the keys twinkle up and down as I pedalled hard below. This instrument left the harmonium for dead! Marmie had a pianola, too, which Dorothy was allowed to play more circumspectly. Another house which we rented was several blocks from Marmie but still close to the beach. This was the house in which we endured Black Friday and the preceding heatwave.

222   Beside the Lake

It took two days to drive to Adelaide. The last part of the journey through the Adelaide Hills was very slow, so Father never attempted to go through in one day. We would stay overnight in a hotel in one of the little towns between Bordertown and Murray Bridge. Murray Bridge was the preferred destination because it was closest to journey's end, and it also had the exciting features of the mighty Murray River with its two big bridges. Once we stayed at Tailem Bend and the hotel there was ever after dubbed 'Slum Alley' by Father, because he was up most of the night dealing with bed bugs in unwashed sheets.

Travelling across a state border was like entering a foreign land. From Kaniva I would be on the lookout for the sign saying 'South Australian Border', with its various stern warnings about grape vines and fruit. Having crossed that invisible line, we then solemnly wound watches back half an hour and magically lived through that thirty minutes of time all over again. After the war broke out, interstate travel was very restricted, but we had at least one more trip to Adelaide because Father was able to get a permit on compassionate grounds to visit his elderly mother. At Bordertown we had to call at the police station to have this pink permit stamped and I was very apprehensive in case the policeman wouldn't let us through. But he did.

The green Chev at the South Australian border post. The car in SA is half an hour behind the trailer in Victoria.

South Australia was different. The road changed colour and stretches of it were still unsealed. Houses were built of stone. There was a 'desert' to negotiate. Brand names were unfamiliar; instead of Peters' we ate Amscol or Alaska icecream. The apples and pears of Ballarat were replaced by the luscious stone fruits of a hot climate. In Adelaide most gardens had their own fruit trees, nectarines, peaches, apricots, grapes, fat plums, and we ate them off the tree, warm and oozy and bursting with flavour. There were vineyards in the suburbs and avenues of almond trees.

The wide beach at Brighton was perfect for small children. There was a 'cockle bank' (sandbank) some way out, creating a warm shallow lagoon for paddling. Father liked swimming, so he would take us into the deeper water. Our bathers were woollen; they sagged and chafed when wet and took ages to dry. We had to wait until after the war for someone to invent cotton swimsuits and later still for lycra and synthetics. We had metal buckets and wooden spades, because there was no plastic. Mother never swam and hated the sun, so she rarely went to the beach.

Mostly I begrudged time spent away from it, but there were certain ritual expeditions which took place on cooler days or in the evening: visits to the Zoo and the Museum in the city centre; a night visit to Belair to see the Lights of Adelaide spread out below like a vast jewel box, this often combined with a stop near the Belair railway gates to watch the Melbourne Express steam through, belching smoke after its long toil up the foothills. Further into the hills, the National Park provided a cricket pitch where we could lash out at our tennis ball, sometimes recruiting other picnickers as fielders. To enter the park we had to go through a gate. This was opened for us by one of the children who lived in the gatehouse, and Father would supply me with two pennies to toss to this infant through the car window, which made me feel like a noblewoman in her carriage. (Georgette Heyer and Baroness Orczy filled their young readers with romantic notions about the aristocracy!)

Marmie's younger sister Florence also lived in Brighton – our Great-Auntie Flo, donor of the croquet set, the game of 'Chook Chook' and similar in name to the Antiflo poultice. While Marmie was quiet and dignified, her three offspring were hilarious and gales of mirth were common when they were gathered together. Uncle Hal took pleasure in using words like 'cantharides' or names like 'Clutterbuck', and Auntie Dod and Father were similarly effervescent. It is tempting to think that this strain of hilarity came from their Irish father, Sam. However,

Marmie's sister Flo was also prone to bouts of helpless mirth; she would go puce in the face and become breathless with laughing, so maybe there was a hilarious streak in that side of the family, too. It certainly showed up in all of us. There were times in Ballarat, especially when some of the relations were staying with us, when we all laughed so much that we had to go and lie down.

'Lying down' (not because of laughing) was something which Marmie and the aunts and Mother did at regular intervals, usually after lunch. This was a sacrosanct time and one didn't visit at that hour. Lying down and rests had something to do with being 'delicate' or having a 'weak heart' it seemed, but they all lived to a ripe old age, nevertheless. Marmie was the youngest to go at seventy-seven! I took all this lying about for granted at the time, but I now suspect that having a rest behind closed doors gave them a chance to ease off their corsets for a while. What a trial it must have been to wear such things even in summer, as well as thick stockings and uncomfortable shoes, but I find it impossible to imagine any of those women wearing joggers, socks, jeans or track pants, as many of their age group do today.

Marmie's house – Spanish marzipan

When Marmie died in 1944, travel was so difficult that Father was the only one from Victoria who went, by train, to Brighton for her funeral. The rest of us hadn't seen her for three years, because of the war. During those years, Father arranged his time table so that his rural rides to the southwest of Victoria were scheduled for January. Our summer holidays in wartime were spent at Portland.

PORTLAND

On our first visit to Portland we stayed at the Clergy Rest House, a rather gloomy residence on a large block, overshadowed on all sides by cypress trees. The very name was redolent of a convalescent home, but while the place might have offered the clergy some rest, I doubt if it did the same for their wives. When we stayed there again after the war, Margaret came with us and she and I had hilarious fun encountering the eccentricities common to holiday houses in those days – curtains which fell down on your head, bedsprings which barked in the night, taps which coughed, sighed and gave up the ghost.

Father took us surfing on the fine beach below the bluff, whisking Elizabeth over the bigger waves when they threatened to swamp her. This new form of swimming (quite unlike the creepy pool at Creswick) was so exhilarating that I had to be dragged home, blue, water-logged and protesting through chattering teeth. The immensely long deep-water pier was so massive that, when I walked on it, I began to lose my post-Macquarie fear of the sight of green water through the gaps.

It was possible to reach Portland in one day from Ballarat, but even so the trip seemed endless. A trunk of bed linen, towels, extra clothing and shoes was sent ahead by rail, but the car was still heavily loaded down with five or six people, suitcases, garden produce, Florrie's cakes and biscuits, buckets and spades and so forth. A perennial packing problem was Mother's hat-box, a cylindrical, blue suitcase which took up an inordinate amount of space. But hats were de rigeur for church, especially for the bishop's wife, and the hat-box had to go. Father owned

Portland, towards the massive pier.
We surfed beyond the bluff.

a genuine pith helmet, which he occasionally wore in summer, so that also went into the box. I don't recall much in the way of beach hats, despite Mother's fear of the sun. I usually had a peeling nose and freckles.

The route along the Glenelg Highway became very familiar as we crawled towards that glorious moment when, emerging from a thick belt of bush, we had our first sight of dark blue ocean.

Portland, I discovered, was even older than Ballarat. In 1834, several years before the Yuilles and their sheep came to the Ballarat swamp, the Hentys had sailed into Portland Bay with their livestock and supplies. They had put up fences, dug a garden and built the first permanent house in what is now the State of Victoria. Before their arrival, sealers and whalers had been active along the shore. Portland was settled from the sea and Major Mitchell, who happened to be passing that way in 1836, was astonished to find a flourishing pastoral settlement and a whaling industry on the southern coastline. Instead of passing through, the Surveyor-General (it is said) sat down on the Hentys' verandah and watched an exciting whale hunt in the bay.

In Portland the magnetic pull was always towards the sea. The bay was like an amphitheatre from Battery Point around to the lighthouse bluff and away beyond to the east, and one's gaze was constantly drawn seawards, as if there were a folk memory of lookouts posted on the headlands, scanning the bay for a sudden arrival of the whales, and of spectators rushing to cliff-top or verandah to watch the launching of the whaleboats from the beach and the wild, dangerous chases over the water after the huge, plunging creatures. It was not very difficult to imagine such scenes in the early 1940s, for the main harbour installations had not yet been built, and the surf rolled in on the town beaches, unhampered by any giant breakwaters. The town was deeply rooted in colonial history, and the legacy of its pioneers and seafarers was visible in bluestone buildings, Victorian Botanical Gardens, giant Norfolk Island pines along the seafront and the old, wind-sculptured cypresses around the squat lighthouse. It was a plain, solid, no-nonsense place.

After that first visit to the Clergy Rest House, we thereafter rented a small weatherboard cottage called St Ives on the cliff-top in the curve of the bay – this because Father didn't want to deprive other clergy of their rest. St Ives was one of a straggle of cottages out of town, towards the Dutton Way – but the magnetism was the same, even stronger. Only a road separated St Ives from the grassy cliff-edge and the sea.

In Newcastle, the ocean lay to the east. Here, at Portland, it lay to the south and I had to learn a whole new orientation. There was no land mass between our clifftop and Antarctica, although on the horizon to the southeast floated Lady Julia Percy Island, sometimes pale and remote, more often looming deep blue. She was coffin-shaped, long and low, and as alluring as our volcanoes at home. From our cliff-top we soaked up the view of dark ocean-blues and white crests, fishing boats, schools of glistening porpoises, and the white gannets patrolling above the bay and hurling themselves like Stuka dive-bombers on to the fish below. We trained Father's binoculars on the plummeting, plundering gannets; at night came the winking flashes of lighthouses along the coast, but we never saw a whale. There were hardly any left to be seen.

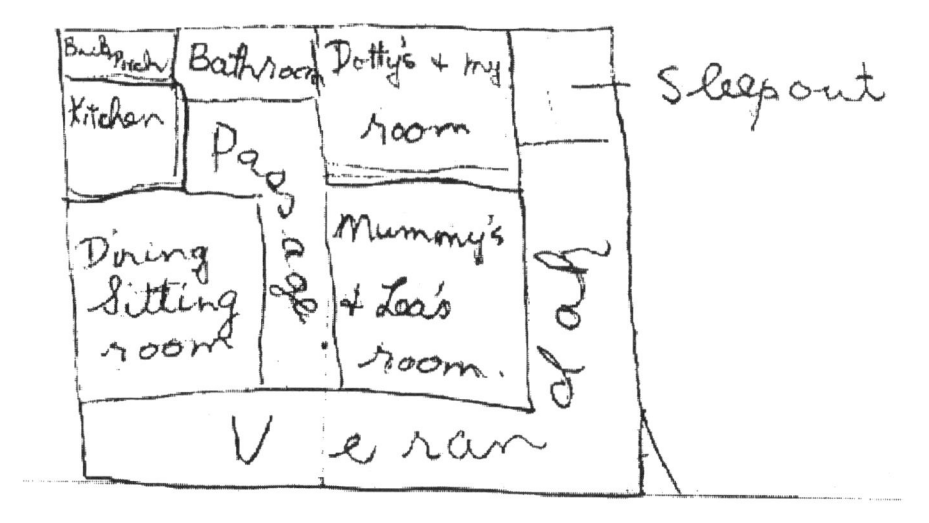

From LM 1942. Plan of St Ives. Daddy also squeezed in with Mummy and Lea.

After the sprawl of the two Bishopscourts, the cottage seemed, and was, confined. I drew a plan of it in one of my letters to Margaret, but memories of its interior are dim as most of my interests lay outside its walls. There was no electricity. Some features still swim into focus, like the tall kerosene lamps under which we played cards and Consequences at night; the outside privy and attendant 'nightman'; the sleepout where we children could sleep close to the wind and boom of the ocean; a miasma of summery holiday smells – of flyspray, kerosene and 'metho', of fragrant pink Q-Tol smeared on our burning skins and calamine lotion blotted on bites and stings, of Phenyle and carbolic soap to counter the lack of 'deep drainage' (as the adults referred to sewerage), of pine-cone smoke from the chip bath-heater and the wood stove, and of the pervasive aroma from the meatworks whenever the wind blew from inland. We groaned about the smelly meatworks, not realising that when the whaling industry was in full swing on the foreshore the smells were probably a good deal worse.

Elizabeth and I had been reared on the urban 'deep drainage' system, as it were, so the 'nightman' and his calling were of great interest to us. He was fascinating because he was never seen and rarely heard; he did indeed call mysteriously and discreetly at night, and only next morning did we confirm that he had been and changed the can. For one whose trade was so earthbound, he was invested with a strangely spectral quality.

At school, one of the choir's most celebrated items was a song called, I think, 'The Nightbells', and the first line of this burst forth as: 'Hark!! I hear the nightbells ringing ... '. It was a simple matter for us to parody this by altering a few words and by substituting 'man' for 'bells'. The rest followed naturally:

... Gaily dancing through the gloaming,
Softly with the winds a-roaming,
Ca-an i-it be-e the Nightman singing,
Singing cheerily?

We performed this often and lustily and the family enjoyed the joke, but Mother was always anxiously poised to suppress us if we showed signs of singing it in public. We hummed a few bars in awkward situations to test her nerve.

Can it be the Nightman, coming again?
Can it be the Nightman, pulling the chain?
Pull-ing mourn-n-full-ee?
(Back to A) HARK! I hear the Nightman singing ...

There was no chain in the privy, of course, but we allowed ourselves a little poetic licence because it rhymed.

Red clay cliffs plunged down to the beach below the cottage. A neighbouring fisherman had cut steep steps down to his boatshed below, and we (not Mother) tackled these several times a day. On the white beach, Father set us to run races in case the cliff climb should leave any vestige of unspent energy, which was not welcome in the tiny cottage. We swam in clear green channels of water between darker, more sinister expanses. From the cliff-top, Dorothy once watched a stingray emerge from the seaweed, cruise around us as we frolicked and then swim lazily off. She told us about it at lunch.

'Our' beach at Portland. Elizabeth surveys the Southern Ocean (left) and samples it (right).

Strange flotsam came ashore – the seahorse which was to adorn my shelf, bird skeletons and pieces of whalebone. There had been a few lucky finds of ambergris in the region, so we investigated all strange brown lumps in the hope of making a fortune, just as we kept watch for gold nuggets at home. The beach was nearly always deserted, such was its distance from town and its steep descent, but sometimes round the headland tripped a party of nuns from the local convent, holidaying, bare-footed nuns, as close to frisky as nuns could be. Elizabeth and I were agog to see them lift the hems of their habits and paddle at the water's edge. We looked for them as you watch for a party of rare water birds, moving carefully around rocks and headlands so as not to disturb them. They would perhaps have been surprised to know that our companion was a bare-footed bishop.

The vicar of Portland was Canon Coupe, an aged Yorkshireman and also an ardent angler. He and Father sometimes managed to set off like truant schoolboys into the backwoods, where the Canon knew all the best streams. One day he piloted us all to an ancient, crumbling ruin called The Woolwash, near the Surrey River. A dim little creek drifted silently below dense, over-arching bush, and here the Canon directed us to fish. We would be catching toupon and gudgeon, he informed us, delicious morsels like large sardines. We spaced ourselves along the bank and the warm, drowsy hush was broken only by the sounds of slapping as we fought off the giant mosquitoes, or the plop of sinkers in the black, velvety water, or our gasps as kingfishers zipped along the stream. Our lines snagged in the overhead thickets, and after a time the Canon moved further away along the bank. 'I'm moving out of earshot, my Lord,' he explained to Father in passing, 'so that the lassies won't be contaminated by my language.' The fish bit well and we had toupon and gudgeon for tea. The Canon caught more than anyone else.

We collected our mail from the Portland Post Office, and I liked to go with Father in case there was a fat letter from Margaret. The Postmaster was the genial Mr Carthew who conducted us to his back garden to meet the kookaburras, cats and the fairy penguin who lived together in perfect amity. Also present, in a convalescent state, was a stone curlew which Mr Carthew was caring for before returning it to the wild. It was beginning to learn from the kookaburras that life in the Postmaster's garden was a whole lot easier than the hurly-burly of the swamp. Elizabeth fell for this mournful bird with the golden eyes. 'Oh,' she sighed, on arriving home to Mother, 'Mr Curlew has such a lovely little carthew!'

It was near Portland that I broke my arm (by falling off a horse) and had to lie about in a cumbersome splint, thereby missing two unexpected episodes. The first was a rescue. On a wild, southerly day we were the first to hear eerie shouts for help and to sight two men clinging to a capsized canoe out on the bay. The family summoned the fisherman, helped him to launch his boat, and took blankets and thermoses to the beach to revive the victims when they were brought ashore. At about the same time, the squalls drove tons of seaweed and flotsam onto the beaches and then it was that the legendary paper nautilis shells 'came in'. I had to stay indoors while everyone else hunted feverishly for these fragile shells; between them they found only one perfect specimen, which sat in Mother's china cabinet for many years thereafter. I felt sure that I could have found more.

Portland then somehow reminded me of Cornwall, where, of course, I had never been. Images of the old world were strangely overlaid on those of the new. How could that be? I suppose I had a vision of Cornwall from stories of smugglers and wreckers which I read in schoolgirl annuals, stories full of sandy coves, Atlantic gales and plain stone cottages. Our rented cottage was called St Ives, probably as a reminder of that Cornish seaside town, and certainly, as I later confirmed, the gorse flowered on the Portland cliffs as brightly as it flowered about Tintagel, and the skylarks sang as loudly there as those above the estuary at Padstow.

CHRISTMAS

At Christmas and Easter, Mother picked suitable blooms from our garden and delivered them to the Cathedral. White and blue were the favoured colours and with any luck there would be several giant delphiniums to pick ('fell' would be a more accurate word), together with Canterbury bells, hydrangeas, Christmas lilies and armfuls of shasta daisies to fill in the gaps. Entering church on Christmas morning we were swept up in the scent of lilies, and among the huge sprays and fantails of flowers I would try to identify those blooms which, until yesterday, had stood in our own flower-beds at home.

Two seductive smells marked the Christmas season, that of the lilies and the resinous scent of the Christmas tree in our front hall. This 'tree' was always composed of cypress branches which Father would help us to cut and arrange in a box weighted down with bricks. We decorated our tree and the hall with chains of home-made streamers and a few paper lanterns, hoarded from year to year. Glass balls and fairy lights were not available in wartime, and even in peacetime too expensive for us, although by the time he had grandchildren Father felt able to afford some fairy lights.

All available surfaces in the front rooms were laden with the Christmas cards which had been arriving in shoals for weeks beforehand. Despatching our own cards was an extensive operation, and when I was competent enough I was allowed to address the envelopes and to make lists of the recipients for the following year. As many of these were dignitaries of church or state, I absorbed useful information about ranks and titles. There were all the reverends – Most (archbishops), Right (bishops), Very (deans) and plain Rev (vicars etc.), as well as the Venerables (archdeacons), and some of them had a Dr tacked on as well. There were one or two His Excellencies (governors) and His Worships (mayors), and in wartime the Colonels, Wing-Commanders and other ranks, in addition to a certain number of Esquires and a large Mr & Mrs collection. Exciting parcels from aunts arrived by mail, too, and were piled under the tree.

Our Christmas Day routine was well ordered. We would attend early church at eight, then come home to a morning of dinner preparation, while Father went to more services. As the morning wore on, Mother and Dorothy supervised the roasting birds while Elizabeth and I fed the survivors. Florrie had holidays, of course, but she had killed and dressed the poultry and made the pudding in advance. We boiled up threepenny bits and buried them in the pudding, helped to make the bread sauce and the custard and to set the festive table, but the presents remained wrapped beneath the tree until well on in the afternoon, for we had to wait until Father was home and dinner was finished before the opening ceremony. It was fun to spin out the excitement and I felt rather sorry for those who had opened everything in bed at six in the morning. As the aroma of roasting poultry and minted peas swirled through the house, we turned on the wireless to hear the ethereal choir of St Paul's Cathedral in distant Melbourne singing the favourite hymns and carols, under the direction of their legendary organist and choirmaster Dr. A.E. Floyd.

On Christmas night we would sometimes hear the live broadcast from the Melbourne Town Hall of Handel's 'Messiah'. This was one of the few substantial musical events we experienced in those days and the only oratorio I ever heard in full, with an orchestra. Church choirs sometimes performed Stainer's 'Crucifixion' or Maunder's 'Olivet to Calvary', but 'Messiah', crackling over the air waves, was in a class of its own.

The End of Childhood

V FOR VICTORY

On 15 August 1945, Father was walking down Sturt Street when he met a man hurrying from the butcher's shop. The man shook his head and gasped, 'They've gone wild in there – they're all kissing one another!' Father, who had of course been listening to the wireless, was able to assure him that the butcher was not conducting orgies amongst the oyster-blade but that the Japanese had surrendered unconditionally and the war was over. The end came suddenly.

BC 16.8.45

At school, we had only just finished one assembly when we were summoned back for another, and the Headmistress, Miss King, announced that the war was at an end and that the Prime Minister, Mr Chifley, had proclaimed a two-day holiday throughout the nation. Assembly broke into the same sort of uproar that was evidently taking place in the butcher's shop and right across the land. Sixth formers and teachers wept, we younger ones shouted. This was the end of another era and I was fourteen.

Later we went into the city to celebrate. Father addressed a Citizens' Service of Thanksgiving at the Alfred Hall, which he described thus in the Church Chronicle (August 1945):

'Every seat was occupied, whilst hundreds stood in the aisles and in the porches and entrances. The service was relayed by means of loud speakers to the immense crowd outside. The singing was led by the Ballarat Choral Society, whose rendering of the Hallelujah Chorus was most stirring. It was a service that none of us will forget.'

The Ballarat Courier (16.8.'45) took up the story:

'In what was probably one of the most stirring scenes in Ballarat's history, thousands of community singers were in front of the City Hall yesterday afternoon. The gathering came as a grand climax to the thanksgiving service, at the close of which returned soldiers, many of them proudly wearing their medals, marched from the Alfred Hall to the City Hall through a dense crowd of spectators. Ballarat's brass bands and pipe bands took part. A spirit of revelry had taken hold of the crowd, and probably Sturt Street has never heard more lusty or spontaneous singing than that in front of the City Hall, which followed. With intense fervour the great gathering sang favourite wartime airs from the first and second world wars, reserving special enthusiasm for 'Pack up your Troubles', and 'There'll always be an England', while the (musical) barrel was rolled out more than once.'

Father took Elizabeth and me back to the street celebrations later in the day. Elizabeth was then aged almost ten and was greatly enjoying herself until a somewhat unsteady youth seized her round the waist and kissed her passionately. She escaped from his clutches and we went home.

When the war ended, Dorothy was working in the Red Cross with sick and wounded servicemen, and she and her colleagues took part in a later Victory March on the back of an army truck, tending to a 'patient' in bed as a sort of tableau. Later still she joined a Red Cross contingent for a victory march through the city of Melbourne.

The release of tension was enormous. Despite the euphoria which followed D-Day in June 1944, when, in another thrilling episode, the Allied armies landed in Normandy to begin the liberation of Northern Europe, the fight had slogged on for over another year. Films had become more honest in depicting the destructive horrors of war, even the firestorm bombing by the Allies of German cities like Dresden, and when the first newsreel footage of Belsen and the other concentration camps was shown in our cinemas, it was hard to believe that this was the same scenario as that of the sanitised 'Mrs Miniver' and the earlier censored newsreels. Berlin was reduced to rubble, Iwo Jima deep in corpses and Hiroshima erased before the Axis powers would surrender. The end was something like Armageddon.

Winning back the islands of the Pacific (BC 16.8.45)

Although the war was over, Austerity continued for years. Dorothy became engaged to Fred, who had been a POW in Germany. (To our excitement, he had actually seen the beastly Heinrich Himmler!) They were married in the chapel at Bishopscourt two years after VP Day, but wedding preparations were severely restricted by shortages and rationing. Florrie more or less 'grew' the entire wedding breakfast – the ducks and vegetables, and eggs for the desserts – and fresh cream came into circulation again just in time, and a supply was sent in from the country. Dorothy wore Mother's wedding dress, while I, as bridesmaid, was garbed in rather peculiar taffeta curtain material which required no coupons. Elizabeth's dress, recycled from an earlier generation, was so old and fragile that she had to behave with unusual restraint.

The end of the war was really the end of my childhood. During my fifteen years of life, the world had moved with appalling rapidity from the early days of wireless to the Nuclear Age, although in 1945 when the Bomb was dropped on Hiroshima, few ordinary people grasped the implications of nuclear power.

Later that year, 1945, I sat for my first public exams (the Intermediate Certificate, now Year 10) on the bentwood chairs in the City Hall. I used my first fountain pen, the acquisition of which, like one's first watch, was a rite of passage. We had dancing classes after school, which led to school dances and (at last) boys! Careers for girls were being taken more seriously since women had proved themselves capable of almost anything during the two wars. They had driven trucks, made armaments, been taken prisoner, worked on farms, kept the economy going. I was drifting towards science, which meant I had to pedal over three kilometres to the Boys' Grammar School and back each day for Physics and Chemistry lessons, as our school had no senior science teacher, but after a year of that I drifted back to the humanities. In 1945 we began sharing a senior English teacher with Clarendon PLC; Miss Bishop opened up the world of literature to us and our enclosed school life also opened up through these contacts with other schools. Such enlarged classes were really a godsend, as there were only four in my Matriculation year at Queens.

As each of us in turn faced the prospect of leaving home and going to study in Melbourne, we became aware of sinister perils which awaited us there. The only drugs we heard about were to be found in Chinese 'opium dens'. There were hushed references to the 'White Slave Trade'; in one ladies' Rest Room in particular we would be at risk, it was said, of being drugged and carried off – who knew where? The term 'White Slave Trade' suggested to me some Middle Eastern destination, amid date palms. We were still relatively innocent and innocence died hard. Dorothy had already survived these hazards, but for me they were still ahead.

When Dorothy married in 1947, I moved into her bedroom on the other side of the swing door. I was then sixteen. In 1949 I went to study in Melbourne, having matriculated twice. The first time I was just seventeen, and it was felt that I was too young for university, so I repeated Year 12 – luckily the syllabus had changed! Elizabeth followed me to Melbourne a few years later. Florrie retired and our parents were often left to themselves in that large house and garden.

Bishopscourt amongst its trees

EPILOGUE

Elizabeth and I were both overseas when Father died unexpectedly in 1960. He had reached the appropriate biblical age of threescore years and ten and he died 'in harness', as the media put it, although he had planned to retire later that year. He and Mother were both worn out and should have laid their harness aside long before.

Several years later, the second Bishopscourt was sold for institutional use. It was too large and unmanageable for our successors and a third house was built for them on the far side of the lake, not far from where the first one had been.

The second house still stands in Sturt Street, but for me it is now no more than a ghostly shell. Suburban houses are well established on the tennis court, the paddock and the Old Ladies' wilderness. The chapel has been gutted and its fittings dispersed. There are no more geese, cows and ducks, trees have been axed, Mother's special flower beds are no more.

I have no wish to revisit my former home, and no need, for I still carry with me an inner map of that house and garden. My ageing muscles still recognise the stairs I bounded up and down, the exact spacing of the steps, the twirl around the landings. I can still bounce on the old couch in the hall after falling off the window sill with Margaret. In the dusk 'The Holy City' resounds from the White bathroom. My arms and legs recall the athletic swing up into the silky oak. My nose inhales the perfume of sweet peas growing against the chapel wall or of the large daphne bush near the front porch. There is Florrie in her pale green overall, spade in hand, heading purposefully towards the potato patch. Elizabeth is halfway up the belfry watching Mother pick red roses. Popeye waits for me at the gate, the canaries are in full chorus and Cocky enquires, 'Where's the bishop?'

Bibliography

Most of the material in this book has been drawn from my own memory or from family memorabilia and records. As I haven't lived in Ballarat for forty years, my memories of that earlier time have remained relatively unaffected by more recent changes and developments to the city and region.

However, some aids to memory have been helpful and certain facts needed to be checked. I acknowledge the following sources for factual information, for quotations as cited, and for pictorial reminders of places and architecture which have aided me with some of my sketches.

Weston Bate: *Lucky City* (MUP, 1978)
——*Life After Gold* (MUP, 1993)
Jan Clarke, Margaret Cochran & Edward Heffernan: *Sovereign City – A Ballarat Tapestry* (Ballarat & Queens Grammar School Parents & Friends' Association, 1974)
Gray, Jenkins & McEvoy: *Latin For Today (First Course)* (Ginn, 1932)
Graham Hawley & John Béchervaise: *Ballarat Sketchbook* (Rigby, 1977)
Home From Dunkirk: Introduction by J.B. Priestley (John Murray, 1940)
W. Jacobs, N. Lewis, E. Vines & R. Aitken: *Ballarat, A Guide to Buildings & Areas 1851 – 1940* (Authors & City of Ballarat, 1981)
John Reid, John Chisholm & Max Harris: *Ballarat – Golden City, A Pictorial History* (Joval, 1989)
T.J.S. Rowland: *Living Things for Lively Youngsters* (Cassell, 1939)
W.C. Sellar & R.J. Yeatman: *1066 And All That* (25th ed. Methuen, 1937)
John Spooner: *The Golden See* (The Anglican Diocese of Ballarat, 1989)
Susanne L. White: *Mainly About Girls – A History of Queen's, Ballarat 1876 – 1972* (Ashwood House, 1990)
Neil Yeates: *Stone on Stone – A Pioneer Family Saga* (Neil Yeates, 1979)

The Church Chronicle for the Diocese of Ballarat, various issues
The Ballarat Courier

Mainly About Girls (School magazine for Queen's CEGGS)
Official Guide to South Street Competitions, 1941

F.D. Johnson: 'Once Upon a Time' (unpublished memoir, 1974)
Unpublished letters of D.M. Thorburn to F.D. Johnson – in possession of the author
Unpublished childhood letters of the author to M. Wilson – in possession of the author

Conversion Tables

Imperial measures were in use in my childhood and have been used in the text. Approximate metric equivalents are as follows:
12 inches = 1 foot = 30.5 cm
1 yard = 3 feet = 91.5 cm
1 mile = 1.61 km
1 acre = 0.405 ha
1 ounce = 31 g
16 ounces = 1 pound = 500 g
2 pounds = 1 kg
1 ton = 0.9 tonne
1 gallon = 2 quarts = 8 pints
1 pint = 0.57 litre
1 gallon = 4.55 litres

Money
£.s.d – 1 pound (£) = 20 shillings (s); 1s = 12 pennies (d)
When Australia changed to decimal currency in 1966: £1 became $2; 10/- (s) became $1; 1/- became 10 cents; 1d became approx. 1 cent

Note: At school we learned tables including now arcane measures such as rods, poles or perches; roods; chains, links and furlongs; bushels and pecks; quarters and hundredweights. These I will not pursue here, except to say that one chain, or 22 yards, is the length of a cricket pitch. There is no equally convenient metric equivalent, which is also true when it comes to measuring the height of a person – cf. 6 feet with 182.9 cm.

Illustrations

In my early childhood, Father owned a Kodak folding camera and the family album was kept reasonably up to date until after Elizabeth was born. There are some early photos taken at Old Bishopscourt, but then follow disappointingly empty pages which can be explained by a marked decrease in leisure time and by the war, when film was scarce or unobtainable.

I took up photography when I was about fifteen. Father let me use the old camera, which was loaded with cumbersome, pink-backed, eight-frame film. Then, in the 1950s, Father was swept up by the rage for 35mm colour photography with its attendant slide evenings. He loved photographing the countryside on his rural rides and some of his shots are included here. I acquired a camera of my own at that time, and most of the photos of the lake, including the cover picture, were taken then. Although these were taken slightly later than the period I have written about, the subject matter had changed very little. All photos not taken by the family and illustrations from other sources are acknowledged as follows:
Sovereign Hill Gold Museum (SHGM), postcard, page 19
Diocese of Ballarat Archives (DBA), pages 24, 34
Rev. C.F. Eggleton (CFE), pages 22, 53, 83, 89
Mainly About Girls (MAG), School Magazine, pages 60, 62.
Official school photo, page 164

From books, journals, newspapers, etc.
The *Ballarat Courier* (BC), pages 87, 90, 233, 235
The *Ballarat Church Chronicle* (BCC), page 142
The Melbourne *Herald* (MH), page 147
Latin for Today, Gray, Jenkins & McEvoy (Ginn 1932), page 172
Living Things for Lively Youngsters, T.J.S. Rowland (Cassell 1939), page 126
Home from Dunkirk, (John Murray 1940), page 109
South Street Competitions Official Guide (1941), page157

From letters
Letters from Aunt Dorothy, Mrs D. Thorburn (LDT), pages 108, 111, 149
Letters to Margaret 1940-46 (LM), pages 116, 123, 179, 196, 198, 201, 227

All other sketches, decorations and maps I have prepared recently for the purposes of this book.

Index

ABC Children's Session 114, 174-5
Abdication 79
Abrams, Fanny 163
Adelaide, SA 8, 12, 13, 17, 82, 84, 221-4
Ah Hung (greengrocer) 186, 207
Alfred Bells (Town Hall) 80
Alfred Hall 67, 74, 80, 157, 219, 234
Alfred, Prince 80, 157
American soldiers 140-3
Angels 91
Argonauts Club 175
Ark Royal, HMS 140
Askgar's Pie Shop 195
Avenue of Honour 49, 81, 161

Ballarat 48-50, 74-5
   Alexandria Tearooms 54
   Alfred Hall q.v.
   Arch of Victory 161
   Art Gallery 159
   Avenue of Honour q.v.
   Baptist Church 162
   Bishops Palace (RC) 162
   Black Hill 75
   Bluebell Hotel 41
   Botanical Gardens q.v.
   The Boulevarde 84
   Bridge St 19, 154
   Chapter House 155
   Chinese Joss House 77, 155
   Christ Church Cathedral 17, 100
   Church of the Little Flower 162
   Cinemas, *see* Picture Theatres

Ballarat (*cont'd*)
   Clarendon PLC 236
   Craig's Hotel 80, 156
   Dana St 155
   Emporia q.v.
   Eureka Stockade 75, 77
   Fairyland 42
   Gaol 156, 162
   Grove St 83, 90, 119, 137, 209
   Guncotton Factory 148
   Lake Wendouree q.v.
   Lindisfarne Ave 84
   Lydiard St 158-9
   Main St 75, 154
   Mair St 60
   Malthouse 138
   Modern Dairy 195
   Pleasant St State School 181
   Queen's CEGGS q.v.
   Railway Station 42, 148, 159
   St Aidan's Drive 84
   St Andrew's Kirk 102, 162
   St John of God Hospital 60
   St Matthew's Church 41
   St Paul's Church 154
   St Peter's Church 111
   Sebastopol 77
   Sovereign Hill 155
   Sturt St 19, 50, 80, 83, 88, 101, 140, 143, 161, 234
   Titanic Bandstand 77
   Town Hall (City Hall) 159, 166, 234, 236
   Victoria St 80, 154
   View Point 205
   Wattle Tearooms 52
   Wendouree 41, 42
   Wendouree Parade 20, 32,

Ballarat (*cont'd*)
   44, 57, 205
   Yarrowee Creek 154, 157
   Zoo 43
Ballarat Grammar School (Boys') 41, 79, 236
Bathtime 30, 95, 147, 191
Batty, Francis de Witt (Bishop) 81, 114
Best, Joseph (Archdeacon) 75
Beaumont, Florrie *see* Florrie
Bickersteth, Julian (Archdeacon) 39
Bicycles 33, 153
Birds 38, 44, 90, 122, 209, 216, 220, 227
Bishop, Edith 236
Bishopscourt, Sturt St (New)
   arrival 88
   description 88-99, 190
   austerity 116
   Pughole 116
   housework 127-30
   backyard 131, 133
   Americans 140-1
   ARP 146
   visitors 188-93
   illness 196
   rabbits 211
   Christmas 231-2
   departure 238
   see also Gardens, Chapel
Bishopscourt, Wendouree (Old)
   arrival 20
   description 22-4, 26-31
   servants 25-6
   move 83-4
   demolition 85

Index

see also Gardens, Chapel
'Black Friday' (1939) 82, 221
Blight, Mr 165
Boatraces 208
Book of Common Prayer 40, 102, 103
Books 70, 98, 175-8, see also Children's Books
Botanical Gardens 45-6, 49
  squirrels, 46
  statues 46, 47
  trees 46
Brazenor, the Misses 52
Brighton, SA 13, 221, 223
British Empire 80-1
Brooke, Rupert (poet) 193
Brown, Miss 156
Bruce, Mary Grant (author) 176, 177, 202
Buick, Miss (Boo) 8-9, 16, 64
Buninyong, Mount 47-8, 211, 212
Burrumbeet, Lake 49, 54
Button, C.N. (Rev. Dr) 102

Cabs (horse) 20, 142
Cannon (from HMAS *Cerberus*) 45
Carey, Clive and Doris (née Johnson, aunt) 81, 107, 168, 191-3
Cars 8, 12, 13, 17, 218
Carthew, Mr (Portland) 230
Cayley, Neville, *What Bird is That?* 220
Cellars 31, 93, 124
Chamberlain, Neville (British Prime Minister) 107
Chapel, Bishopscourt 38-9, 85, 88-9, 103, 127, 189, 235, 238
Charles, Father (SSM) 189
Chifley, Ben (Prime Minister) 234
Children's Books 9, 10, 65, 68, 70, 78, 81, 175-8, 187, 202, 207, 208, 223
Children's games, see Play
Children's parties 10-11, 52
Chooks 38, 117, 120-2
Christmas 231-2
Churchill, Sir Winston (British Prime Minister) 110, 112, 115
Churchgoing 5, 100-4, 231
Cinema, see Picture Theatres

Clarendon PLC 236
Clergy Rest House, Portland 225
Cooper, Robert (violinist) 66
Coronation (1937) 79
Coward, Noel 104
Coupe, Canon 229
Creswick 204
Cricket 175
Crimean War 77
Cudmore, Anniette (Aunt Nettie) 53

Davis, the Butcher 185
de Chair, Sir Dudley 14
de Chair, Ernest (grandfather) 14
Depression, The 7, 25, 150
Dingley Dell 212
Diocese of Ballarat 51, 84, 216-21
Divinity 69-70
Domestic Service 6-7, 25-6, 29-30, 92, 94, 96, 115-16
Domestic Staff
  Alexander, E. (Nursie) 92
  Brown, B. (Nursie) 92
  Doris 6, 17, 25, 26
  Florrie q.v.
  Jean 25, 31, 32, 92
  Lilian 25, 92
  Nellie 25
  Scruse 25, 35, 58, 85, 92, 94
  Stan 115, 135, 210-11
  Thelma 25, 92, 107
  Veta 5, 6, 26
Dorothy, Aunt see Thorburn, Dorothy
Dunkirk 109, 158

Easter 70
Eddy, Nelson (film star) 99, 158
Edward VIII 79, 161
Edwards' Hair Salon 185
Education, formal
  'Boo's' School 8-9
  Ballarat 21
  Grades I-II 60-3
  Grades III-V 63-6
  Middle school 163-8
  Upper school 236
  Art 66, 168
  Current Affairs 108

Drama 68, 155, 173
Eng. Lit. 171-3
Geography 167
Grammar 66, 172
Handwriting 8, 61, 64
History 76-8, 168
Languages 171-2
Latin 46, 74, 79, 171-2
Music 169
Poetry 173
Religious Instruction 5, 69-70, 101-2
Science 167-8
Spelling 9, 64
Sport 63, 167
Education, informal, see whole book
Empire Day, 24th May 79, 80
Emporia 155-6
Exams 65, 166, 236

Facts of life 125-6, 183
Fairbairn, Rene 149
Favourites' Club 134
Fisher, Geoffrey (Archbishop of Canterbury, later Lord Fisher) 189
Flags 143-4
Flight from Pompeii 47
Flo, Auntie see Stokes, Florence
Florrie (Beaumont) 116, 117-21, 124, 132, 141, 194, 200, 211, 212, 216, 225, 232, 236, 237
Food 5, 25, 58, 63, 70, 120, 188, 190, 193-5, 209, 211-12, 216, 223, 232, 236

Games, see Play
Gardens
  New Bishopscourt 88, 90, 118-20, 135-6, 231, 238
  Old Bishopscourt 23, 27, 32-6
  See also Botanical Gardens, Pleasure Gardens
George V 78
George VI and family 79-80
Gill's Boatshed 206
Girl Guides 212-13
Gold mining 75
Gone with the Wind 126, 171
Gordon, Adam Lindsay 43, 156

Graham, Dorothy (née Johnson, q.v.)
Graham, Frederick 207, 235
Grampians, The 218
Green, Arthur Vincent (Bishop) 24
Guns 33, 210
Guy Fawkes 77, 82

Harmonium 39
Head, Edith 188
Heating 28, 30, 31, 93-4, 116, 134-5, 165, 188
Henty family 226
Herbert's Grocery 185-6
Hiller, Ray 64
Holiday houses 221, 225, 226-8
Housework 6-7, 127-30
Hunt, Holman, *The Light of the World* 101
Hymns 68-9, 104-6, 111, 144

Illness 14, 51-2, 196-202
Illustrated London News 78, 109, 110, 112
Invergowrie Homecraft Hostel 139
Ironing 93, 129

James, G. (Dr) 198
Jenkin, Elma ('Jenks') 62-5, 70, 77, 101, 109, 146
Johnson, Dorothy (later Graham, sister)
  birth 17
  childhood 2-3, 7, 8, 16
  Ballarat 19, 20, et seq.
  marriage 235-6
Johnson, Elizabeth (later Wood, sister)
  birth 3, 16
  babyhood, 12, 16, 17, 21, 28, 29, 52
  childhood 92, 95, et seq.
Johnson, Frances Dymphna (née de Chair, mother)
  background 14-15, 53, 81, 108
  in Newcastle 6, 8, 10, 12
  official duties 19
  servants, housework 25-6, 93, 115-16, 127-9, 194
  at Old Bishopscourt 31, 38, 53, 84

as gardener 27, 45, 90, 135, 231
as mother 16-17, 33, 53, 66, 97-8, 103, 124, 125-6, 181-3, 197, 228
entertaining 131, 190-1
war 139, 140-1, 145, 151
shopping 156, 185, 215
Johnson, Harry (Uncle Hal) 20, 107
Johnson, Mabel (grandmother 'Marmie') 12, 46, 82, 191, 221, 223-4
Johnson, Mary (later Steele, author)
  birth 2, 16
  Newcastle 2 et seq.
  at Old Bishopscourt 19 et seq.
  starts school 60
  education, formal, q.v.
  at New Bishopscourt 88, et seq.
Johnson, Samuel (grandfather) 13, 223
Johnson, William Herbert (father)
  Dean of Newcastle 2
  background 13, 81
  as bishop 21, 51, 101-3
  Anglophile 81, 143
  travels 17-18, 51, 216-19, 222
  re Old Bishopscourt 83-4, 88
  War I 50, 77, 97
  War II 114, 140, 143, 145, 151, 153, 234
  as father 8, 10, 13, 17, 33, 127, 132, 182, 183, 209-12, 215, 216, 219, 220
  domestic duties, 29, 128
  recreation 210-12, 229-30
  humour 13, 163, 223
  death 238

King, Emily 171, 234
Kitchens 30, 96, 117
'Kongbool', Balmoral 216-17
Krome, Victoria 65, 68, 108, 171, 181

Lake Macquarie 8
Lake Wendouree 20, 203-9
  flood 32
  'Fairyland' 42

steamers 43, 206, 207
birds 44, 208
history 49, 204
cf. Lake Burrumbeet 55
tram route 57
leeches 204
walks 204-5
View Point 205
reeds 206
boats 206-7
boatraces 208
scenery 209
Lantern lectures 68-9
Larkins, Violet ('Larks') 72, 146
Laundry 7, 94, 128-9
Lending Library 177
'Lucas Girls' 161

McKay, Pat (later Fitzgibbon) 207
MacDonald, Jeanette (film star) 99
Mail 41, 81, 108, 232
Manifold family 40
Manifold House 61, 146
Marseillaise, La 110
Maxwell Gumbleton, M.H. (Bishop), and Mrs 25, 40, 81
Melbourne 214-6
Menzies, Sir Robert (Prime Minister) 107
Milne, A.A. (author) 10, 78
Misdemeanours 19, 53, 58, 102-3, 131, 163, 164, 180-1, 182, 207, 217, 228
Mitchell, Major (explorer) 218, 226
Mitchell, Mrs 195
Monarchy 78-80
Money 59
Moorabool Reservoir 209
Motor cars, *see* Cars
Mrs Miniver (film) 158, 235
Murphy Miss 67
Music 62, 66-7, 168-70, 215, 219, 221

Natimuk 103
Nerrina 186, 187, 213
Nettie, 'Aunt' *see* Cudmore, Anniette
Newcastle, NSW 2-12, 45
  Cathedral 2-4
  Deaneries 2-3, 5 et seq.

Index

Nightman, the 228
Nursery 92-3

O'Farrell, H.J. 80
'Old Ladies', the (Misses Williamson) 137

Pantomime 215
Pearl Harbour 139
Pern, S. (Dr) 177, 206
Pets 24, 38, 85, 122-5, 125, 192, 216
Picnics 8, 209, 212
Picture Theatres 126, 158, 170, 171, 215, 235
  Britannia 158
  Her Majesty's 158
  Newsreel 215
  Plaza 158
  Regent 158
  Savoy 215
Play
  Imaginative 6, 22, 32-4, 72, 91, 97, 98-9, 133-4, 178
  Indoor 38, 89-90, 91-2, 96-9, 131, 133-4, 178-80
  Outdoor/school 37, 44-5, 54-5, 71-2, 132-3, 135-6, 137-8, 206
  Effects of war on 150, 153
Pleasure Gardens 42-5
  'Fairyland' 42, 44
  kiosk 43, 44, 45
  maze 43
  naval cannon 45
  steamers 43
  zoo 43-4
Pocket money 59
Polio epidemic 51, 197
Portland 225-31
  Clergy Rest House 225
  'St Ives' 226-7
  nightman 228
  whales 226
  Canon Coupe 229-30
  'The Woolwash' 229
  Carthew, Mr 230
Powell, Mrs (Sheep Hills) 216
Propriety 16, 125-6, 183-4
'Pughole', The 116, 140, 146, 194

Queen's CEGGS, 60-66, 68-73, 77, 110, 145-6, 151, 163-8, 169, 171-3, 180-1, 183, 234, 236
  acting 68
  assembly 68
  concert 66
  'Fort' 72
  library 177
  Manifold House 61
  playground (the quad) 61, 71
  'Pringles' 72
  rules 73
  VP Day 234
  effects of war 108, 110, 146, 166-7
  Teachers, *see* Abrams, F., Bishop, E., Hiller, R., Jenkin, E., King, E., Krome, V., Larkins, V., Woodbridge, F.W., Wright, N.E.
  See also Education, formal
Queen Victoria 80

RAAF base 140, 145, 148
Rabbiting 209-11
Railways 42, 148, 159
Rationing 152
Refisch, S. (violin teacher) 66, 169
Religious Instruction 5, 69-70, 101-2
Retreats 191
Richardson, Henry Handel, *The Fortunes of Richard Mahony* 24, 176
River Plate, Battle of the 109
Rotheram, Margaret (née Wilson, q.v.)
Rules 56, 72-3, 180, 182

St Aidan 84
St Aidan's College 23, 24, 25, 84, 85
St Cuthbert 84
St Paul's Cathedral, Melbourne 17, 232
Sargent, Sir Malcolm (conductor) 62
School, *see* Education, formal and Queen's CEGGS
Sectarianism 60, 102, 184
Sellar, W.C. & Yeatman, R.J., *1066 and All That* 76

Servants, *see* Domestic service/staff
Shopping 41, 155-6, 185-6, 195
Smyth, Sir Nevill & Lady 216-17
Snow Goose, The, (Paul Gallico) 109
South Australia 221-3
South Street Competitions 67, 157
Statues 46, 47, 80, 161
Stokes, Florence (Auntie Flo, great aunt) 36, 176, 223

Taylor's Boatshed 206
Tea parties 130-1
Tennyson, Alfred Lord (poet) 78, 173
Thompson, Tilly 161
Thorburn, Dorothy (née de Chair, Aunt Dorothy) 81, 107-8, 139, 149
Thornton, Samuel (Bishop) 24, 84, 137
Tim the Toyman 215
Toys 2, 11, 32-3, 192
Tradesmen 26, 41, 150, 185-7
Trafalgar Day 77
Trams 55-59, 74, 77, 140, 142, 159
Trees 34-5, 46, 49-50, 71, 85, 135-6
Trollope, Anthony, *The Barchester Chronicles* 23
Turner, Ethel, *Seven Little Australians* 177, 202

Uncle Remus Stories (Joel Chandler Harris) 10
Union Jack 143
Urquhart, W.S. (surveyor) 49
US Army, *see* American soldiers

Victoria Coffee Palace (Melbourne) 214
Victoria, Queen 80
Volcanos 47-8

Warrenheip, Mount, 47-8, 80
Wars, *see* World Wars I and II
Wartime songs 170-1
Washing, *see* Bathtime, Laundry

Wendouree, *see* Ballarat, Lake Wendouree
White Slave Trade 236
Wilson family 54, 139, 143, 183, 201
Wilson, Margaret (later Rotheram) 54, 61, 89, 98-9, 123-4, 131, 133-4, 137, 149, 153, 154-5, 158, 163, 202, 203, 206, 211, 212
    letters and writing, 178-80, 197, 227, 230
Windsor Hotel (Melbourne) 214
Winter 28, 31-2, 93-4
Wireless 114-15, 166, 174-5
Wood, Elizabeth (née Johnson, q.v.)

Woodbridge, F.W. 167
World War I 50, 77, 97, 102, 161
World War II 86
    in Europe 107 et seq.
    in Pacific 139 et seq.
    wireless 114-15
    effect on domestic service 115-16, 142
    Americans 139-43
    flags 143
    ARP 145-6
    war effort & austerity 149-53, 209, 235
    effect on schools 166-7
    effect on music 169-71
    effect on motoring 152-3, 219
    effect on travel 222, 224
    VP Day, 233-4
Wright, Nancy 167-8
Writing, creative 178-80

Yabbying 211
Yeates family 14
Yuille family, Yuille's Swamp 24, 74, 204, 226

Zoos, Ballarat 43-4, Taronga Park, Sydney 9, 44